THE
♥Love Your
HEART
Italian
(Low Cholesterol)
C·O·O·K·B·O·O·K

by
CAROLE KRUPPA

Surrey Books

Chicago

THE LOVE YOUR HEART ITALIAN (LOW CHOLESTEROL) COOKBOOK is published by Surrey Books, Inc., 230 E. Ohio St., Suite 120, Chicago,IL 60611.

First edition: 1 2 3 4 5

This book is manufactured in the United States of America.

Library of Congress Cataloging-in-Publication data:

Kruppa, Carole.
    The love your heart Italian (low cholesterol) cookbook /
  by   Carole Kruppa. — 1st ed.
    360 p.   cm.
    Includes index.
    ISBN 0-940625-81-4 (paper) : $12.95
    1. Low-fat diet—Recipes.   2. Reducing diets—Recipes.
  3. Cookery, Italian.   I. Title.
RM237.7.K779   1994
641.5'63—dc20   93-44576
                                                                 CIP

Editorial and production: *Bookcrafters, Inc., Chicago*
Art Director: *Hughes & Co., Chicago*
Front cover illustration by *Jean Holabird*
Back cover photos courtesy *California Olive Industry*

For free catalog and prices on quantity purchases, contact Surrey Books at the address above.

This title is distributed to the trade by Publishers Group West.

Other titles in the "Love Your Heart" cookbook series:

The Love Your Heart (Low Cholesterol) Cookbook
The Love Your Heart Mediterranean (Low Cholesterol) Cookbook

CONTENTS

♥

I dedicate this book to my husband, Harvey Stern, and good friend, Kim Graff, tasters *straordinàrio*.

I wish to thank my friend and publisher, Susan Schwartz, whose vision has been without fault.

I wish also to thank Florence Guido for allowing me to use two recipes in honor of her deceased husband, the chef and owner of Guido's Restaurant in Waconda, Illinois. His Chicken Piccata and Fettuccine Alfredo are not to be forgotten.

I also wish to thank Philibert Gentilini of Restaurant Le Scampi in Paris, France, for his recipes for Saltimbocca and Pepper Steak. His is the finest restaurant on the rue de Penthievre.

And last but not least, my editor, Gene DeRoin, who brings my visions into reality.

INTRODUCTION

Italians have a unique ability to turn any meal into a celebration. Perhaps it is because Italian meals feature an extravaganza of flavor, color, and texture. Perhaps it is because the Italians can turn such basic ingredients as flour, vegetables, water, and spices into fantastic feasts. Whatever the reasons, the influence of Italian cuisine on American food tastes has been substantial.

Without leaving the mainstream of those marvelous flavors, the recipes in this book have been "lightened" to reflect today's concern for healthful, nutritious eating. The goal was to retain the great tastes while reducing the fat and controlling calories, cholesterol, and sodium. We also have attempted to adhere to American Heart Association guidelines of no more than 30 percent of calories from fat, bearing in mind that this rule should apply to an entire day's intake rather than a single meal. Additionally, in meat recipes the percentage of calories from fat may actually be as high as 49 percent, but if consumed with a balance of fruits, vegetables, and low-fat dairy products, the entire meal will likely be under the 30 percent guideline.

Italian foods are robust and hearty, high in fiber and complex carbohydrates. We have maintained this dimension, and most of the recipes use plenty of vegetables, pasta, grains, or fruit. To slim down the dishes, we have substituted many newly available low-fat items, such as yogurt and evaporated skim milk, for butter and cream. We also recommend vegetable cooking spray as a replacement for oil in many recipes. However, olive oil, a mainstay of Italian cooking, is used in moderation for its incomparable flavor and because, as a monounsaturated vegetable oil, it is thought to stimulate the body's production of HDL, the "good" cholesterol that inhibits artery-blocking materials.

As in the two previous "Love Your Heart" cookbooks, the recipes have been simplified to save preparation time. Also, they call for easy-to-obtain ingredients that may be found in neighborhood supermarkets at modest prices. Simplicity, convenience, and economy are hallmarks of Italian cuisine just as they are of our own.

Today, everyone charged with the responsibility of cooking for others wants meals that are as nourishing as they are delicious. Nutritional data follow each recipe so you'll know how many calories you are eating, as well as the amounts of fat, cholesterol, carbohydrate, protein, and sodium. Diabetic exchanges are also given to guide those on more rigorous diets. But please understand that nutritional data are not infallible: the sizes of vegetables, specific components of packaged ingredients, differences among brands, and other variables make it impossible to assure total accuracy. Where alternate ingredients are listed, the first ingredient was used in our calculations. Optional ingredients were not figured into the nutritional data.

May you find these updated and slimmed down Italian recipes as delicious as their traditional counterparts, just as economical, and much easier to make. *Mangia bene! Vivi bene!*—eat well! live well!

The Italian Pantry

♥

The following items are some of the staple ingredients you might wish to keep on hand at all times.

Pantry Items

Beans   Dry white beans, lentils, and chickpeas may be stored in bulk.

Canned Goods   Tomato paste and Italian peeled tomatoes are ever useful, as are cans of cannellini, garbanzo, and kidney beans. Cans of water-packed tuna for salads and anchovy fillets for antipasti should be available, along with green and black olives, extra virgin olive oil, red wine and balsamic vinegar, and a jar each of capers and peppercorns.

Cornmeal   I keep two kinds for making polenta: coarse cornmeal, which needs to cook for 45 minutes and must be stirred constantly, and instant 5-minute cornmeal, which is more convenient.

Pasta Store dry pasta in several of your favorite shapes so you will have the right one to pair with your sauce de jour. A good assortment would include: fettuccine, fusilli, lasagna, linguine, pappardelle, tagliatelle, and tortellini.

Porcini Mushrooms These keep well and can be used in any number of recipes.

Rice Besides regular white and brown rice, keep on hand Italian arborio rice for risotto and to use in soups.

Vegetables Mushrooms, zucchini, onions, eggplant, lemons, and—of course—tomatoes are necessaries.

Refrigerator Items

Cheese A wedge of Parmesan is an essential ingredient; wrap it tightly in foil and refrigerate. Grate it fresh as needed. Mozzarella and fontina are also good to have on hand.

Espresso Coffee Store ground coffee in a tightly lidded glass jar; if you grind your own, the beans should also be kept in the fridge.

Nuts Almonds, pine nuts, and walnuts should be kept in the freezer compartment, as they will remain fresher there.

Pancetta Italian bacon—a large whole piece—should be on hand for slicing when the need arises.

Pastes Anchovy, tomato, and garlic paste tubes provide quick flavorings and little goes to waste.

Pesto Sauce Keep this in a jar or plastic container to add to pasta, sauces, soups, or even spread on bread.

Prosciutto A thick chunk may be sliced as needed.

Stock Chicken, beef, and vegetable stock are best kept in the freezer compartment, ready for thawing and use in risotto, soups, and sauces.

Herbs and Spices

Basics Basil, oregano, garlic, bay leaves, and assorted peppers are fundamental to Italian cooking. You can now buy many herbs fresh at farmers' markets or in the produce section of your supermarket. You may even wish to plant a small herb garden, either outdoors or in countertop pots. Snipping your own herbs is a singular pleasure.

Saffron Keep this pricey spice available for risotto, soups, and meat dishes.

Spike This brand-name item is a combination of many natural, dried spices and herbs. It comes with or without salt. I like to use the no-salt variety to add flavor to a whole spectrum of dishes. Spike may be found in most supermarkets and health food stores.

1
CONDIMENTS
(CONDIMENTI)

In traditional Italian homes condiments such as vinegar, infused oils, sun-dried tomatoes, preserved herbs, and the like are all made from scratch. Summer is a great time to begin making vinegars and oils using fresh herbs from your garden. It is also a good time to prepare sun-dried tomatoes because tomatoes are so plentiful.

Once you make your own vinegars and sun-dried tomatoes, you will never buy them again. The intense flavor enhances all the food made with these condiments. Vinegars are easy to make and make wonderful gifts by adding a pretty label and including some recipes.

1

BASIL VINEGAR

All year long I save large wine bottles for summer vinegar-making. I give them a good scrubbing and scalding, and then I stuff them with fresh herbs, such as basil, lemon balm, tarragon, and the like. I use a funnel and pour in white vinegar or wine vinegar, filling the bottles to the brim. I let them steep for weeks so the herbs flavor the vinegar. Almost any fresh herb can be used this way. I like combining herbs, too, for thyme-lemon vinegar or parsley-chive vinegar. I use these vinegars on salads, in marinades, and to deglaze chicken and veal dishes.

  1 bottle of basil sprigs
  1 clove garlic
4–5 whole peppercorns
     White vinegar or red wine vinegar
     Glass bottle and cap or cork, sterilized

Wash and dry basil sprigs, placing them in bottle. With a knife make a small slit in the garlic clove and add it to bottle. Fill with vinegar. Cap or cork the bottle and place it in the sun, indoors or out.

Ripen for two weeks or longer. Strain vinegar and return to bottle. Add fresh sprig of herb and let stand for 1 month before using.

WINE VINEGAR

Italians make good vinegar by leaving wine exposed to air for several weeks. The yeast in the wine is still active and with the help of enzymes in the air, a "mother" forms and turns the wine to good vinegar.

Often trying to make vinegar from Italian wine in America, the "mother" does not form, probably from the absence of enzymes in the air or perhaps because the wine may have been pasteurized, killing the active yeast. Put bread in the wine to reintroduce yeast and cause the wine to become good vinegar.

4 cups dry red wine
1 cup white bread, crusts removed

Pour wine into a jar and add bread. Place a lid loosely over the jar to allow some air to enter. Let stand for about 4 weeks, at which time the "mother" should be formed. Once formed, the "mother" will continue to grow as more wine is added, and pieces of it may be cut off and used to make other barrels or bottles of vinegar.

Keep wine vinegar in a small wooden barrel and add wine as needed for a fresh supply of wine vinegar. You may safely add as much as three times the amount of wine as the quantity of wine vinegar left in the barrel. With an active "mother," new wine will turn to good vinegar in less than a week.

Makes 4 cups

FRUIT VINEGAR

Fruit vinegar enhances any fresh fruit salad or dessert.

- 1 qt. cider or white wine vinegar
- 2 cups fresh or frozen cranberries, blueberries, raspberries, strawberries, not in syrup, thawed if frozen
- ½ cup light honey
- Cinnamon sticks

Combine vinegar and 1 cup of berries in a medium-size saucepan. Boil, then lower the heat and simmer, uncovered, for 2 minutes. Stir in honey and remove from heat. Pour berry mixture through a fine-mesh strainer into a large measuring cup. Don't press berries. Discard berries.

Divide the remaining 1 cup berries between two 16-ounce bottles or four 8-ounce bottles. Place one 6-inch cinnamon stick in each 16-ounce bottle or one 3-inch cinnamon stick in each 8-ounce bottle. Pour warm vinegar into bottles to within 1 inch of the top. Allow flavors to mellow for at least 1 week.

Makes 1 quart

BASIL OIL

I make this oil during summer, when herbs are plentiful. Pinch off the tops of your basil plants so they will become bushy.

- 1 bottle of basil sprigs
- 1 clove garlic, peeled
- Extra-virgin olive oil
- Clear wine bottle and new cork, sterilized

Wash and dry the basil, putting 3 or 4 sprigs into bottle. With a small knife, make a slit in the garlic clove and add it to bottle. Fill bottle with olive oil and cork it.

Store oil in refrigerator and use within 3 weeks. Bring oil to room temperature before using. You will have oil with a beautiful basil flavor, and the leaves stay perfectly preserved.

This oil can be used like any other in salads, marinades or for sautéing meats, but it is wonderful on pasta.

PRESERVED HERBS

This method for making herbs last all year was used by the ancient Egyptians, Greeks, and Romans. It is good for basil, sage, rosemary, oregano, and lemon balm.

> Fresh basil, oregano, sage, or rosemary
> Coarse sea salt
> Pint jars, sterilized

Gently wash herbs and dry well. Discard stems (or leave short stems if you like).

Cover bottom of each jar with ¼-inch layer of salt. Add a few herb leaves, then a layer of salt, and continue making alternate layers of herbs and salt until the jar is three-quarters full. Seal jars, and place in refrigerator.

To use, remove desired amount of herbs and rinse and dry them well. Make sure remaining herbs are covered with salt before resealing. The color may be a little lighter, but the flavor will be as fresh as when you picked the herb.

2
APPETIZERS
(ANTIPASTI)

When I was growing up, appetizers always meant a celebration. The recipes in this chapter are for parties, birthday dinners, and holiday festivities. In this chapter are recipes for vegetarian feasts, luncheons that feature fish, hearty appetizers, and light appetizers. All are spectacular.

With the emphasis on lighter meals today, I think it is best to forgo large amounts of appetizers before a meal. Instead I like to serve one, beautifully prepared as a first course. This shortens the cocktail period before dinner, and your guests will eat your dinner instead of gorging on finger foods.

Some recipes, such as Baked Clams or Marinated Tortellini, are easy to prepare, while others, such as Camponata, take more time but are worth every minute. Try one or try them all. Most importantly, have fun the next time you entertain.

BAKED ASPARAGUS WITH HAM

Demonstrate the versatility of Italian food by serving this as an appetizer, lunch, or supper.

- 1½ lbs. asparagus
- 8 thin slices boiled ham
- ¼ cup Parmesan cheese, freshly grated
- 2 tablespoons white wine

Preheat oven to 350 degrees. Spray an 11-by-7-inch baking dish with vegetable cooking spray. Cut off tough asparagus ends. Tie asparagus together in 1 or 2 bunches with string. Pour cold salted water 2 to 3 inches deep in an asparagus cooker, tall stockpot or old coffeepot. Place asparagus upright in water and boil.

Cover and cook over high heat 6 to 8 minutes, depending on size. Drain on paper towels; remove string.

Divide asparagus into 4 bundles. Wrap 2 ham slices around each bundle. Arrange wrapped asparagus bundles in a single layer in baking dish. Sprinkle with Parmesan cheese and pour white wine around asparagus. Bake 8 to 10 minutes or until cheese is melted.

Serves 4

NUTRITIONAL DATA

PER SERVING		EXCHANGES	
calories	114	milk	0.0
% calories from fat	29	vegetable	1.5
fat (gm)	3.9	fruit	0.0
sat. fat (gm)	1.8	bread	0.0
cholesterol (mg)	19.9	meat	1.5
sodium (mg)	464	fat	0.0
protein (gm)	12.6		
carbohydrate (gm)	7.7		

♥

VEGETABLE PLATTER WITH VINAIGRETTE

2 small ripe fresh tomatoes, sliced
1 small cucumber, thinly sliced
1 small carrot
2 small zucchini, thinly sliced
2 cloves garlic, minced
¼ teaspoon Dijon-style mustard
¼ cup Tomato Vinaigrette (see index)

Arrange tomatoes around the edge of a serving plate. Arrange cucumber slices and then zucchini slices on plate, overlapping rows. Using a vegetable peeler, cut carrot into long strips. Place carrot strips in center of plate. Just before serving, drizzle vinaigrette over vegetables.

Serves 8

NUTRITIONAL DATA

PER SERVING		EXCHANGES	
calories	30	milk	0.0
% calories from fat	8	vegetable	1.0
fat (gm)	0.3	fruit	0.0
sat. fat (gm)	0.1	bread	0.0
cholesterol (mg)	0	meat	0.0
sodium (mg)	76	fat	0.0
protein (gm)	1.3		
carbohydrate (gm)	6.3		

BAKED CHEESE

½ cup Basic Tomato-Basil Sauce (see index) or
purchased garden-style spaghetti sauce
6 oz. part skim mozzarella cheese
1 teaspoon lemon juice
¼ teaspoon cracked pepper
6 hard rolls, sliced or melba toast

Pour sauce into a 10- or 12-ounce ovenproof baking dish. Using a pastry brush, brush cheese with lemon juice. Sprinkle with cracked pepper.

Place cheese atop sauce in the dish. Bake, uncovered, in a 375-degree oven for 6 to 8 minutes or until cheese is just heated and softened.

To serve, spread warm cheese and sauce on sliced rolls or melba toast.

Serves 6

NUTRITIONAL DATA

PER SERVING		EXCHANGES	
calories	237	milk	0.0
% calories from fat	25	vegetable	0.5
fat (gm)	6.8	fruit	0.0
sat. fat (gm)	3.3	bread	2.0
cholesterol (mg)	15.9	meat	1.0
sodium (mg)	498	fat	0.5
protein (gm)	12.3		
carbohydrate (gm)	32.7		

MARINATED TORTELLINI

8 oz. packaged cheese tortellini

2 medium carrots, cut into ½-inch long julienne strips (about ⅔ cup)

½ of a green or red sweet pepper, cut into ½-inch-long julienne strips (about ½ cup)

⅓ cup Pesto Sauce (see index)

Parmesan cheese

4 teaspoons lemon juice

Cook tortellini according to package directions. Drain well. Rinse with cold water, drain again.

In a large bowl combine tortellini, carrot strips, pepper strips, pesto, Parmesan cheese and lemon juice. Toss till coated. Cover and chill 4 to 24 hours. Let stand at room temperature 30 minutes before serving.

Serves 6

NUTRITIONAL DATA

PER SERVING		EXCHANGES	
calories	84	milk	0.0
% calories from fat	21	vegetable	0.0
fat (gm)	2.1	fruit	0.0
sat. fat (gm)	1.7	bread	1.0
cholesterol (mg)	8.6	meat	0.0
sodium (mg)	111	fat	0.5
protein (gm)	3.9		
carbohydrate (gm)	13		

MARINATED PASTA

This is an easy dish to tote to a potluck dinner.

- 4 oz. fusilli or spaghetti
- 1 6-oz. jar marinated artichoke hearts
- ½ small yellow summer squash
- ½ cup mozzarella cheese, shredded (4 oz.)
- ¼ cup pitted ripe olives
- 2 tablespoons grated Parmesan cheese
- ¼ cup Italian vinaigrette
- 8 romaine or Boston lettuce leaves

Break fusilli or spaghetti in half. Cook and drain immediately. Rinse with cold water, and drain again.

Drain and cut artichoke hearts. Cut zucchini and yellow squash in half lengthwise. Then cut into slices.

In a large bowl combine artichokes, zucchini slices, yellow squash, mozzarella cheese, olive oil, Parmesan cheese, and pasta. Gently toss. Pour dressing over salad. Gently toss to coat. Cover and chill for 4 to 24 hours. Serve on lettuce-lined plates.

Serves 8 as appetizer, or 4 as main dish.

NUTRITIONAL DATA

PER SERVING		EXCHANGES	
calories	117	milk	0.0
% calories from fat	29	vegetable	1.0
fat (gm)	3.9	fruit	0.0
sat. fat (gm)	1.9	bread	0.5
cholesterol (mg)	9.2	meat	1.0
sodium (mg)	186	fat	0.0
protein (gm)	7.1		
carbohydrate (gm)	13.6		

ARTICHOKE HEARTS

Pull off dark green outer leaves to reveal pale green heart.

Cut about ⅓ inch off top; trim stems. Rub all over with lemon or soak in water.

Place trimmed hearts in saucepan with lightly salted water to cover. Boil until just tender, about 5 minutes. Drain, pat thoroughly dry, and put in a clean bowl or jar. Cover completely with olive oil. Oil-covered hearts can be stored, covered, in refrigerator for up to a month.

Peeling, Seeding, and Chopping Tomatoes

1. Use a paring knife to core the tomatoes.
2. Turn tomatoes over and slit the skin in an X-shaped cut.
3. Put the tomatoes in a pan containing enough boiling water to cover them and boil for 15 seconds. Remove them with a slotted spoon and put them in a bowl of cold water for a few seconds.
4. Remove them from the cold water and use a paring knife to pull off skins.
5. Halve tomatoes horizontally with a chopping knife. Hold each half over a bowl, cut side down, and squeeze to remove seeds.
6. Chop tomatoes into small pieces.

TOMATO CROSTINI

The secret to the success of these crostini is to use ripe plum tomatoes and fresh basil. I like to serve these in summer for a barbecue because I can serve them while the rest of the meal is cooking.

- 1½ cups fresh plum tomatoes (about 3 medium tomatoes), seeded and chopped
- 12 slices Italian bread (from narrow baguette-type loaf)
- 2 large cloves garlic, peeled
- 2 tablespoons olive oil
- 12 tablespoons fresh basil, minced
- 1 tablespoon fresh oregano, minced
  Spike, to taste
  Black pepper, freshly ground, to taste

Put tomatoes in colander and set aside to drain.

Grill or toast bread slices. Rub each slice with garlic, and drizzle each one with olive oil.

Place tomatoes in a bowl and top with remaining ingredients. Stir to mix well. Divide mixture evenly among bread slices and serve immediately.

Serves 6

NUTRITIONAL DATA

PER SERVING		EXCHANGES	
calories	140	milk	0.0
% calories from fat	31	vegetable	0.0
fat (gm)	4.7	fruit	0.0
sat. fat (gm)	0.7	bread	1.0
cholesterol (mg)	0	meat	0.0
sodium (mg)	157	fat	1.0
protein (gm)	3.6		
carbohydrate (gm)	20.3		

ROASTED RED PEPPERS

2 red bell peppers
1 clove garlic, finely minced
2 tablespoons olive oil
1 teaspoon fresh oregano, minced
   Spike, to taste

Hold peppers over an open gas flame or charcoal fire, or place them under a broiler. Turn often until blackened on all sides. Transfer peppers to a paper bag; close and set aside until cool (15 to 20 minutes).

Peel peppers; halve; remove stem and seeds. Lay halves flat and use dull side of small knife to scrape away black bits of skin and stray seeds. Slice into ¼-inch strips.

Put sliced peppers in a medium bowl; add garlic, olive oil, and oregano. Add Spike to taste. Toss to blend and let marinate at room temperature for 1 hour before using.

MARINATED PEPPERS
(Peperonata)

*S*weet peppers stewed slowly with tomatoes, herbs, and garlic are a popular summer first course in southern Italy. Serve them with crusty bread to mop up the aromatic juices, or offer peperonata as part of an antipasto platter.

 2 tablespoons garlic, minced
½ yellow onion, minced
 2 red bell peppers
 2 green bell peppers
 2 yellow bell peppers
 2 tomatoes, peeled, seeded, and coarsely chopped
10 fresh basil leaves, chopped

2   teaspoons Spike
¼   cup fresh oregano leaves
½   red onion, in paper thin slices, garnish
1   tablespoon capers, garnish
2   tablespoons parsley, minced, garnish
2   tablespoons olive oil (optional)

In a large skillet sprayed with vegetable spray, over medium heat add garlic and yellow onion. Sauté, stirring until lightly colored (about 3 minutes).

Halve peppers; remove seeds, and trim away white ribs. Cut lengthwise into strips ½-inch wide. Add all peppers to skillet at one time and stir to blend with garlic-onion mixture. Add tomatoes, basil, and Spike; mix gently. Place oregano leaves on top. Cover and simmer slowly until peppers are soft (about 12 to 15 minutes). Remove from heat, and transfer to serving bowl to cool.

Serve peppers at room temperature, garnishing top with sliced red onion, capers, and minced parsley. If desired, drizzle with the 2 tablespoons olive oil (not included in Nutritional Data) just before serving.

Makes about 3½ cups
Serves 8

NUTRITIONAL DATA

PER SERVING		EXCHANGES	
calories	36	milk	0.0
% calories from fat	7	vegetable	1.5
fat (gm)	0.3	fruit	0.0
sat. fat (gm)	0.1	bread	0.0
cholesterol (mg)	0	meat	0.0
sodium (mg)	5	fat	0.0
protein (gm)	1.4		
carbohydrate (gm)	8.2		

MARINATED VEGETABLES

These are wonderful in antipasti or as hostess gifts.

1⅓ cup red or white wine vinegar
2⅔ cups water
26 cups vegetables: broccoli, cauliflower, bell peppers, carrots, onions, etc., cut up
4 or 5 peppercorns (or pinch red pepper flakes)

Combine the vinegar, water, and salt in a bowl large enough to hold the vegetables. Add vegetables and pepper. Place a plate in bowl on top of vegetables to hold them down. Cover with plastic wrap and refrigerate for 2 to 3 days.
Makes 6 cups pickled vegetables
Serves 24 (4 servings per cup)

NUTRITIONAL DATA

PER SERVING		EXCHANGES	
calories	49	milk	0.0
% calories from fat	5	vegetable	2.0
fat (gm)	0.3	fruit	0.0
sat. fat (gm)	0.1	bread	0.0
cholesterol (mg)	0	meat	0.0
sodium (mg)	22	fat	0.0
protein (gm)	2.1		
carbohydrate (gm)	11.4		

MIXED MARINATED VEGETABLES

*C**an be used as antipasto or as a salad on a bed of lettuce.*

- ⅓ cup Italian Vinaigrette (see index)
- 2 large bulbs fennel, cut into 1-inch pieces
- 1 lb. fresh broccoli, separated into florets
- 4 oz. part skim mozzarella cheese, cut into ½-inch cubes
- 2 jars (6 oz. each) marinated artichoke hearts, drained
- 1 jar (12 oz.) marinated mushrooms, drained
- 10 Italian black olives, pitted and sliced

Toss vegetables into large bowl. Pour dressing over vegetables; toss. Cover and refrigerate about 2 hours or until chilled. Toss well before serving.

Serves 8

NUTRITIONAL DATA

PER SERVING		EXCHANGES	
calories	97	milk	0.0
% calories from fat	27	vegetable	2.0
fat (gm)	3.4	fruit	0.0
sat. fat (gm)	1.6	bread	0.0
cholesterol (mg)	8	meat	0.5
sodium (mg)	378	fat	0.5
protein (gm)	7.8		
carbohydrate (gm)	11.9		

SUN-DRIED TOMATOES

These tomatoes have a unique flavor and the texture of the sun-dried tomatoes sold in gourmet shops. They are wonderful in salads, pizza, pasta dips, and spreads. Tomatoes can be dried in oven or a dehydrator. If using a dehydrator, follow the manufacturer's instructions.

     6 lbs. fresh plum tomatoes
       Fresh basil leaves
     3 cloves garlic, peeled
    15 whole peppercorns
     2 teaspoons extra-virgin olive oil
       Pint jars, sterilized

Wash and dry tomatoes. Cut in half lengthwise and place cut-sides down on wire racks set on baking sheets. Place racks in a 200-degree oven and let tomatoes dry until they are the consistency of dried apricots. This may take up to 12 hours depending on size of tomatoes.

Layer tomatoes into 2 jars, adding one clove of garlic per jar, 5 peppercorns and 2 basil leaves. Cover with extra-virgin olive oil. Don't pack too many tomatoes in a jar. Cap jars and place them in a cool spot overnight.

If tomatoes absorb oil and are poking through it, add oil to submerge tomatoes. Check jars 2 or 3 more times, adding oil if necessary, before capping them for the final time.

Store in cool place for at least 6 weeks before using. Refrigerate after opening; bring tomatoes to room temperature before serving.

Makes 3 pints
Serves 4 per pint

NUTRITIONAL DATA

PER SERVING		EXCHANGES	
calories	57	milk	0.0
% calories from fat	20	vegetable	2.0
fat (gm)	1.5	fruit	0.0
sat. fat (gm)	0.2	bread	0.0
cholesterol (mg)	0	meat	0.0
sodium (mg)	21	fat	0.0
protein (gm)	2.1		
carbohydrate (gm)	11.3		

CAPONATA

This tangy eggplant dip can be served as a topping for crostini, on lettuce as a salad, or as part of an antipasto tray.

1 medium eggplant, peeled and cut into ½-inch cubes (about 1 lb.)

¾ cup onion, chopped

⅓ cup celery, chopped

1 14½-oz. can chunky tomatoes

3 tablespoons wine vinegar

2 tablespoons tomato paste

1 teaspoon sugar

½ teaspoon Spike

   Dash ground red pepper

1 tablespoon parsley, snipped

1 tablespoon basil

1 teaspoon oregano

1 teaspoon lemon juice

In a large skillet, cook eggplant, onion, and celery in olive oil, covered, over medium heat for 5 to 8 minutes or till just tender.

Stir in tomatoes, wine vinegar, tomato paste, sugar, Spike, and red pepper. Cook, uncovered, over low heat for 5 minutes, stirring occasionally. Remove from heat.

Stir in parsley, basil, oregano, and lemon juice. Cool. Cover and refrigerate. Let stand at room temperature for 30 minutes before serving.

Serves 10

NUTRITIONAL DATA

PER SERVING		EXCHANGES	
calories	30	milk	0.0
% calories from fat	7	vegetable	1.5
fat (gm)	0.3	fruit	0.0
sat. fat (gm)	0.04	bread	0.0
cholesterol (mg)	0	meat	0.0
sodium (mg)	74	fat	0.0
protein (gm)	1.1		
carbohydrate (gm)	7.1		

TOMATOES WITH PESTO

6 ripe tomatoes (all about same size if possible)
  Spike
1 cup Pesto Sauce (see index)
3 tablespoons olive oil (optional)

Cut tomatoes in half horizontally, and cut out any green parts where stems had been. Sprinkle liberally with Spike. Turn them upside down, and let them stand for about ½ hour.

Spread a little pesto over each tomato. Some of it will sink in; when it does, add a little more to form a thin layer of pesto over each tomato. At serving, drizzle olive oil (not included in Nutritional Data) over each.

Serves 5

NUTRITIONAL DATA

PER SERVING		EXCHANGES	
calories	62	milk	0.0
% calories from fat	32	vegetable	1.5
fat (gm)	2.4	fruit	0.0
sat. fat (gm)	1.3	bread	0.0
cholesterol (mg)	5.7	meat	0.0
sodium (mg)	120	fat	0.5
protein (gm)	4		
carbohydrate (gm)	7.5		

ONION-AND-OLIVE FOCACCIA

2¾ to 3¼ cups all-purpose flour, divided
1 package active dry yeast
½ teaspoon salt
1 cup warm water (120 to 130 degrees)
2 tablespoons olive oil, divided
4 medium sweet onions, halved and sliced (4 cups)
2 cloves garlic, minced
2 teaspoons fresh rosemary, snipped, or ¾ teaspoon dried rosemary, crushed
½ cup ripe olives, sliced

Combine 1¼ cups of the flour, yeast, and salt in large bowl. Add warm water and 1 tablespoon olive oil. Beat with electric mixer on low speed for 30 seconds, scraping bowl constantly. Beat on high speed for 3 minutes. Using a spoon, stir in as much of remaining flour as you can. Turn out onto a lightly floured surface. Knead in enough remaining flour to make a moderately stiff dough that is smooth and elastic (6 to 8 minutes total). Cover; let rest 10 minutes.

Meanwhile, cook onion, garlic, and rosemary in 1 tablespoon olive oil, covered, over low heat about 15 minutes or till very tender, stirring occasionally. Remove from heat. Stir in olives; set aside.

Turn dough out on lightly floured surface. Divide in half. Roll each portion into a 10-inch circle. Transfer to a lightly greased baking sheet. Press slight indentations all over in dough rounds with fingertips. Evenly top with onion mixture. Cover; let rise in warm place till nearly double (30 to 40 minutes).

Bake in a 375-degree oven about 25 to 30 minutes or till golden. Cut into wedges; serve warm or at room temperature.

Serves 24

NUTRITIONAL DATA

PER SERVING		EXCHANGES	
calories	83	milk	0.0
% calories from fat	25	vegetable	0.0
fat (gm)	2.3	fruit	0.0
sat. fat (gm)	0.3	bread	1.0
cholesterol (mg)	0	meat	0.0
sodium (mg)	138	fat	0.5
protein (gm)	2.0		
carbohydrate (gm)	13.7		

MARINATED AUTUMN VEGETABLES

*M*ake this a day or two before serving to allow flavors to mellow. This is especially good with crusty bread to mop up the sauce. This can also be part of an antipasto platter.

1½ lbs. mushrooms

1 head cauliflower (about 2 lbs.)

6 ribs celery

¼ cup fresh lemon juice

½ cup white wine vinegar

5 cups water

1 tablespoon fresh oregano or 1 teaspoon dried oregano

¼ cup fresh basil leaves

1 teaspoon Spike

>   2 tablespoons dried lemon thyme or ¼ cup fresh
>   lemon verbena leaves
>   ¼ cup Italian Vinaigrette (see index)
>   Additional minced basil and oregano for garnish
>   Lettuce leaves for serving (romaine, Boston, etc.)

Trim, clean, and quarter mushrooms. Break cauliflower into bite-size florets. Trim celery into 3-inch pieces.

In a large saucepan combine mushrooms, lemon juice, vinegar, water, oregano, basil, Spike, and lemon thyme. Simmer gently 5 minutes. With a slotted spoon, transfer mushrooms to a bowl. Add cauliflower to liquid, and cook until crisp-tender. With a slotted spoon, remove to mushroom bowl.

Raise heat to high and reduce liquid to 1½ cups. Remove from heat, strain. Add Spike to taste. Pour dressing over vegetables in bowl. Garnish with additional basil and oregano leaves.

To serve, arrange lettuce leaves on 8 salad plates and top with vegetables.

Serves 8

NUTRITIONAL DATA

PER SERVING		EXCHANGES	
calories	62	milk	0.0
% calories from fat	8	vegetable	2.5
fat (gm)	0.7	fruit	0.0
sat. fat (gm)	0.1	bread	0.0
cholesterol (mg)	0	meat	0.0
sodium (mg)	38	fat	0.0
protein (gm)	4.3		
carbohydrate (gm)	13.3		

CREAM CHEESE ON SHIITAKE MUSHROOMS

L ook for shiitake mushrooms in oriental mar-
kets or in the produce section of your
supermarket.

6 large (2½-3-inch diameter) fresh shiitake
   mushrooms
8 oz. Kraft Free cream cheese
1 recipe Cilantro Tomato Sauce (see index) or
   purchased tomato sauce
1 tablespoon Pesto Sauce (see index) or purchased
   Fresh cilantro (optional)

Clean mushrooms; cut off stems and discard. In a lightly greased
shallow baking pan, arrange mushroom caps, stem sides up. Place a
tablespoon of cheese on each cap. Bake uncovered, in a 450-degree
oven for 6 to 8 minutes or until mushrooms are tender and cheese is
slightly soft.

To serve, pour warm cilantro tomato sauce onto 6 appetizer
plates; top with stuffed mushrooms. Top each cheese round with 1
teaspoon of pesto. Garnish with cilantro.

Serves 6

NUTRITIONAL DATA

PER SERVING		EXCHANGES	
calories	59	milk	0.0
% calories from fat	5	vegetable	1.5
fat (gm)	0.3	fruit	0.0
sat. fat (gm)	0.1	bread	0.0
cholesterol (mg)	7.1	meat	0.5
sodium (mg)	239	fat	0.0
protein (gm)	6.3		
carbohydrate (gm)	7.1		

MUSHROOM, TOMATO, AND BREAD KEBABS

16 ¾-inch thick slices of country bread
2 tablespoons olive oil
2 garlic cloves, minced
1 tablespoon fresh rosemary, finely chopped
1 teaspoon fresh sage, finely chopped
   Pepper, freshly ground
12 shiitake mushrooms, about 2½ inches in diameter, stems discarded
8 cherry tomatoes

Preheat the oven to 225 degrees. Toast bread in oven for 10 minutes.

In a small bowl, combine olive oil with garlic, rosemary, and sage. Season with pepper. Lightly brush mushroom caps and bread with herb oil, stuffing seasonings in mushroom undersides. Alternately thread 3 mushrooms, 2 tomatoes, and 4 slices of bread on a skewer, beginning and ending with a bread slice. Thread another skewer alongside to secure. Repeat the process with remaining bread and mushrooms. Brush with remaining herb oil.

Light broiler. Lightly spray a baking sheet with vegetable cooking spray. Broil skewers for 3 to 5 minutes, turning until golden brown on all sides.

Serves 4

NUTRITIONAL DATA

PER SERVING		EXCHANGES	
calories	501	milk	0.0
% calories from fat	22	vegetable	1.0
fat (gm)	12.6	fruit	0.0
sat. fat (gm)	1.8	bread	5.5
cholesterol (mg)	0	meat	0.0
sodium (mg)	778	fat	2.0
protein (gm)	15.0		
carbohydrate (gm)	82.6		

Stuffed Mushrooms

20 large mushrooms

1 small onion, finely chopped

¼ cup parsley, chopped

2 tablespoons white wine

2 tablespoons pimiento, chopped

½ cup dry bread crumbs

¼ cup grated Parmesan cheese

¼ teaspoon Spike

¼ teaspoon pepper

Clean mushrooms. Remove and chop stems.

In a large skillet sprayed with vegetable cooking spray, cook mushrooms, stems, onion, and parsley till onion is tender. Stir in wine, pimiento, bread crumbs, Parmesan cheese, Spike, and pepper.

Arrange mushrooms in a shallow baking pan. Spoon cheese mixture into mushroom caps. Bake in a 350-degree oven for 15 minutes or till mushrooms are tender and cheese mixture is heated through.

Serves 10

NUTRITIONAL DATA

PER SERVING		EXCHANGES	
calories	80	milk	0.0
% calories from fat	18	vegetable	0.5
fat (gm)	1.6	fruit	0.0
sat. fat (gm)	0.6	bread	1.0
cholesterol (mg)	2	meat	0.0
sodium (mg)	158	fat	0.0
protein (gm)	3.4		
carbohydrate (gm)	12.7		

WILD MUSHROOMS MARINARA

2 large tomatoes, peeled, seeded, and chopped
1 small yellow onion, finely minced
1 small clove garlic, peeled
1 bay leaf
½ cup white wine or dry vermouth
¼ cup fresh basil leaves, torn
12 oz. fresh wild mushrooms (trumpet, shiitake, oyster, etc.)
1 teaspoon olive oil
1 clove garlic, minced
1 tablespoon fresh parsley, minced
Spike, to taste
Pepper, freshly ground, to taste

Begin by making marinara sauce. Combine tomatoes, onion, garlic, bay leaf, white wine, and basil in saucepan. Boil, then reduce heat and simmer for 35 minutes, stirring frequently.

While sauce is cooking, brush mushrooms lightly with a damp cloth, but do not wash them. Slice mushrooms lengthwise, leaving stems on. Warm oil over medium heat in sauté pan. Add garlic and parsley, and sauté for 1 to 2 minutes. Then add sliced mushrooms; sauté over high heat until tender. Season with Spike and pepper to taste. Place on a serving plate and garnish with marinara sauce (not included in Nutritional Data).

Serves 4

NUTRITIONAL DATA

PER SERVING		EXCHANGES	
calories	66	milk	0.0
% calories from fat	24	vegetable	2.5
fat (gm)	1.2	fruit	0.0
sat. fat (gm)	0.3	bread	0.0
cholesterol (mg)	0	meat	0.0
sodium (mg)	13	fat	0.0
protein (gm)	2.8		
carbohydrate (gm)	9.7		

BAKED CLAMS

T his is one of my favorite ways to prepare fresh clams.

12 clams in shells
¾ cup dry bread crumbs
6 tablespoons white wine
¼ cup parsley, chopped
3 cloves garlic, finely chopped
½ teaspoon Spike
½ teaspoon pepper

Open clams over bowl; remove clam muscle. Reserve clam juice and shells. Scrub shells under cold running water and place in a single layer in a shallow baking pan.

In a mixing bowl, stir together bread crumbs, wine, parsley, garlic, Spike, and pepper. Place 1 clam in each shell in baking pan. Spoon bread crumb mixture over clams. Bake uncovered in a 375-degree oven for 15 to 20 minutes or until brown.

Serves 6

NUTRITIONAL DATA

PER SERVING		EXCHANGES	
calories	70	milk	0.0
% calories from fat	12	vegetable	0.0
fat (gm)	1	fruit	0.0
sat. fat (gm)	0.2	bread	0.5
cholesterol (mg)	9.6	meat	0.5
sodium (mg)	16	fat	0.0
protein (gm)	5		
carbohydrate (gm)	11.5		

BABY SHRIMP WITH OIL AND LEMON

Y ou can serve this with a selection of salads for a low-calorie luncheon party.

    2 lbs. precooked baby, bay shrimp
       Juice of 2 lemons
    1 teaspoon mustard
       Spike, to taste
       Pepper, freshly ground, to taste
    2 tablespoons olive oil
    6 tablespoons white wine
    3 tablespoons parsley, chopped
    2 cloves garlic, minced
    8 lettuce leaves

Pat shrimp dry with paper towels and place in large salad bowl.

Combine lemon juice, mustard, Spike, and pepper in medium bowl. Add oil, wine, parsley, and garlic; mix until blended. Taste and adjust for seasoning.

Pour lemon dressing over shrimp. Toss lightly until shrimp are coated with dressing. Refrigerate until ready to use.

Wash and dry lettuce thoroughly. Serve shrimp at room temperature garnished with lettuce.

Serves 8

NUTRITIONAL DATA

PER SERVING		EXCHANGES	
calories	154	milk	0.0
% calories from fat	28	vegetable	0.0
fat (gm)	4.7	fruit	0.0
sat. fat (gm)	0.8	bread	0.0
cholesterol (mg)	221	meat	3.0
sodium (mg)	263	fat	0.0
protein (gm)	23.9		
carbohydrate (gm)	1.1		

ESCARGOTS FLORENTINE

1   teaspoon unsalted butter

12 canned snails, washed

2   cups (firmly packed) fresh spinach, well rinsed and stemmed

    Black pepper, freshly ground

1   oz. blue cheese, crumbled

2   tablespoons yogurt

2   teaspoons Parmesan or Romano cheese, freshly grated

    Lemon wedges

Melt butter in a sauté pan over medium heat. Add snails and spinach. Add black pepper to taste. Sauté over medium heat for about 3 to 4 minutes until spinach begins to wilt. Add blue cheese.

Reduce heat and simmer for 4 to 6 minutes until cheese is melted. Add yogurt and mix well.

Transfer mixture to 2 individual gratin dishes or ramekins. Sprinkle grated Parmesan or Romano cheese on top and place under broiler for 2 to 3 minutes until cheese is lightly browned.

Garnish with lemon wedges. Serve immediately.

Serves 2

NUTRITIONAL DATA

PER SERVING		EXCHANGES	
calories	215	milk	0.0
% calories from fat	32	vegetable	2.0
fat (gm)	7.5	fruit	0.0
sat. fat (gm)	4.5	bread	0.0
cholesterol (mg)	73.5	meat	3.0
sodium (mg)	466	fat	0.0
protein (gm)	26.5		
carbohydrate (gm)	10		

SEA SCALLOPS WITH MINT, MOZZARELLA, AND CAPELLINI

    1 lb. capellini (angel hair pasta)
    2 cups evaporated skim milk
    6 oz. part-skim mozzarella cheese, shredded
 1½ teaspoons black pepper, coarsely cracked
  18 oz. large sea scallops
 1½ tablespoons fresh mint
 1½ tablespoons fresh parsley, chopped
    2 tablespoons olive oil
       Spike, to taste

Cook pasta in large pot of boiling water. Capellini will cook very quickly, in about 45 seconds in fresh. Do not overcook. Drain well and chill.

In a large saucepan, gently simmer milk and mozzarella cheese. Do not boil. Reduce to about 1½ cups. Add pepper and scallops. Turn off heat, and cover pan. The scallops will poach in 1 minute. Check for desired doneness. Add 1 tablespoon of mint and 1 tablespoon of parsley and stir.

Add oil to another large saucepan and add drained pasta. Toss with remaining mint and parsley.

Divide pasta among 6 serving plates. Bring sauce to a boil. Add Spike to taste.

Serves 6

NUTRITIONAL DATA

PER SERVING		EXCHANGES	
calories	534	milk	1.0
% calories from fat	21	vegetable	0.0
fat (gm)	12.5	fruit	0.0
sat. fat (gm)	3.9	bread	3.0
cholesterol (mg)	130	meat	4.0
sodium (mg)	467	fat	0.5
protein (gm)	43.3		
carbohydrate (gm)	61.7		

3
HIGH OMELETS
(FRITTATE)

Frittate are high omelets that incorporate ingredients such as vegetables, herbs, and meats and are rather different from thin omelets that are stuffed with such ingredients and then rolled. After illustrating the basic technique of making a frittata, examples of recipes from different parts of Italy follow. *Frittata profumata,* herb-flavored and made with mixed fresh basil, mint, and parsley, is one of the favorites of southern Italian cooking.

How to Season Pan

Before making the frittate recipes that follow, it is important that the pans when new be well-seasoned. The pans may be iron, aluminum, or stainless steel. Copper is beautiful for serving, but not for making a frittata.

1. Place pan over medium heat with about 2 tablespoons of salt (not coarse). Add about 1 tablespoon of vegetable oil to pan.
2. When the oil is warm, but not hot, use paper towel to rub salt and oil into bottom of pan and then sides.
3. Continue rubbing pan over medium heat for 2 or 3 minutes. Remove pan from heat, and wipe it out thoroughly with a clean towel. The pan is now ready to use. Sauté pans may also be seasoned this way.

How to Prepare Frittate

Break eggs into large crockery bowl. The number of eggs or egg substitute varies. See individual recipes below. If omelet pan is new, be sure to season it first (see above).

1. With a fork, break yolks and beat them lightly so no air bubbles or foam begins to form.
2. Place 10-inch omelet pan over medium heat. Spray pan with vegetable spray. When the pan is hot, add beaten eggs or egg substitute. Keep puncturing bottom with fork as eggs set to allow liquid on top to move to bottom. This helps eggs set uniformly.
3. When eggs are well set and frittata is well detached from bottom of pan, put upside-down plate over pan.
4. Hold plate firmly.
5. Reverse pan.
6. Turn frittata out onto plate.
7. Return pan to heat and carefully slide frittata into pan and cook other side. When eggs are well set on second side (about 1 minute), reverse frittata onto a serving plate.

ARTICHOKE FRITTATA

T his is a favorite frittata. The artichokes, cut into wedges and sautéed until golden, are a perfect complement to the eggs. This dish is typical of Tuscan cooking.

    8 medium artichoke hearts
    1 tablespoon lemon
    4 tablespoons flour
   12 egg whites or 2 cartons egg substitute
    1 teaspoon Spike
    1 tablespoon Italian seasoning
      Pepper, freshly ground

Place artichoke hearts in bowl of water with lemon juice. Drain artichokes well, and pat them dry. Dredge artichoke hearts in flour. Spray 10-inch skillet with vegetable cooking spray, and sauté them, a few at a time, until crisp and golden. Drain on paper towels. Continue until all artichokes are sautéed.

Beat eggs in mixing bowl until light and frothy, and season with Spike, Italian seasoning, and pepper. Using same skillet, spread artichokes evenly on bottom of pan, and add eggs. Reduce heat to low, and continue to cook until bottom of omelet begins to brown.

Place pan under broiler for a couple of minutes to brown top and set eggs. Serve hot or at room temperature.

Serves 6

NUTRITIONAL DATA

PER SERVING		EXCHANGES	
calories	74	milk	0.0
% calories from fat	2	vegetable	1.0
fat (gm)	0.2	fruit	0.0
sat. fat (gm)	0	bread	0.0
cholesterol (mg)	0	meat	1.0
sodium (mg)	146	fat	0.0
protein (gm)	9		
carbohydrate (gm)	9.5		

FRITTATA FIESOLE STYLE

*I n this recipe the eggs are beaten lightly before
being added to the pan. They float on top of
the vegetables and are actually steamed. This
makes a superb, light, and digestible omelet.*

- 2 cloves garlic, minced
- 1 lb. Swiss chard (or spinach), washed, stems
  removed, and roughly chopped (2 cups)
- 12 egg whites or 2 cartons egg substitute
  Spike, to taste
  Pepper, freshly ground, to taste

Heat large skillet sprayed with vegetable cooking spray. Add garlic, and sauté over medium heat for 1 minute. Add chard, mix well, and cook until tender, about 10 to 15 minutes. Do not add water. When chard is tender, distribute it evenly to cover bottom of pan.

Beat eggs very briefly. Pour eggs on top of chard. Do not mix them together. Season with Spike and pepper, reduce heat to low, and cover skillet. Cook for 5 minutes, then remove from heat, keeping top on pan until eggs are firm, about 15 minutes. Eggs should be cooked but not hard and dry. Serve hot or at room temperature.

Serves 6

NUTRITIONAL DATA

PER SERVING		EXCHANGES	
calories	38	milk	0.0
% calories from fat	0	vegetable	0.0
fat (gm)	0	fruit	0.0
sat. fat (gm)	0	bread	0.0
cholesterol (mg)	0	meat	1.0
sodium (mg)	132	fat	0.0
protein (gm)	7.3		
carbohydrate (gm)	1.5		

PASTA FRITTATA

1 lb. dried pasta, such as penne
¼ cup liquid Butter Buds
5 sprigs Italian parsley, leaves only
5 sprigs oregano
12 egg whites or 2 cartons egg substitute
¼ cup Parmesan cheese, freshly grated
10 fresh mint leaves
8 large basil leaves
  Spike, to taste
  Black pepper, freshly ground, to taste
1 scant tablespoon olive oil

Boil large pot of cold water. Add pasta and cook according to package directions until al dente. Drain pasta and put it in large bowl with butter. Toss very well so that Butter Buds coat cooked pasta. Cover bowl, and let stand for about 15 minutes.

Finely chop parsley and oregano.

In large bowl, beat eggs with fork, adding grated Parmesan, mint leaves, 3 basil leaves, parsley, and oregano. Add Spike and pepper to taste. Add cooked pasta, and mix thoroughly.

Place 10-inch omelet pan sprayed with vegetable cooking spray over medium heat. Prepare frittata following directions (see p. 36). When frittata is on serving platter, spread remaining whole basil leaves over it and serve.

Serves 6

NUTRITIONAL DATA

PER SERVING		EXCHANGES	
calories	340	milk	0.0
% calories from fat	14	vegetable	0.0
fat (gm)	4.9	fruit	0.0
sat. fat (gm)	1.4	bread	3.5
cholesterol (mg)	3.3	meat	1.0
sodium (mg)	313	fat	0.5
protein (gm)	19.2		
carbohydrate (gm)	51.5		

FRITTATA PROFUMATA
(From Southern Italy)

10 Sprigs Italian parsley, leaves only
15 fresh basil leaves, torn into thirds
15 whole mint leaves
12 egg whites or 2 cartons egg substitute
    Spike, to taste
    Black pepper, freshly ground, to taste

Wash parsley, basil, and mint, and dry on paper towels. Finely chop parsley on board. Begin to make frittata, following directions above. Then add chopped parsley, basil, mint, Spike, and a little pepper to beaten eggs. Mix with fork.

Finish making frittata and sprinkle with a little more black pepper before serving. Frittata may be served hot or at room temperature.
Serves 6

NUTRITIONAL DATA

PER SERVING		EXCHANGES	
calories	41	milk	0.0
% calories from fat	3	vegetable	0.0
fat (gm)	0.1	fruit	0.0
sat. fat (gm)	0	bread	0.0
cholesterol (mg)	0	meat	1.0
sodium (mg)	112	fat	0.0
protein (gm)	7.4		
carbohydrate (gm)	2.1		

Red Onion Frittata

12 egg whites or 2 cartons egg substitute
1 tablespoon water
½ teaspoon black pepper, freshly ground
2 medium red onions, cut into ¼-inch slices and separated into rings
1 tablespoon balsamic or red wine vinegar

In bowl, beat eggs with water to blend, then beat in pepper. Set aside.

Spray vegetable cooking spray on 10-inch omelet pan with ovenproof handle, and place over medium heat. Add onions; cook, stirring, until softened (about 8 minutes). Spread onions evenly in pan. Pour in egg mixture. Cook, puncturing eggs with fork to let uncooked portion flow underneath, until eggs begin to set on top but are still moist (about 5 minutes).

Remove frittata from heat, then broil about 6 inches below heat until puffy and lightly browned (about 2 minutes). Slide onto plate, and cut into wedges to serve.

Serves 6

NUTRITIONAL DATA

PER SERVING		EXCHANGES	
calories	52	milk	0.0
% calories from fat	1	vegetable	0.5
fat (gm)	0.1	fruit	0.0
sat. fat (gm)	0	bread	0.0
cholesterol (mg)	0	meat	1.0
sodium (mg)	112	fat	0.0
protein (gm)	7.5		
carbohydrate (gm)	4.8		

ROASTED TOMATO FRITTATA

1½ lbs. Roma-type tomatoes, cored and cut into halves lengthwise

1 small onion, finely chopped

12 egg whites or 2 cartons egg substitute

1 tablespoon water

½ teaspoon pepper

½ teaspoon nutmeg

¼ cup Parmesan cheese, freshly grated

½ cup lightly packed small fresh basil leaves

¼ cup lightly packed oregano sprigs

Place tomatoes, cut side up, in 9 × 13-inch baking dish sprayed with vegetable cooking spray. Bake, uncovered, in 450-degree oven for 20 minutes; sprinkle with onion, and continue to bake until tomatoes are browned at edges and bubbly on top (about 20 more minutes).

Spray vegetable cooking spray on 10- to 12-inch nonstick frying pan with oven-proof handle, and place over medium heat. Arrange tomato mixture in pan, placing tomato halves cut side down.

In bowl, beat eggs with water to blend; then beat in pepper, nutmeg, cheese, basil, and oregano. Pour mixture over tomatoes. Cook, lifting edges with wooden spoon to let uncooked portion flow underneath until eggs begin to set on top but are still moist (about 5 minutes).

Transfer frittata to broiler; broil about 6 inches below heat until puffy and slightly browned (about 2 minutes). Slide onto plate, and cut into wedges to serve.

Serves 6

NUTRITIONAL DATA

PER SERVING		EXCHANGES	
calories	92	milk	0.0
% calories from fat	18	vegetable	1.5
fat (gm)	1.9	fruit	0.0
sat. fat (gm)	0.9	bread	0.0
cholesterol (mg)	3.3	meat	1.0
sodium (mg)	200	fat	0.0
protein (gm)	10.3		
carbohydrate (gm)	9.2		

ZUCCHINI-PARMESAN FRITTATA

12 egg whites or 2 cartons egg substitute
 1 tablespoon water
½ teaspoon black pepper, freshly ground
½ teaspoon nutmeg
 1 medium zucchini, thinly sliced
 1 small red bell pepper, seeded and cut into ½-inch squares
¼ cup Parmesan cheese, freshly grated

In bowl, beat eggs with water to blend, then beat in pepper and nutmeg. Set aside.

Spray vegetable cooking spray on 10-inch omelet pan with oven-proof handle, and place over medium heat. Add zucchini and bell pepper; cook, stirring until softened (about 8 minutes).

Spread vegetables evenly in pan. Pour in egg mixture. Cook, puncturing eggs with fork to let uncooked portion flow underneath, until eggs begin to set on top but are still moist (about 5 minutes).

Remove frittata from heat; sprinkle with cheese, then broil about 6 inches below heat until puffy and lightly browned (about 2 minutes). Slide onto plate and cut into wedges to serve.
    Serves 6

NUTRITIONAL DATA

PER SERVING		EXCHANGES	
calories	61	milk	0.0
% calories from fat	21	vegetable	0.5
fat (gm)	1.4	fruit	0.0
sat. fat (gm)	0.9	bread	0.0
cholesterol (mg)	3.3	meat	1.0
sodium (mg)	188	fat	0.0
protein (gm)	9.2		
carbohydrate (gm)	2.5		

OMELET FLAN

*I*n this hearty dish, Italian herb omelets are combined with tomato sauce and cheese and baked. This is a nice buffet dish, and you can make substitutions, such as bechamel sauce for tomato, and vary the cheeses.

12 egg whites or 2 cartons egg substitute
 2 tablespoons flour
¼ cup skim milk
½ teaspoon Spike
    Pepper, freshly ground, to taste
 2 tablespoons parsley, chopped
 2 tablespoons basil, chopped
 2 tablespoons chives, chopped
 1 oz. Gruyère or fontina cheese, grated
¼ cup Parmesan cheese, freshly grated
1½ cups Basic Tomato-Basil Sauce (see index) or
    purchased
 1 tomato, sliced
 8 fresh basil leaves

Beat eggs, flour, milk, Spike, and pepper together in mixing bowl until eggs are light and frothy. Add chopped herbs, mix well, and set aside.

Spray a 8- or 9-inch omelet pan with vegetable cooking spray. Add ¼ cup of egg batter, tip pan to distribute, and cook over low heat until browned on bottom. Then turn omelet and brown other side. Transfer omelet to plate, and continue until all omelets are prepared, adding butter to pan as necessary.

To assemble stack, spray baking dish slightly larger in diameter than diameter of omelets with vegetable cooking spray. Combine Gruyere or fontina and Parmesan in mixing bowl. Place omelet in bottom of dish; cover with 2 tablespoons of tomato sauce and 2 tablespoons of cheese mixture. Repeat until all ingredients are used. Cover top omelet with remaining tomato sauce and then the cheeses, allowing sauce to spill over the sides.

Bake in preheated 350-degree oven for 15 minutes, until cheese is melted and begins to brown. Remove from oven, and transfer to heated serving platter. Garnish with tomato slices and basil. Serve hot, cutting stack in wedges like a cake.

Serves 8

NUTRITIONAL DATA

PER SERVING		EXCHANGES	
calories	117	milk	0.0
% calories from fat	30	vegetable	1.5
fat (gm)	4	fruit	0.0
sat. fat (gm)	1.9	bread	0.0
cholesterol (mg)	13.3	meat	1.5
sodium (mg)	322	fat	0.0
protein (gm)	11.9		
carbohydrate (gm)	8.7		

BAKED OMELETS WITH RICOTTA AND MUSHROOMS

OMELETS

12 egg whites or 2 cartons egg substitute

¼ cup skim milk

2 tablespoons flour

1 teaspoon Spike

Pepper, freshly ground, to taste

FILLING

Vegetable cooking spray

¾ lb. mushrooms, washed, trimmed, and thinly sliced

2 cloves garlic, minced

½ lb. ricotta cheese

2 tablespoons Parmesan cheese, freshly grated

3 tablespoons fresh parsley, chopped

Pinch of nutmeg

TOPPING

Mock Béchamel Sauce (see index)

2 tablespoons Parmesan cheese, freshly grated

To make Omelets: Beat eggs in mixing bowl with milk and flour until light and frothy, and season with Spike and pepper.

Spray 8-inch skillet with vegetable cooking spray, and add ¼ cup of egg mixture; cook as you would crepes. Tip pan to distribute eggs evenly, and turn omelet when browned on one side to cook the other.

Transfer cooked omelet to plate and repeat, adding spray to pan as necessary, until all eggs are cooked. You will end up with 12 omelets. Set aside.

To make Filling: Spray saucepan with vegetable spray. Add mushrooms and garlic, and sauté over high heat until mushrooms begin to brown, about 5 minutes. Remove from heat and set aside.

Spray an 8×12-inch baking dish. Combine ricotta and 2 tablespoons of Parmesan and parsley in mixing bowl, add nutmeg and mushrooms, and combine thoroughly. Place about 2 tablespoons of filling on each omelet, roll them up, and place them in sprayed baking dish.

To make Topping: Make Mock Béchamel Sauce (see index), and distribute 2 tablespoons evenly over omelets. Sprinkle with Parmesan, and bake in 350-degree oven for 20 minutes, until top begins to brown. Serve hot from baking dish.

Serves 6

NUTRITIONAL DATA

PER SERVING		EXCHANGES	
calories	192	milk	0.5
% calories from fat	31	vegetable	0.5
fat (gm)	6.6	fruit	0.0
sat. fat (gm)	4.1	bread	0.5
cholesterol (mg)	23.9	meat	2.0
sodium (mg)	387	fat	0.0
protein (gm)	18.1		
carbohydrate (gm)	14.6		

4
SALADS & DRESSINGS
(INSALATE)

Italian salads usually reflect the season. Some feature the tender, young vegetables of spring, some have summer's tomatoes and zucchini, and winter salads contain beets and turnips.

Salads can serve as first courses, main dishes, side dishes with main dishes, or as desserts. Be broad-minded and you will find salad makings in every season. Be inventive and create salads with originality.

Olive Oil

Basics needed to make great salads include good olive oil and vinegar. Some of the best olive oil comes from Italy. Although some northern dishes are made with butter, it is olive oil that gives most Italian cooking its characteristic flavor.

The flavor of the oil varies according to the type of olives it is pressed from, the region where the olives are grown, and the method of pressing. The best oils have a clean, fruity aroma, a full but not heavy body, and a fruity or peppery flavor.

Olive oils are categorized according to acidity and the procedure used to make them. To qualify for the top four categories, oil must be pressed from olives that have received no chemical treatment.

Extra-Virgin oil contains no more than 1 percent oleic acid.

Super-fine Virgin olive oil contains no more than 1.5 percent oleic acid.

Fine Virgin olive oil contains no more than 3 percent oleic acid.

Virgin olive oil contains no more than 4 percent oleic acid.

Olive oil that contains more than 4 percent oleic acid is considered unfit for human consumption. Some large olive oil manufacturers treat this oil with chemical solvents to reduce the acid below 4 percent, then add some virgin oil to improve the flavor. The result is called pure olive oil.

Heat changes the character of olive oil. For frying or sautéing, it makes little sense to use an expensive extra-virgin oil because you would not notice the benefits. Use a good-tasting less expensive one, and save your best oils for uncooked dishes or for drizzling on cooked dishes at the end of the cooking.

Store all olive oils in a cool, dark place; they go rancid when exposed to heat and light. All oils should be used within a year.

Vinegar

In the past, plain white vinegar was traditional in Italy. Within the last 10 years, however, more vinegars are being used: raspberry, tarragon, sherry, and lately cider, a delicious light vinegar with little acidity, yet a full and developed flavor. Both red and white vinegar are commonly used.

Balsamic Vinegar is made from the cooked and concentrated must of Trebbiano white grapes, exists in two forms, one common and one scarce. The first is labeled, simply *aceto balsamico* (balsamic vinegar), with the characteristic flavor of a little caramelized sugar. It has a sweet yet vinegary fragrance, and it is a beautiful dark brown color glinting with gold. This is the balsamic vinegar found in Italian shops and good supermarkets in America. It is a good product that can be used without qualms in most recipes presented here.

The other, rarer balsamic vinegar is called *aceto balsamico tradizionale,* and by law it can only be given this name when it has been aged for at least 10 years. This balsamic vinegar is similar in color to the first, but its flavor is full and velvety, a perfect balance between sweet and sour, with a more subtle, elegant fragrance. Made on a very small scale in and around Reggio Emilia and, above all, Modena, *aceto Balsamico tradizionale* is the object of a gastronomic cult.

ITALIAN MIXED SALAD
(Insalata Mista)

T he typical Italian green salad is simply the freshest seasonal greens in a light oil-and-vinegar dressing. The range of salad greens used in Italy is enormous.

Arrange 6 cups of greens in a bowl (combine endive, butter lettuce, dandelion, purple kale, arugula, and romaine)

- 1 cup chive blossoms
- 1 red onion, sliced thinly
- 1 recipe Italian Vinaigrette (see p. 69)
- 2 tablespoons Parmesan cheese, freshly grated

Place greens, chive blossoms, and onion in a bowl. Toss lightly. Pour dressing over greens, and toss again.

Note: Tomato Vinaigrette (see p. 70) is also excellent on this salad.

Serves 6

NUTRITIONAL DATA

PER SERVING		EXCHANGES	
calories	46	milk	0.0
% calories from fat	16	vegetable	2.0
fat (gm)	0.9	fruit	0.0
sat. fat (gm)	0.4	bread	0.0
cholesterol (mg)	1.6	meat	0.0
sodium (mg)	54	fat	0.0
protein (gm)	2.5		
carbohydrate (gm)	6.6		

FENNEL SALAD

T *he clean, fresh flavor of raw fennel is welcome after a hearty meal.*

4 medium fennel

1 tablespoon parsley, chopped

1 teaspoon of dried oregano

¼ teaspoon Spike

Pepper, freshly ground, to taste

¼ cup Italian Vinaigrette (see p. 69)

Cut off and discard tops of fennel and trim base. Discard tough outer layers. Rinse well under cold water. Cut fennel horizontally into slices ⅛ to ¼ inch thick and place them in salad bowl.

Combine remaining ingredients in mixing bowl, and mix well. Pour over fennel, toss, and serve.

Serves 6

NUTRITIONAL DATA

PER SERVING		EXCHANGES	
calories	17	milk	0.0
% calories from fat	9	vegetable	0.5
fat (gm)	0.2	fruit	0.0
sat. fat (gm)	0	bread	0.0
cholesterol (mg)	0	meat	0.0
sodium (mg)	73	fat	0.0
protein (gm)	0.9		
carbohydrate (gm)	2.9		

SPRING SALAD

  4 small carrots
 12 radishes
  2 heads romaine lettuce
  1 bunch arugula
 ¼ cup Italian Vinaigrette (see p. 69)
 12 slices Italian bread
  2 tablespoons Parmesan cheese, coarsely grated

Scrub carrots and radishes. Grate them coarsely by hand or in food processor. Wash and dry romaine; remove outer leaves and reserve for another use. Wrap hearts in damp paper towels and refrigerate until ready to use. Wash and dry arugula; wrap in damp towels and refrigerate.

Add carrots and radishes to bowl and toss to coat with dressing. Marinate at room temperature for about 20 minutes.

To serve, arrange Romaine hearts, bread, and arugula on individual plates. Top with vegetables, spooning some of vegetables and dressing over bread rounds. Garnish with Parmesan.

Serves 4

NUTRITIONAL DATA

PER SERVING		EXCHANGES	
calories	331	milk	0.0
% calories from fat	4	vegetable	3.0
fat (gm)	1.5	fruit	0.0
sat. fat (gm)	0.6	bread	3.5
cholesterol (mg)	2.5	meat	0.0
sodium (mg)	555	fat	0.0
protein (gm)	13.4		
carbohydrate (gm)	63.4		

SUMMER SALAD OF ZUCCHINI AND TOMATOES

The mint in this dish implies that its origin was Roman. This is excellent spooned onto hard crusty rolls for a summer sandwich.

- ½ lb. small, firm green zucchini
- ½ lb. small yellow crookneck squash
- 4 tomatoes, peeled, seeded, and diced
- ¼ cup Tomato Vinaigrette (see p. 70)
- 3 tablespoons fresh parsley, minced
- 1 tablespoon fresh chives, minced
- 1 tablespoon fresh mint, minced
- 1 head butter lettuce
- 1 head red leaf lettuce
  Spike, to taste
- 1 teaspoon black pepper, freshly ground
  Additional mint leaves for garnish

Grate zucchini and squash coarsely. Add tomatoes. Add parsley, chives, and mint to dressing; pour over salad and set aside.

Wash and dry lettuces; tear into bite-sized pieces. Arrange on a large serving platter. Season with Spike and pepper. Pile vegetables onto platter; garnish with mint leaves.

Serves 4

NUTRITIONAL DATA

PER SERVING		EXCHANGES	
calories	128	milk	0.0
% calories from fat	11	vegetable	5.0
fat (gm)	1.9	fruit	0.0
sat. fat (gm)	0.3	bread	0.0
cholesterol (mg)	0	meat	0.0
sodium (mg)	172	fat	0.0
protein (gm)	6.1		
carbohydrate (gm)	26.2		

♥

WHITE BEAN SALAD WITH PEPPERS

The combination of white beans and peppers can be found all over Italy. It can be used as a picnic salad, as an antipasto, or as a side dish. Dress them while they're warm so that they absorb the flavors of lemon, oil, and onion.

    2 cups dried white beans
    ½ white onion, stuck with 2 cloves
    1 bay leaf
    1 large sprig fresh thyme
    1 large sprig fresh parsley
    2 teaspoons Spike
    ¼ cup Italian Vinaigrette (see p. 69)
    ½ cup tomatoes, peeled, seeded, and diced
    2 green onions, minced
    2 sun-dried tomatoes (from jar), slivered
    2 tablespoons lemon juice
    1 tablespoon white wine vinegar
    1 recipe Marinated Peppers (Peperonata) (see index)
       Lettuce leaves (optional)
    4 thick slices bread, brushed with olive oil and
       grilled or toasted

Cover beans with cold water and soak 1 hour. Drain; place beans in large kettle. Add onion, bay leaf, thyme, parsley, and Spike. Cover with water; bring to a boil. Reduce heat; simmer until beans are just tender, about 45 minutes. Drain; discard onion, bay leaf, thyme, and parsley.

Cool beans slightly; place in a stainless steel, glass, or ceramic bowl. Add vinaigrette, tomatoes, green onions, sun-dried tomatoes, lemon juice, and vinegar. Cool to room temperature; taste and add Spike if needed.

Stir in marinated peppers, then serve salad as is or atop lettuce leaves. Serve with warm bread.

Serves 4

NUTRITIONAL DATA

PER SERVING		EXCHANGES	
calories	480	milk	0.0
% calories from fat	25	vegetable	3.0
fat (gm)	13.7	fruit	0.0
sat. fat (gm)	2	bread	4.0
cholesterol (mg)	0	meat	0.0
sodium (mg)	179	fat	2.5
protein (gm)	19.8		
carbohydrate (gm)	73.7		

ROMAN POTATO AND ONION SALAD

*D*ress potatoes while they're still warm so they will absorb the maximum flavor. This salad is ideal for picnics.

    3 tablespoons white wine vinegar
    1 tablespoon lemon juice
      Rind of 1 lemon, grated
    2 tablespoons fresh oregano, finely minced
    2 tablespoons small capers, drained
    4 green onions, sliced
    ½ cup white wine
    1 large white onion, sliced in ¼-inch rounds
 1½ lbs. red potatoes
    3 tablespoons parsley, minced
    ½ tablespoon lemon rind, grated

In large bowl, combine vinegar, lemon juice, lemon rind, oregano, capers, and green onions. Whisk in wine. Add onion slices and mix thoroughly.

Bring large pot of water to a boil. Add potatoes and boil until tender. Drain, and when cool enough to handle, slice potatoes ¼ inch thick.

Immediately add potatoes to dressing and toss to mix well. Cool to room temperature, then taste and adjust seasoning. Garnish with minced parsley and lemon rind.

Serves 4

NUTRITIONAL DATA

PER SERVING		EXCHANGES	
calories	191	milk	0.0
% calories from fat	2	vegetable	2.0
fat (gm)	0.3	fruit	0.0
sat. fat (gm)	0.1	bread	2.0
cholesterol (mg)	0	meat	0.0
sodium (mg)	11	fat	0.0
protein (gm)	3.9		
carbohydrate (gm)	40		

TORTELLINI SALAD

A great picnic salad, this can be made a day ahead and left to marinate in the refrigerator.

1 package (16 oz.) uncooked fresh or dried tortellini (cheese or spinach is best)
¼ cup Balsamic Vinaigrette (see p. 71)
   Spike, pinch
   Pepper, pinch
2 tablespoons capers, drained
2 green onions with tops, sliced thinly
2 medium carrots, sliced
2 cups cherry tomatoes, cut in half
2 tablespoons Italian parsley, chopped
¼ cup fresh basil, chopped
   Several sprigs fresh oregano, chopped
2 tablespoons Parmesan cheese

Cook tortellini as directed on package. Rinse with cold water, and drain well. Set aside. In mixing bowl, combine remaining ingredients except Parmesan cheese. Mix well. Pour dressing over tortellini and refrigerate until ready to serve. Before serving, toss well and top with Parmesan cheese.
Serves 8

NUTRITIONAL DATA

PER SERVING		EXCHANGES	
calories	133	milk	0.0
% calories from fat	18	vegetable	1.5
fat (gm)	2.8	fruit	0.0
sat. fat (gm)	2.3	bread	1.0
cholesterol (mg)	11.2	meat	0.0
sodium (mg)	146	fat	0.5
protein (gm)	5.8		
carbohydrate (gm)	22.1		

TOMATO AND POTATO SALAD WITH HERBS

1 lb. small red potatoes

5 fresh plum tomatoes, cut into quarters

½ cup fresh basil, chopped

⅓ cup fresh sage, chopped

⅓ cup fresh mint, chopped

1 small onion, finely chopped (about ¼ cup)

¾ cup Italian Vinaigrette (see p. 69)

Boil potatoes in enough water to cover about 20 minutes or until tender; drain and cool.

Peel potatoes; cut into ½-inch slices. Mix potatoes, tomatoes, basil, sage, mint, and onion. Pour vinaigrette over potato mixture; toss.

Cover and refrigerate about 2 hours, stirring occasionally, until chilled.

Serves 6

NUTRITIONAL DATA

PER SERVING		EXCHANGES	
calories	109	milk	0.0
% calories from fat	5	vegetable	1.5
fat (gm)	0.7	fruit	0.0
sat. fat (gm)	0.1	bread	1.0
cholesterol (mg)	0	meat	0.0
sodium (mg)	14	fat	0.0
protein (gm)	2.9		
carbohydrate (gm)	23.7		

MUSHROOM SALAD

1½ lbs. fresh mushrooms
   Lemon juice
½ cup part-skim mozzarella cheese*
¼ cup Italian Vinaigrette (see p. 69)
 2 tablespoons parsley, finely chopped
   Spike, to taste
   Pepper, freshly ground, to taste
 6 large leaves Boston lettuce
 1 cup herb seasoned croutons

Wash mushrooms, and rub caps with lemon juice. Slice them thin and place in mixing bowl. Cut cheese into 1-inch squares roughly ⅛-inch thick. Place cheese in bowl with mushrooms. Add parsley, Spike, and pepper to vinaigrette, and pour over salad. Mix well, and refrigerate for about 45 minutes. Before serving, top with croutons and mix well.

When ready to serve, place one lettuce leaf on each of 6 salad plates, and divide the mushroom salad among them or serve salad on a large serving platter with the lettuce leaves overlapping around the border.

*Note: Bel Paese, a cheese from Lombardy, is a relatively recent arrival in America. It is a mild, semisoft cheese that is low in butterfat, and it can be substituted for mozzarella.

Serves 6

NUTRITIONAL DATA

PER SERVING		EXCHANGES	
calories	100	milk	0.0
% calories from fat	30	vegetable	1.0
fat (gm)	3.6	fruit	0.0
sat. fat (gm)	2	bread	0.5
cholesterol (mg)	10.7	meat	0.5
sodium (mg)	156	fat	0.5
protein (gm)	8		
carbohydrate (gm)	10.3		

HARLEQUIN SALAD

This is a rich salad that is best served as a main dish or as an antipasto or first course.

½ cup Dijonaise Sauce (see p. 286)
3 medium firm tomatoes, sliced and seeded
4 oz. part-skim mozzarella cheese, shredded
1 small cucumber, peeled and sliced
¼ cup white wine
2 tablespoons lemon juice
¼ teaspoon prepared mustard
¼ teaspoon Spike
2 tablespoons capers
6 fresh basil leaves, chopped
Fresh oregano sprigs

On one end of an oval or round serving dish, place one slice of tomato. Spread 1 teaspoon of the Dijonaise sauce on it. On top of that, overlapping tomato but not covering it completely, place a slice of mozzarella. On top of mozzarella, without covering completely, place 1 cucumber slice. Repeat in an attractive pattern, starting with the tomato slice until all the ingredients are used.

Make dressing by combining in mixing bowl wine, lemon juice, mustard, and Spike. Add capers and basil, and combine. When ready to serve, garnish plate with oregano, placing some in center if you are using a round serving platter. Drizzle dressing over salad and serve.

Serves 6

NUTRITIONAL DATA

PER SERVING		EXCHANGES	
calories	92	milk	0.0
% calories from fat	32	vegetable	2.5
fat (gm)	3.6	fruit	0.0
sat. fat (gm)	2	bread	0.0
cholesterol (mg)	10.7	meat	0.0
sodium (mg)	315	fat	0.5
protein (gm)	5.7		
carbohydrate (gm)	10		

SICILIAN MIXED SALAD

1 large head romaine or Boston lettuce, washed and
  dried

2 medium, ripe tomatoes, cut in wedges

1 cup cucumber, peeled and thinly sliced

¼ cup Italian black olives, pitted and roughly
  chopped

2 tablespoons parsley, coarsely chopped

1 medium red onion, thinly sliced

¼ cup Italian Vinaigrette (see p. 69)

1½ cups garlic-flavored croutons

Divide whole lettuce leaves into two equal portions. Arrange half
around rim of salad bowl. Tear remaining leaves into small pieces
and place them in salad bowl. Distribute tomatoes, cucumber
slices, and olives over torn lettuce and set vegetables aside.

When ready to serve, distribute onions over vegetables, top with
croutons, pour dressing over all, sprinkle with parsley, and toss
well.

Serves 8

NUTRITIONAL DATA

PER SERVING		EXCHANGES	
calories	54	milk	0.0
% calories from fat	27	vegetable	1.5
fat (gm)	1.7	fruit	0.0
sat. fat (gm)	0.2	bread	0.0
cholesterol (mg)	0	meat	0.0
sodium (mg)	214	fat	0.5
protein (gm)	1.8		
carbohydrate (gm)	8.3		

ARTICHOKE SUMMER SALAD

2 packages (20 oz. each) frozen artichoke hearts
1 cup Balsamic Vinaigrette (see p. 71)
1 tablespoon flat fillets of anchovy in oil, finely chopped
1 teaspoon fennel seed, crushed
¼ teaspoon Spike
¼ teaspoon pepper, freshly ground
1 head romaine, torn into bite-size pieces
¼ cup fresh parsley, chopped
1 tablespoon capers, drained

Cook artichoke hearts as directed on package; drain and cool. Mix ¾ cup of dressing with fillet of anchovy in jar with tight-fitting lid. Shake well. Combine artichokes with remaining ingredients in large bowl. Pour dressing over salad, and serve.
Serves 6

NUTRITIONAL DATA

PER SERVING		EXCHANGES	
calories	74	milk	0.0
% calories from fat	8	vegetable	3.0
fat (gm)	0.8	fruit	0.0
sat. fat (gm)	1.1	bread	0.0
cholesterol (mg)	1.1	meat	0.0
sodium (mg)	169	fat	0.0
protein (gm)	4.9		
carbohydrate (gm)	15.1		

PIQUANT SALAD

½ lb. fresh green beans
1 head radicchio
1 teaspoon capers, drained
2 small bulbs fennel, cut into quarters
1 head Boston lettuce, torn into bite-size pieces
1 jar (6 oz.) marinated artichoke hearts, drained
½ cup Tomato Vinaigrette (see p. 70)
½ teaspoon fresh mint, chopped
½ teaspoon fresh sage, chopped
½ teaspoon fresh oregano, chopped
½ teaspoon Spike
¼ teaspoon pepper
1 clove garlic, chopped

Boil green beans in enough water to cover about 10 minutes or steam until crisp and tender, about 8 minutes. Drain and cool. Arrange radicchio leaves around edge of large platter. Mix beans, capers, fennel, Boston lettuce, and artichoke hearts; place in center of radicchio-lined platter. Mix remaining ingredients; pour over salad.

Serves 4

NUTRITIONAL DATA

PER SERVING		EXCHANGES	
calories	96	milk	0.0
% calories from fat	7	vegetable	4.0
fat (gm)	0.9	fruit	0.0
sat. fat (gm)	0.1	bread	0.0
cholesterol (mg)	0	meat	0.0
sodium (mg)	370	fat	0.0
protein (gm)	5.6		
carbohydrate (gm)	18.7		

BEAN-STUFFED TOMATOES

T his is a wonderful barbecue recipe. It goes well with steak, shrimp, or chicken.

- 1 9-oz. package frozen Italian green beans
- 6 medium-large fresh tomatoes
- 1 cup mushrooms, sliced
- ⅓ cup Italian Vinaigrette (see p. 69)
- 4 green onions, sliced
- ¼ teaspoon Spike
- ¼ teaspoon pepper, freshly ground
- 6 large Boston lettuce leaves
- 6 large fresh basil leaves

Cook green beans according to package directions. While green beans are cooking, cut thin slice from tops of 6 medium tomatoes. Scoop out center, leaving shell about ¼-inch thick. Invert on paper towels to drain; chill.

Drain beans thoroughly, and place in bowl with mushrooms and green onion. Pour on dressing, and toss well. Add green beans, and toss again.

At serving time season shells with Spike and pepper, and fill with bean mixture. Place 1 tomato on top of a Boston lettuce leaf and top tomato with basil leaves.

Serves 6

NUTRITIONAL DATA

PER SERVING		EXCHANGES	
calories	53	milk	0.0
% calories from fat	9	vegetable	2.0
fat (gm)	0.7	fruit	0.0
sat. fat (gm)	0.1	bread	0.0
cholesterol (mg)	0	meat	0.0
sodium (mg)	21.5	fat	0.0
protein (gm)	2.4		
carbohydrate (gm)	11.3		

RICE SALAD
(Insalata di Riso)

Although it may come as a surprise to some, cooked rice is excellent in salads. It complements raw vegetables and responds well to vinaigrette dressing.

1½ cups Italian or long-grain rice
⅓ cup Italian Vinaigrette (see p. 69)
3 scallions, chopped
1 tablespoon parsley, chopped
1 tablespoon basil, chopped
⅓ cup red or green bell pepper, diced
⅓ cup celery, diced
⅓ cup cucumber, peeled and diced
2 large firm tomatoes, seeded and diced
¼ cup chopped Italian hot marinated peppers
2 tablespoons capers
¼ cup Italian black olives, pitted and chopped
   Spike, to taste
   Pepper, freshly ground, to taste
1 large firm tomato, seeded and cut into wedges
   Black or green olives
   Parsley sprigs

Bring 4 cups of water to boil, add rice, reduce heat, and simmer for 15 minutes, until rice is cooked al dente. Drain, and place rice in mixing bowl. Add vinaigrette and scallions. Combine well. Set aside to cool.

When cooled, add remaining salad ingredients, toss to mix thoroughly, and adjust for taste with Spike and pepper. Mound salad on serving platter, and garnish with tomato wedges, olives, and parsley.

Serves 6

NUTRITIONAL DATA

PER SERVING		EXCHANGES	
calories	273	milk	0.0
% calories from fat	28	vegetable	1.0
fat (gm)	8.7	fruit	0.0
sat. fat (gm)	1.9	bread	2.5
cholesterol (mg)	3.5	meat	0.0
sodium (mg)	335	fat	1.5
protein (gm)	5.2		
carbohydrate (gm)	41.8		

CHICKEN, SPINACH, AND TOMATO SALAD

1 small onion, chopped (about ½ cup)

6 skinless, boneless chicken breast halves (about 1½ lbs.)

½ cup dry white wine

¾ cup Italian Vinaigrette (see 69)

1 lb. spinach leaves

6 medium tomatoes, sliced

¼ cup Parmesan cheese, freshly grated

Several fresh rosemary sprigs and basil leaves (for garnish)

Spray a skillet with vegetable cooking spray, and sauté onion over medium-high heat. Reduce heat to medium; add chicken breasts. Cook uncovered about 5 minutes, turning frequently, until chicken is brown; add wine. Cover, and simmer about 10 minutes or until chicken is done. Refrigerate until cold.

Cut chicken into strips. Set aside. Arrange one-third of the spinach on large platter; top with one-third of tomatoes and chicken. Repeat twice with remaining spinach, tomatoes, and chicken; drizzle with vinaigrette. Sprinkle with cheese. Garnish with fresh rosemary, and basil if desired.

Serves 6

NUTRITIONAL DATA

PER SERVING		EXCHANGES	
calories	184	milk	0.0
% calories from fat	19	vegetable	2.0
fat (gm)	4	fruit	0.0
sat. fat (gm)	1.5	bread	0.0
cholesterol (mg)	49	meat	2.5
sodium (mg)	196	fat	0.0
protein (gm)	22		
carbohydrate (gm)	12.1		

ITALIAN VINAIGRETTE

This is a basic vinaigrette. It is good to keep a bottle of this on hand.

¼ cup lemon juice

¼ cup red wine vinegar

¼ cup white wine

1 teaspoon oregano

1 teaspoon basil

½ teaspoon dry mustard

½ teaspoon onion powder

1 clove garlic, minced

1 tablespoon chives, chopped

1 teaspoon thyme

½ teaspoon rosemary

Combine all ingredients. Chill for an hour or two to allow herbs to blend.

Makes ¾ cup

Serves 12 (1 tablespoon per serving)

NUTRITIONAL DATA

PER SERVING		EXCHANGES	
calories	7.4	milk	0.0
% calories from fat	5	vegetable	0.0
fat (gm)	0.1	fruit	0.0
sat. fat (gm)	0	bread	0.0
cholesterol (mg)	0	meat	0.0
sodium (mg)	3	fat	0.0
protein (gm)	0.1		
carbohydrate (gm)	1.2		

TOMATO VINAIGRETTE

U *se this no-oil version on greens, cold meats, or fish.*

1 can (14½ oz.) chunky tomatoes
2 tablespoons white wine
2 tablespoons white wine vinegar
½ teaspoon basil
½ teaspoon thyme
½ teaspoon Dijon mustard

Combine all ingredients in blender or food processor. Blend on medium speed for about 15 seconds or until combined. Will keep, refrigerated, for 2 days. Shake well before using.

Makes ⅓ cup
Serves 4

NUTRITIONAL DATA

PER SERVING		EXCHANGES	
calories	28	milk	0.0
% calories from fat	9	vegetable	1.0
fat (gm)	0.3	fruit	0.0
sat. fat (gm)	0.1	bread	0.0
cholesterol (mg)	0	meat	0.0
sodium (mg)	176	fat	0.0
protein (gm)	1.0		
carbohydrate (gm)	5.1		

BALSAMIC VINAIGRETTE

¾ cup water
¼ balsamic vinegar
3 teaspoons capers
2 teaspoons Dijon mustard
1 teaspoon tarragon
1 teaspoon thyme
1 tablespoon fresh parsley, chopped

Combine all ingredients. Adjust vinegar to taste; you may feel that it has a strong flavor. Store in a covered container.
Makes about 1 cup
Serves 16 (1 tablespoon per serving)

NUTRITIONAL DATA

PER SERVING		EXCHANGES	
calories	5	milk	0.0
% calories from fat	10	vegetable	0.0
fat (gm)	0.1	fruit	0.0
sat. fat (gm)	0	bread	0.0
cholesterol (mg)	0	meat	0.0
sodium (mg)	9.2	fat	0.0
protein (gm)	0.1		
carbohydrate (gm)	1		

SPRING GARDEN DILL DRESSING

- ½ cup low-fat cottage cheese
- ½ cup low-fat yogurt
- 2 tablespoons fresh dill, minced, or 1 tablespoon dried dill
- 1 tablespoon fresh parsley, minced
- ½ teaspoon Dijon mustard
- 1 tablespoon lemon juice

Combine all ingredients in food processor or blender and process on medium speed for 30 seconds. Chill before serving. Will keep, refrigerated, for 1 week.

Stir before serving.

Makes 1 cup

Serves 8

NUTRITIONAL DATA

PER SERVING		EXCHANGES	
calories	21	milk	0.0
% calories from fat	17	vegetable	0.0
fat (gm)	0.4	fruit	0.0
sat. fat (gm)	0.2	bread	0.0
cholesterol (mg)	1.5	meat	0.5
sodium (mg)	73	fat	0.0
protein (gm)	2.6		
carbohydrate (gm)	1.8		

DIJON DRESSING

1 cup low-fat cottage cheese
4 tablespoons skim milk
3 teaspoons Dijon mustard
3 teaspoons lemon juice
2 tablespoons chives, minced

Combine all ingredients in blender. Process until smooth.
Makes about 1 cup
Serves 16 (1 tablespoon per serving)

NUTRITIONAL DATA

PER SERVING		EXCHANGES	
calories	15	milk	0.0
% calories from fat	20	vegetable	0.0
fat (gm)	0.3	fruit	0.0
sat. fat (gm)	0.2	bread	0.0
cholesterol (mg)	1.3	meat	0.0
sodium (mg)	72	fat	0.0
protein (gm)	2.1		
carbohydrate (gm)	0.8		

CREAMY BLUE CHEESE DRESSING

Rich and creamy, this dressing is excellent for salad greens or sandwiches.

- 1 cup non-fat cottage cheese
- 2 tablespoons blue cheese, crumbled
- 2 tablespoons skim milk
- 1 clove garlic, minced

Place ingredients in blender or food processor. Process for about 20 seconds. (The blue cheese will still be chunky.)
Keeps for 1 week in a tightly covered jar in refrigerator.
Makes 1 cup
Serves 8

NUTRITIONAL DATA

PER SERVING		EXCHANGES	
calories	42	milk	0.0
% calories from fat	23	vegetable	0.0
fat (gm)	1.1	fruit	0.0
sat. fat (gm)	1.3	bread	0.0
cholesterol (mg)	6.2	meat	1.0
sodium (mg)	107	fat	0.0
protein (gm)	6.3		
carbohydrate (gm)	1.6		

STRAWBERRY DRESSING

This is a unique dressing to serve with fruit and vegetable salad combinations.

- ½ cup low-fat yogurt
- ⅓ cup red onions, chopped
- ¼ cup strawberries, sliced
- 3 tablespoons lemon juice
- 2 teaspoons tarragon vinegar
- 1 teaspoon honey
- 1 teaspoon paprika
- ½ teaspoon lemon rind, grated
- Dash of dry mustard

Place all ingredients in blender. Process on medium speed until smooth. Store tightly covered in refrigerator. Will keep for 3 to 5 days. Stir before serving.

Makes 1 cup
Serves 8

NUTRITIONAL DATA

PER SERVING		EXCHANGES	
calories	18	milk	0.0
% calories from fat	13	vegetable	0.5
fat (gm)	0.3	fruit	0.0
sat. fat (gm)	0.2	bread	0.0
cholesterol (mg)	0.9	meat	0.0
sodium (mg)	10	fat	0.0
protein (gm)	0.9		
carbohydrate (gm)	3.4		

5
SOUPS
(ZUPPE)

Whether light or hearty, offered as a first course or a main meal, nourishing soups are a cornerstone of Italian cuisine. Soup can provide a very creative outlet, for the cook can use vegetables without concern, add herbs without restraint, add pasta, rice, beans, meat, fish, or a little of each, and still feed a crowd on a shoestring.

While recipes are flexible, delicious soups depend on the best basic ingredients. The stock is the soul of the soup. Because today's busy cooks may not be able to savor broths for long periods, modern soups often rely on meat or vegetable broth for a flavorful foundation.

While homemade broth is the first choice, top quality canned broth works well, too. If you need to cut down on sodium, you may want to try a low-sodium brand or dilute canned broth by half with water.

Add your favorite vegetables, meats, pasta, or anything that strikes your fancy. Make it your own soup, and just dip in your spoon and enjoy.

VEGETABLE BROTH

     2 tablespoons olive oil
     3 onions, chopped
     2 stalks celery, with leaves, chopped
     2 leeks, white and green parts, chopped
     3 carrots, chopped
     2 cups cabbage, shredded
     ½ cup lentils
     1 cup potatoes, peeled and diced
     ½ teaspoon dried thyme
     ½ cup parsley, chopped
     ¼ cup basil, chopped
8 to 10 whole peppercorns
     3 cloves garlic
     2 bay leaves
     1 teaspoon Spike
       Pinch of nutmeg

Heat oil in stockpot, and sauté together onion, celery, leeks, and carrots for a few minutes, until the onions begin to color. Stir in all remaining ingredients, add 3 quarts of water, and bring to a boil. Reduce heat, and simmer, covered, for 2 hours. Remove from heat and use as required.

Note: Keep a stock of this broth on hand to use in flavoring other dishes, such as potatoes, vegetables, soup, and vegetarian dishes. For a light cream of vegetable soup, puree the vegetables, add evaporated skim milk, and serve. The broth will keep up to a week in the refrigerator or may be frozen.

Makes 13 cups
Serves 13

NUTRITIONAL DATA

PER SERVING		EXCHANGES	
calories	92	milk	0.0
% calories from fat	22	vegetable	1.5
fat (gm)	2.4	fruit	0.0
sat. fat (gm)	0.3	bread	0.5
cholesterol (mg)	0	meat	0.0
sodium (mg)	21	fat	0.5
protein (gm)	3		
carbohydrate (gm)	16		

TORTELLINI SOUP

2 cloves garlic, minced
2 medium stalks celery, chopped
1 small onion, chopped
1 medium carrot, chopped
4 cups low-salt chicken broth
4 cups water
2 packages (10-oz. each) dried cheese-filled tortellini
2 tablespoons fresh parsley, chopped
10 fresh basil leaves, shredded
1 tablespoon fresh oregano, chopped
1 teaspoon Spike
½ teaspoon black pepper, freshly ground
Parmesan cheese

Spray large pot with vegetable cooking spray. Add garlic, celery, onion, and carrot. Cook over medium heat for 10 minutes. Stir in chicken broth and water. Heat to boiling; reduce heat.

Stir in tortellini; cover and simmer 20 minutes, stirring occasionally, or until tortellini are tender. Stir in parsley, basil, and oregano. Season with Spike and pepper.

Cover and cook 10 minutes. Top each serving with Parmesan cheese (not included in Nutritional Data).

Serves 10

NUTRITIONAL DATA

PER SERVING		EXCHANGES	
calories	109	milk	0.0
% calories from fat	19	vegetable	1.0
fat (gm)	2.4	fruit	0.0
sat. fat (gm)	2	bread	1.0
cholesterol (mg)	10	meat	0.0
sodium (mg)	136	fat	0.5
protein (gm)	5.3		
carbohydrate (gm)	16.9		

PASTA E FAGIOLI

*P*erhaps the only soup that's better than a good pasta e fagioli *is a* pasta e fagioli *the second day. If you make it a day ahead, wait to add the pasta until just before you serve it.*

    2 cups dried Great Northern white beans or
      cannellini beans
    2 tablespoons olive oil
    1 cup onion, coarsely chopped
    ½ cup celery, diced
    ½ cup carrot, diced
    1½ tablespoons garlic, minced
    9 cups water
    4½ cups tomatoes, peeled, seeded, and diced
      Spike, to taste
      Black pepper, freshly ground, to taste
    5 oz. pasta, macaroni or small shells

Soak beans overnight in water to cover (no need to refrigerate). Next day, heat olive oil in large stockpot over moderate heat. Add onion and sauté until soft and translucent (about 3 minutes). Add celery, carrot, and garlic, and sauté gently another 5 minutes, stirring occasionally.

Drain beans and add to pot along with 9 cups fresh water and tomatoes. Cover and simmer 1½ hours or until beans are tender. Season to taste with Spike and pepper. If you are using homemade pasta, add it to soup and cook until tender. If you are using dried pasta, cook it until tender in boiling water; drain it well, add to soup, and heat through.

Cool soup slightly before serving. Serve it in warm bowls, topped with a sprinkle of Parmesan cheese (not included in Nutritional Data).

Makes 12 to 14 cups

Serves 12

NUTRITIONAL DATA

PER SERVING		EXCHANGES	
calories	124	milk	0.0
% calories from fat	21	vegetable	1.0
fat (gm)	3.1	fruit	0.0
sat. fat (gm)	1.1	bread	1.0
cholesterol (mg)	10.2	meat	0.0
sodium (mg)	18	fat	0.5
protein (gm)	5		
carbohydrate (gm)	20.4		

MILANESE VEGETABLE-RICE SOUP

RISOTTO

    4 qts. chicken broth (low-salt if canned), divided

1½ cups onion, diced, divided

    1 lb. arborio rice

SOUP

    2 tablespoons olive oil

    1 cup carrots, finely diced

    2 cups spinach, torn into small pieces

    ½ lb. green beans, trimmed and cut into 1-inch pieces

    1 cup zucchini, finely diced

    ½ cup peas

    ½ cup tomato, diced

    1 teaspoon black pepper, freshly ground

    Parmesan cheese, freshly ground

To make Risotto: Simmer 2 quarts chicken broth in a large pot. In a heavy-bottomed saucepan, sprayed with vegetable cooking spray, cook ½ cup onion until just soft. Add rice, and stir well. Begin adding additional broth, a cup at a time, stirring over medium-low heat. As broth is absorbed, add more. Mixture should never be soaked or dry. Continue adding broth and stirring until rice is fairly soft, 18 to 20 minutes. Spread rice in a baking pan lined with wax paper, and allow to cool.

To make Soup: Heat olive oil in pot or large casserole. Add remaining 1 cup onion and carrots and cook over low heat until onions are transparent, 3 to 5 minutes. Add remaining 2 quarts broth and bring to a boil. Add spinach and green beans, and simmer, uncovered, for 20 minutes. Add zucchini, peas, and tomato. Simmer for an additional 10 minutes. Season to taste with pepper. (Soup may be made ahead to this point.)

Place 5 cups of risotto in a large saucepan. Add hot broth and stir gently. Adjust seasoning as desired. Serve in large bowls. Pass Parmesan at the table (not included in Nutritional Data).

Serves 10

NUTRITIONAL DATA

PER SERVING		EXCHANGES	
calories	230	milk	0.0
% calories from fat	14	vegetable	1.0
fat (gm)	3.5	fruit	0.0
sat. fat (gm)	0.5	bread	2.5
cholesterol (mg)	0	meat	0.0
sodium (mg)	44	fat	0.5
protein (gm)	5.6		
carbohydrate (gm)	43.9		

MUSHROOM SOUP

*D*ried *Italian mushrooms called porcini add an earthy flavor to this rustic Piedmonese soup. Save any leftover soaking liquid to flavor other soups, sauces, or stews.*

- 1 oz. dried Italian porcini mushrooms
- 1½ cups hot water
- 1½ tablespoons garlic, minced, plus 1 clove, cut
- ¾ cup onion, thinly sliced
- 2 teaspoons flour
- 6 tablespoons dry white wine
- 4 cups chicken stock
- 4 oz. fresh mushrooms, cleaned and quartered
- 1 teaspoon fresh rosemary
  Spike, to taste
  Black pepper, freshly ground, to taste
- 6 bread rounds, about 2 inches in diameter and ⅓-inch thick, cut from dense, day-old country-style bread
  Olive oil
- ½ cup fresh lemon pulp, chopped
- ½ cup Italian parsley, minced

Soak porcini in hot water 20 minutes. Carefully remove mushrooms with slotted spoon. Strain liquid through cheesecloth and reserve. Pick through porcini carefully to remove grit. Chop coarsely.

Spray a skillet with vegetable cooking spray and place over medium heat. Add onion and garlic and sauté until onion is soft and translucent, about 5 minutes. Add flour and wine; cook gently 5 minutes. Add stock, porcini, and 2 tablespoons of the reserved porcini liquid. Cook 5 minutes. Add fresh mushrooms and cook until they are very tender. Add fresh rosemary, Spike, and black pepper.

Preheat oven to 350 degrees. Rub bread rounds with the cut clove of garlic, brush lightly with olive oil, and toast in oven until browned. Add lemon pulp and half of parsley to soup; reheat gently. Put a bread round in bottom of each of 6 warm bowls, ladle soup over, and garnish with remaining parsley.

Serves 6

NUTRITIONAL DATA

PER SERVING		EXCHANGES	
calories	90	milk	0.0
% calories from fat	10	vegetable	2.0
fat (gm)	1	fruit	0.0
sat. fat (gm)	0.1	bread	0.5
cholesterol (mg)	0	meat	0.0
sodium (mg)	86	fat	0.0
protein (gm)	3.7		
carbohydrate (gm)	14.9		

MINESTRONE PRIMAVERA
(Spring Minestrone)

A *chunky soup chock-full of vegetables often opens an Italian meal, or it can be the meal.*

- 2 tablespoons olive oil
- 1 cup onion, minced
- 2 small leeks, white part only, well washed and thinly sliced
- 3 cups cabbage leaves, coarsely shredded
- 4 cups tomatoes, peeled, seeded, and quartered
- 12 small new potatoes, quartered
- 5 cups chicken broth, divided
- 2 cups carrots in ½-inch thick rounds
- ¾ cup bulb fennel*, chopped
- 1 cup garbanzo beans (chickpeas), cooked and drained
- 1 cup fresh green beans, in 1-inch pieces
- 2 cups tiny cauliflower florets
- 2 cups small shell pasta or macaroni, cooked and drained
- 2 cups fresh shelled peas
  Black pepper, freshly ground, to taste
- 2 tablespoons fresh basil, chopped
- 1 tablespoon fresh oregano, chopped
- ½ cup Italian parsley, minced
  Parmesan cheese, grated

Heat oil in large stock pot. Add onion and leeks, and cook 5 minutes or until onion is soft and translucent but not browned. Add cabbage. Stir to coat cabbage with oil, then sauté 1 minute. Add tomatoes, potatoes, and 3 cups of broth. Simmer 10 minutes. Add carrots, fennel, and ½ cup more stock. Simmer 10 minutes more.

Add remaining stock, garbanzo beans, green beans, cauliflower, and pasta. Simmer 10 minutes. Add peas. Continue simmering until potatoes are fully cooked and peas are crisp-tender. Pasta should be cooked slightly beyond al dente.

Season to taste with pepper. Stir in basil, oregano, and parsley. Serve soup in warm bowls, garnishing with Parmesan cheese (not included in Nutritional Data). Pass additional Parmesan at table if desired.

*Note: To prepare fennel, cut off and discard tops; remove bruised or discolored outer ribs; trim base. Halve bulbs and core them; slice thinly lengthwise.

Serves 8

NUTRITIONAL DATA

PER SERVING		EXCHANGES	
calories	338	milk	0.0
% calories from fat	17	vegetable	4.0
fat (gm)	6.8	fruit	0.0
sat. fat (gm)	1.2	bread	2.5
cholesterol (mg)	1.5	meat	0.0
sodium (mg)	189	fat	1.0
protein (gm)	11.5		
carbohydrate (gm)	61.4		

CREAM OF SPINACH SOUP

This soup may be made with any combination of leaf vegetables, which determine the flavor.

- 2 tablespoons olive oil
- 2 tablespoons fresh parsley, chopped
- 4 cloves garlic, minced
- 1 large leek, thinly sliced
- 1 lb. fresh spinach, torn into bite-size pieces
- 1 cup plain low-fat yogurt
- 3 cups evaporated skim milk
- 2 cups chicken broth
- 1 tablespoon lemon juice
- 1 teaspoon nutmeg, freshly grated
- 1 teaspoon Spike
- ½ teaspoon black pepper, freshly ground

Heat oil in 4-quart Dutch oven over medium-high heat. Sauté parsley, garlic, and leek in oil. Add spinach; cook uncovered over low heat 10 minutes, stirring frequently. Stir in yogurt and milk.

Stir well, and add chicken broth and lemon juice. Heat to near boiling; reduce heat. Cover and simmer 1 hour, stirring occasionally. Stir in remaining ingredients.

Serves 6

NUTRITIONAL DATA

PER SERVING		EXCHANGES	
calories	203	milk	1.5
% calories from fat	26	vegetable	1.5
fat (gm)	6	fruit	0.0
sat. fat (gm)	1.3	bread	0.0
cholesterol (mg)	7.4	meat	0.0
sodium (mg)	249	fat	1.0
protein (gm)	14.7		
carbohydrate (gm)	24.2		

TUSCAN LENTIL SOUP

This is a very inexpensive and popular meal.

- 1 lb. lentils
- 4 cups chicken broth
- 3 cups water
- 2 tablespoons olive oil
- 1 large onion, diced
- 1 sweet red pepper, diced
- 2 cloves garlic
- 4 carrots, diced
- 1 16-oz. can crushed tomatoes
- Spike, to taste
- Black pepper, freshly ground, to taste
- Parmesan cheese

Put lentils, broth, and water in a large soup pot. Bring to a boil, and simmer for 1 hour and 15 minutes.

In a small skillet, gently sauté onion, red pepper, and garlic in the olive oil until tender. Add this and carrots to cooking lentils. Add tomatoes, and simmer for 30 minutes more, or until lentils are very tender. Add Spike and pepper to taste. Serve with sprinkle of Parmesan cheese (not included in Nutritional Data).

Serves 10

NUTRITIONAL DATA

PER SERVING		EXCHANGES	
calories	211	milk	0.0
% calories from fat	15	vegetable	1.5
fat (gm)	3.6	fruit	0.0
sat. fat (gm)	0.5	bread	1.5
cholesterol (mg)	0	meat	1.0
sodium (mg)	409	fat	0.5
protein (gm)	13.3		
carbohydrate (gm)	33.6		

PAY DAY SOUP

M *y Italian neighbor created this soup about 20 years ago when we entered a contest to see who could produce the least expensive meal to serve for pay day, when no one had any money.*

- 2 cloves garlic, minced
- 2 tablespoons olive oil
- 2 medium onions, chopped
- 2 large potatoes, peeled and diced
- 2 cups arborio rice (or your favorite rice will do)
- 2 cups garbanzo beans (chickpeas)
- 4 cups chicken broth
- 4 cups water
- 2 tablespoons fresh parsley, chopped
- 2 tablespoons grated Parmesan cheese

Gently sauté garlic in oil until golden brown. Add onion, potatoes, rice, garbanzo beans, broth, water, and parsley. Stir, bring to boil, and let simmer for 1 hour, stirring occasionally.

Just before serving, stir in the grated cheese.

This is best served immediately with additional cheese sprinkled on top of each serving.

Serves 8

NUTRITIONAL DATA

PER SERVING		EXCHANGES	
calories	359	milk	0.0
% calories from fat	21	vegetable	3.0
fat (gm)	8.5	fruit	0.0
sat. fat (gm)	2	bread	3.0
cholesterol (mg)	4.3	meat	0.0
sodium (mg)	206	fat	1.5
protein (gm)	9.5		
carbohydrate (gm)	61		

♥

ITALIAN MUSHROOM BARLEY SOUP

This is a wonderful low-fat soup that you can serve again and again. It freezes well too.

1½ cups barley
 3 tomatoes, chopped
 2 carrots, chopped
 1 medium onion, chopped
 2 cloves garlic, minced
 6 cups chicken stock
 2 cups tomato juice
 4 fresh basil leaves, chopped
 1 teaspoon fresh oregano, chopped
 1 cup mushrooms, thinly sliced
    Pepper, to taste
    Low-fat yogurt

In a soup pot combine barley, tomatoes, carrots, onion, garlic, chicken stock, tomato juice, and herbs. Stir. Bring to a boil. Lower heat, and cover, but not completely, leaving lid slightly ajar. Stir occasionally. Simmer 1 hour, then stir in mushrooms. Add pepper and let simmer 1 more hour. Ladle into hot soup bowls and top each with a spoonful of yogurt.
    Serves 10

NUTRITIONAL DATA

PER SERVING		EXCHANGES	
calories	135	milk	0.0
% calories from fat	7	vegetable	1.5
fat (gm)	1.1	fruit	0.0
sat. fat (gm)	0.2	bread	1.5
cholesterol (mg)	0	meat	0.0
sodium (mg)	208	fat	0.0
protein (gm)	5.3		
carbohydrate (gm)	27.7		

♥

GREEN VEGETABLE SOUP

½ cup green cabbage, chopped
1 medium onion, chopped
½ cup celery, chopped
½ cup broccoli, chopped
½ cup green beans, cut into 1-inch pieces
½ cup zucchini, diced
2 tablespoons Italian parsley, chopped
2 tablespoons fresh basil, chopped
4 cups water
1 medium potato, diced
1 tablespoon safflower oil
   Salt, to taste
   Black pepper, freshly ground, to taste
½ cup ditali or other small-cut pasta
2 tablespoons Pesto Sauce (see index)

Put all ingredients except the pasta and pesto in a pot and bring to a boil. Cover, and boil gently about 1 hour. Add pesto, and turn off the heat. Bring a large pot of water to a boil, add the pasta, and cook until al dente. Do not overcook. Drain and rinse in cold water. Add to soup. Serve at once with garlic bread.
   Serves 6

NUTRITIONAL DATA

PER SERVING		EXCHANGES	
calories	96	milk	0.0
% calories from fat	26	vegetable	1.5
fat (gm)	2.8	fruit	0.0
sat. fat (gm)	0.4	bread	0.5
cholesterol (mg)	0.7	meat	0.0
sodium (mg)	29	fat	0.5
protein (gm)	2.9		
carbohydrate (gm)	15.6		

White Bean Soup With Spinach

This soup is a meal in a bowl. Serve with bread and a salad.

1½ cups dry white beans (use navy or Great Northern)
2 teaspoons olive oil
1 large onion, chopped
2 cloves garlic, minced
6 cups chicken bouillon, reconstituted from cubes or granules, divided
2 cups water
¼ cup pearl barley
2 large carrots, sliced
2 large stalks celery, sliced
2 large bay leaves
1 teaspoon dried marjoram leaves
1 teaspoon dried basil
½ teaspoon thyme leaves
   Dash cayenne pepper
1 16-oz. can chunky tomatoes
1 10-oz. package chopped frozen spinach, thawed and drained
   Spike, to taste

Cover beans with water in a bowl, and let sit overnight. Place beans in Dutch oven or soup pot. Cover with 2 inches of water, and boil over high heat. Lower heat, and boil 2 minutes. Remove from heat, cover, and let stand 1 hour.

Drain beans in colander, discarding water. In same pot, combine olive oil, onion, garlic, and 3 tablespoons of bouillon. Cook mixture over medium heat, stirring frequently, 4 to 5 minutes or until onion is soft. If liquid begins to evaporate, add a bit more bouillon.

Add remaining bouillon and beans to pot. Add water, barley, carrots, celery, bay leaves, marjoram, basil, thyme, cayenne pepper. Bring to a boil. Reduce heat, and simmer 1 hour and 35 minutes or until beans are tender.

Remove pot from heat. Remove and discard bay leaves. With large spoon, skim fat from top of soup and discard. Add tomatoes and spinach, stirring in and distributing spinach with large spoon. Bring soup to a boil, reduce heat, and simmer, stirring occasionally about 4 to 7 minutes or until spinach is tender. This soup keeps in refrigerator 3 or 4 days.

Serves 8

NUTRITIONAL DATA

PER SERVING		EXCHANGES	
calories	115	milk	0.0
% calories from fat	14	vegetable	3.0
fat (gm)	1.9	fruit	0.0
sat. fat (gm)	1	bread	0.5
cholesterol (mg)	0	meat	0.0
sodium (mg)	806	fat	0.0
protein (gm)	5.4		
carbohydrate (gm)	20.9		

♥

TUSCAN TOMATO SOUP

E very Tuscan cook has a favorite recipe for this regional soup, but each version has two basic elements: ripe tomatoes and crusty bread. To keep this recipe low in fat, the olive oil, usually drizzled on just before serving, has been eliminated.

Light olive oil

1 large onion, chopped

2 cloves garlic, chopped

3 lbs. very ripe tomatoes, peeled, cored, seeded, and coarsely chopped

4 cups chicken broth

1 cup lightly packed fresh basil leaves, coarsely chopped

Spike, to taste

Pepper, to taste

6 slices crusty Italian bread (each about 3 inches wide, 5 inches long, and ½ inch thick)

Heat 2 tablespoons oil in 4- or 5-quart pan over medium heat. Add onion and garlic and cook, stirring occasionally, until onion is golden (about 15 minutes). Stir in tomatoes, then broth. Bring mixture to a boil over high heat; reduce heat and simmer, uncovered, until tomatoes are very soft when pressed (about 20 minutes).

In a food processor or blender, whirl tomato mixture (a portion at a time, if necessary) just until coarsely pureed. Stir in basil; season to taste with Spike and pepper.

While soup is cooking, place bread slices in a single layer on a baking sheet and broil about 4 inches below heat until golden brown on top (1 to 2 minutes). Turn slices over, brush each lightly with olive oil, and broil until golden brown on other side (1 to 2 more minutes).

Place one slice of toasted bread in the bottom of each of 6 wide shallow soup bowls. Ladle soup over bread and serve immediately.

Serves 6

NUTRITIONAL DATA

PER SERVING		EXCHANGES	
calories	195	milk	0.0
% calories from fat	25	vegetable	3.0
fat (gm)	5.6	fruit	0.0
sat. fat (gm)	0.8	bread	1.0
cholesterol (mg)	0	meat	0.0
sodium (mg)	199	fat	1.0
protein (gm)	6.3		
carbohydrate (gm)	31.4		

VEGETABLE SOUP WITH PESTO

*I*n Italy, minestrone *means something different to everyone, but the literal name, "big soup," implies a recipe generously laden with vegetables, grains, beans, and herbs. In the basil-loving town of Genoa, the addition of pungent pesto distinguishes the local version.*

- 2 cups Pesto Sauce (see index)
- 2 large leeks
- 3 qts. chicken broth
- 2 large carrots
- 3 stalks celery, thinly sliced
- 2 cans (about 15 oz. each) cannellini beans, drained and rinsed
- 2 cups dry elbow macaroni
- 1 lb. yellow crookneck squash or yellow zucchini, cut into ½-inch chunks
- 1 large red bell pepper, seeded and chopped
- 1 large yellow bell pepper, seeded and chopped
- 1 cup frozen tiny peas, thawed

Prepare pesto; set aside.

Trim root ends and tough green tops from leeks; split lengthwise, rinse thoroughly, and thinly slice crosswise.

In an 8- to 10-quart pan, combine leeks, broth, carrots, and celery; boil over high heat. Reduce heat, cover, and simmer until vegetables are tender to bite (about 15 minutes). Add beans, macaroni, squash and bell peppers; cover and simmer until macaroni is just tender to bite (about 10 minutes). Add peas; bring to boil. Stir in ½ cup of pesto.

Serve soup hot, at room temperature, or cold. To serve, ladle into bowls and offer remaining pesto to season soup to taste. If made ahead, let cool; then cover and refrigerate until next day. Bring to room temperature or reheat before serving, if desired.

Serves 12

NUTRITIONAL DATA

PER SERVING		EXCHANGES	
calories	224	milk	0.0
% calories from fat	19	vegetable	1.0
fat (gm)	5.2	fruit	0.0
sat. fat (gm)	5	bread	2.0
cholesterol (mg)	23.8	meat	1.0
sodium (mg)	1269	fat	0.0
protein (gm)	14		
carbohydrate (gm)	37.6		

SPRING SOUP

T his soup is best when all the ingredients are fresh, as they are in the spring.

 1 tablespoon olive oil
 1 tablespoon safflower oil
 ½ cup onion, finely chopped
 1 cup tomatoes, fresh if possible (drain if canned), chopped
 1 tablespoon Italian parsley, finely chopped
 4 cups water
 1 cup peas (about ¾ lb.)
 1 cup potatoes, diced
 4 tablespoons long-grain rice
 1½ cups asparagus, cut into 1-inch pieces
 1 cup whole scallions, coarsely chopped
   Spike, to taste
   Black pepper, freshly ground, to taste

Heat two oils in medium pot. Add onion, and sauté until it begins to brown. Add tomatoes, and cook over moderate heat about 5 minutes. Add parsley and water, cover, and bring to a boil. Add peas and potatoes. Boil gently for about 5 minutes.

Add rice, and cook about 6 minutes. Add asparagus and scallions. Add Spike and pepper to taste, and boil gently until rice is done, about 20 more minutes. Test to be sure rice is done.

Serves 6

NUTRITIONAL DATA

PER SERVING		EXCHANGES	
calories	151	milk	0.0
% calories from fat	29	vegetable	1.5
fat (gm)	5	fruit	0.0
sat. fat (gm)	0.6	bread	1.0
cholesterol (mg)	0	meat	0.0
sodium (mg)	32	fat	1.0
protein (gm)	4.6		
carbohydrate (gm)	23.6		

♥

SICILIAN SUMMER TOMATO SOUP

T his tomato soup is unusual because of the addition of herbs, sugar, and orange. I like to make it in the summer, when tomatoes are best.

      2 tablespoons olive oil
      2 red onions, finely chopped
      2 yellow onions, finely chopped
      1 bunch green onions, minced
    ½ cup carrot, minced
    ½ cup celery, minced
      1 cup mushrooms, sliced
    ¼ cup garlic, minced
      1 cup parsley, coarsely chopped
      2 tablespoons tomato paste
  1½ lbs. fresh spinach
    18 plum tomatoes, peeled and chopped
      1 teaspoon sugar
         Rind of 1 orange, grated
    ¼ cup orange juice
      4 cups chicken stock
      1 cup dry white wine
    ½ cup fresh basil leaves
         Spike, to taste
         Black pepper, freshly ground, to taste

Warm olive oil in large pot over moderate heat. Add red and yellow onions; sauté about 5 minutes, until soft and translucent. Add green onion, carrot, celery, mushrooms, garlic, parsley, and tomato paste. Cook for 5 minutes.

Wash spinach and remove stems. Blanch leaves briefly in boiling water. Place spinach in bowl of ice water to stop cooking. Drain well; chop coarsely.

Add chopped tomatoes, spinach, sugar, orange rind, and orange juice to pot. Add stock and wine. Simmer 10 to 15 minutes. Stir in basil and remove from heat. Puree soup in a blender in batches. Return to pot; season to taste with Spike and pepper. Reheat and divide among warm bowls to serve.

Serves 10 as a first course

NUTRITIONAL DATA

PER SERVING		EXCHANGES	
calories	146	milk	0.0
% calories from fat	22	vegetable	4.0
fat (gm)	4.1	fruit	0.0
sat. fat (gm)	0.6	bread	0.0
cholesterol (mg)	0	meat	0.0
sodium (mg)	103	fat	1.0
protein (gm)	5.8		
carbohydrate (gm)	22.2		

STRACCIATELLE WITH TINY MEATBALLS

This is a wonderful soup, with many textures and colors. Stracciatelle *means "torn rags," which is what the eggs look like when you stir them into the hot broth.*

SOUP

- 1 qt. low-salt chicken broth
- 2 cups water
- ½ cup pastina
- 1 teaspoon fresh parsley, chopped
- 1 carrot, sliced thin
- ½ cup celery, sliced
- ½ cup onion, sliced
- ½ lb. spinach (just leafy part, julienne cut)

MEATBALLS

- ½ lb. ground turkey
- 2 tablespoons flavored bread crumbs
- 1 teaspoon grated Parmesan cheese
- 2 teaspoons fresh parsley, chopped
- 1 small onion, minced
- 2 tablespoons tomato paste

- 2 egg whites
  Parmesan cheese, grated

In soup pot, combine soup ingredients and bring to a low boil. Mix meatball ingredients in bowl, make tiny meatballs, and drop into boiling broth mixture. Simmer 20 minutes.

In small bowl, beat egg whites. Remove soup from heat. With a wooden spoon, stir soup as you slowly drop in egg whites, stirring constantly. Cover and let stand 2 minutes.

Serves 8

NUTRITIONAL DATA

PER SERVING		EXCHANGES	
calories	87	milk	0.0
% calories from fat	28	vegetable	1.0
fat (gm)	2.7	fruit	0.0
sat. fat (gm)	0.7	bread	0.0
cholesterol (mg)	10.8	meat	1.0
sodium (mg)	94	fat	0.0
protein (gm)	7.3		
carbohydrate (gm)	8.8		

RED CLAM CHOWDER

- 2 tablespoons olive oil
- 1 large onion, chopped
- 2 cloves garlic, minced
- 2 stalks celery, diced
- 1 medium green pepper, chopped
- 4 medium potatoes, peeled and diced
- 4 carrots, diced
- 2 6½-oz. cans chopped clams, including juice
  Water
- 2 6-oz. bottles clam juice
- 1 14½-oz. can chunky tomatoes
- 2 cups tomato juice
  Dash cayenne pepper
- 1 bay leaf
- 1 tablespoon fresh basil, chopped
- 1 teaspoon fresh oregano, chopped
- ½ teaspoon sugar
- ⅛ teaspoon black pepper, freshly ground

In a large, heavy saucepan or Dutch oven, heat olive oil and add onion, garlic, celery, and green pepper. Cook vegetables over medium heat, stirring frequently, until onion is tender, about 8 minutes. If vegetables begin to stick, lower heat. Add potatoes and carrots to pot and cook for about 20 minutes.

Drain liquid from clams (reserving clams) into a measuring cup and add enough water to make 1¾ cups of liquid. Add this liquid to pan, along with clam juice, tomatoes, and tomato juice. Stir in pepper, bay leaf, basil, oregano, sugar, and black pepper. Bring to a boil.

Cover, lower heat, and simmer 10 to 12 minutes, stirring occasionally, or until potato is tender. Add clams, cover, and bring to a boil. Lower heat, and simmer about 5 minutes longer, until flavors are well blended. Remove and discard bay leaf.

Serves 8

NUTRITIONAL DATA

PER SERVING		EXCHANGES	
calories	162	milk	0.0
% calories from fat	23	vegetable	2.5
fat (gm)	4.4	fruit	0.0
sat. fat (gm)	0.7	bread	1.0
cholesterol (mg)	28.7	meat	0.0
sodium (mg)	408	fat	0.5
protein (gm)	6.9		
carbohydrate (gm)	26.7		

CLAM SOUP

You can make this dish with mussels as well.

- 2 tablespoons olive oil
- 3 large garlic cloves
- 4 dozen clams (littlenecks or cherrystones), well-scrubbed
- 1 cup tomato sauce
- 1 cup dry white wine
- ¼ cup parsley, minced
- 1 teaspoon dried hot red pepper flakes or Tabasco
- 1½ teaspoons dried oregano
- 1 teaspoon thyme
  Spike, to taste
  4 to 8 slices Italian bread, toasted

Heat oil in a deep kettle. Add garlic and cook until garlic is browned; discard garlic. Add clams, tomato sauce, wine, parsley, red pepper, oregano, thyme, and a little Spike. Bring to the boiling point over high heat and cook for about 5 minutes or until clams have opened.

With a slotted spoon, distribute the clams among 4 large bowls or soup plates. Pour broth over each serving of clams. Serve immediately with toasted Italian bread on the side.

Serves 4

NUTRITIONAL DATA

PER SERVING		EXCHANGES	
calories	275	milk	0.0
% calories from fat	26	vegetable	0.0
fat (gm)	7.9	fruit	0.0
sat. fat (gm)	1.1	bread	2.0
cholesterol (mg)	28.9	meat	2.0
sodium (mg)	575	fat	0.5
protein (gm)	15.2		
carbohydrate (gm)	25.9		

FISH SOUP

A long the Tuscan coast, each town boasts its own incomparable fish soup. The pride of Livorno is known as cacciucco. *Although many versions can be found, each usually holds a touch of hot red pepper and five different kinds of seafood, one for each of the c's in the dish's name. If you prefer, you can use just two kinds of fish. This soup is hearty enough for a main dish.*

3 cloves garlic, minced

2 cloves garlic, cut in half
  Light olive oil

2 medium-size onions, chopped

¾ teaspoon crushed red pepper flakes

2 tablespoons Italian parsley, chopped

1 cup dry red wine, such as Chianti

3 lbs. very ripe tomatoes, peeled, cored, seeded, and chopped; or 2 large cans (about 28 oz. each) plum tomatoes

4 cups chicken broth

6 slices crusty Italian bread (each about 3 inches wide, 5 inches long and ½ inch thick)
  Black pepper, freshly ground, to taste

1½ lbs. mixed boneless, skinless fish fillets, such as sole, flounder, rockfish, snapper, tuna, and halibut

4 oz. medium-size shrimp, shelled and deveined

2 tablespoons fresh Italian parsley

2 tablespoons fresh oregano

2 tablespoons fresh sage

2 tablespoons fresh rosemary

In a 5- to 6-quart pan, heat 2 tablespoons olive oil over medium heat. Add minced garlic and onions; cook, stirring occasionally, until onions are tender and golden (about 15 minutes). Stir in red pepper flakes and the 2 tablespoons parsley. Cook, stirring often, for 5 minutes. Add wine, and cook for about 2 minutes.

Add tomatoes (if using canned tomatoes, cut up tomatoes and add to pan along with their liquid). Add broth and bring to a boil over high heat. Reduce heat, cover, and simmer until tomatoes are very soft when pressed (about 20 minutes).

Meanwhile, place bread slices in a single layer on a baking sheet and broil about 4 inches below heat until golden brown on top (1 to 2 minutes). Turn slices over and brush each lightly with olive oil, and broil until golden brown on other side (1 to 2 minutes).

Remove toasted bread from broiler. Rub one side of each slice with reserved garlic cloves; sprinkle with black pepper. Place one slice in the bottom of each of 6 wide shallow soup bowls. Set aside.

Rinse fish and shrimp; pat dry. Cut fish into about ¾-inch chunks. Stir fish and shrimp into soup, and cook, uncovered, until opaque in thickest part; cut to test (about 5 minutes).

Ladle soup into bowls over bread. Sprinkle evenly with herbs.
Serves 6

NUTRITIONAL DATA

PER SERVING		EXCHANGES	
calories	337	milk	0.0
% calories from fat	19	vegetable	2.5
fat (gm)	7.1	fruit	0.0
sat. fat (gm)	1.1	bread	1.5
cholesterol (mg)	82.2	meat	3.0
sodium (mg)	337	fat	0.0
protein (gm)	28.6		
carbohydrate (gm)	33.7		

FISH SOUP WITH VEGETABLES

This soup is delicious served with a loaf of crusty bread.

     2 tablespoons olive oil
     1 onion, chopped
     4 cloves garlic, minced
     2 celery stalks, chopped
     2 carrots, sliced
     1 green pepper, chopped
     1 cup mushrooms, sliced
     2 28-oz. cans tomatoes, crushed
     1 16-oz. low-sodium tomato sauce
     1 6-oz. bottle clam juice
     3 medium potatoes, peeled and diced
     ½ teaspoon black pepper, freshly ground
     1 teaspoon oregano
     6 fresh basil leaves, chopped
     ½ lb. halibut, cut into bite-size pieces
     ½ lb. sole, cut into bite-size pieces
     ½ lb. snapper, cut into bite-size pieces
     1 cup dry white wine
   3-4 tablespoons fresh parsley, chopped
     6 fresh basil leaves

Place oil in large pot, and sauté onion, garlic, celery, carrots, green pepper, and mushrooms just until al dente.

Add tomatoes, tomato sauce, clam juice, and potatoes. Cook over medium heat for 5 minutes. Add pepper, oregano, and basil. Cover and simmer for 20 minutes, or until potatoes are done.

Add fish and wine, cover and continue simmering for 10 minutes. Sprinkle with chopped parsley and fresh basil before serving.

Serves 8

NUTRITIONAL DATA

PER SERVING		EXCHANGES	
calories	245	milk	0.0
% calories from fat	19	vegetable	2.5
fat (gm)	5.2	fruit	0.0
sat. fat (gm)	0.8	bread	1.0
cholesterol (mg)	32.8	meat	2.0
sodium (mg)	275	fat	0.0
protein (gm)	20.3		
carbohydrate (gm)	25.1		

6
PASTA

Pasta is often served as a first course in Italy. As an appetizer, smaller portions are served, usually six to the pound. As the main course, a pound serves only four, generously. Pasta can be low calorie and low fat if caution is used when preparing sauces. In Italy sauces are never heaped on, but a small amount is added and the sauce and pasta thoroughly tossed.

You can serve pasta on an Italian light menu, but you should balance your choices. For example, if you start with a pasta appetizer, you may wish to serve fish, chicken, or a vegetable dish as the main course. Italians love vegetables and reserve them for a special course, and vegetables are low in calories. If you are serving pasta as the main course, you may wish to start with a clear soup and serve a fruit-based dessert. This is truly an Italian meal. You will find pasta an indispensable part of meal planning.

Making your own pasta is fun, and the results are magnificent. Fresh pasta cooks so quickly that you will find yourself cooking it more often. If you don't have the time to make your own pasta, consider imported products, which cost only a little more and are well worth the money. Either kind should be cooked in deep boiling water, about 6 quarts to the pound, with two teaspoons of salt and a little oil to prevent sticking. Be sure not to overcook; pasta must never be mushy, but firm enough to resist the teeth—*al dente*. Stir several times with a wooden fork or spoon; do not rinse.

Hot Pasta Tips

To keep pasta piping hot the way you like it, consider these hints.

- Use a warm serving dish to serve pasta. To warm the serving dish, fill it with hot water, then let it stand for about 8 minutes. Drain the pasta in a colander. Empty the pasta bowl, dry it, and add the pasta. Serve immediately.
- Drain pasta quickly. Shake the colander so the pasta drains as quickly as possible.
- If you can't serve the pasta right away, place it in the pan in which it was cooked. For a delay of 10 minutes or more, leave the pasta in the colander, then place the colander over a pan containing a small amount of boiling water. Keep the water simmering. Coat pasta with a little oil to prevent sticking. Cover the colander. Serve the pasta as soon as possible.

BASIC PASTA

1¼ cups plus 1 tablespoon all-purpose flour, divided
¼ teaspoon salt
2 eggs, lightly beaten
3 qts. boiling water

Handmade Method

Combine 1 cup four and salt in bowl; stir well. Make indentation in center of mixture; add eggs, stirring to form dough. Turn dough out onto a lightly floured surface; shape into ball.

Knead until smooth and elastic (10 to 15 minutes); add enough of remaining flour, 1 tablespoon at a time, to prevent dough from sticking to hands. Dust dough lightly with flour, and wrap in plastic wrap; let rest 10 minutes.

Food Processor Method

Position knife blade in food processor bowl; add 1¼ cups flour and salt. Pulse 3 times or until combined. With processor running, slowly add eggs through food chute until dough forms a ball leaving sides of bowl. Turn dough out onto a lightly floured surface. Shape into ball.

Knead dough until smooth and elastic (about 10 to 15 minutes). Add enough of remaining flour to prevent dough from sticking to hands. Dust dough lightly with flour, and wrap in plastic wrap; let rest 10 minutes.

NUTRITIONAL DATA

PER SERVING		EXCHANGES	
calories	187	milk	0.0
% calories from fat	14	vegetable	0.0
fat (gm)	2.9	fruit	0.0
sat. fat (gm)	0.8	bread	2.0
cholesterol (mg)	106.5	meat	0.5
sodium (mg)	165	fat	0.5
protein (gm)	7.4		
carbohydrate (gm)	31.6		

Fettuccine

Divide dough into 4 equal portions. Working with each portion separately, pass dough through smooth rollers of pasta machine on widest setting. Continue moving width gauge to narrower settings; pass dough through rollers once at each setting, dusting dough with flour, if needed. Roll dough to desired thinness (about 1/16th inch). Pass each dough sheet through the fettuccine cutting rollers of machine. Hang pasta on wooden drying rack (dry no longer than 30 minutes).

Cook pasta in boiling water 2 minutes. Drain; serve immediately.
Serves 4 (See Basic Pasta, above, for Nutritional Data)

Cannelloni

Divide dough into 7 equal portions. Working with each portion separately, pass dough lengthwise through rollers of pasta machine on widest setting. Continue moving width gauge to narrower settings; pass dough through rollers once at each setting. Turn dough crosswise at setting #2 and #3, dusting with flour, if needed. Hang pasta on a wooden drying rack (dry no longer than 30 minutes). Repeat procedure with remaining portions of dough.

Cook pasta in boiling water 2 minutes or until al dente. Drain. Cut each cooked noodle in half crosswise.
Serves 4 (See Basic Pasta, above, for Nutritional Data)

Lasagna

Divide dough into 4 equal portions. Working with each portion separately, pass dough through smooth rollers of pasta machine on widest setting. Continue moving width gauge to narrower settings, pass dough through rollers once at each setting, dusting dough with flour, if needed. Repeat procedure with remaining portions of dough.

Cut dough portions into a total of 16 (11x2-inch) strips. Hang pasta on a wooden drying rack (dry no longer than 30 minutes). Cook pasta in boiling water 2 minutes or until al dente. Drain.

Serves 4, 4 noodles each (See Basic Pasta, above, for Nutritional Data)

FETTUCCINE ALFREDO

1 cup 2% milk
2 tablespoons all-purpose flour
2 tablespoons margarine
½ teaspoon salt
3 cloves garlic, minced
¼ cup Parmesan cheese, freshly grated
1 lb. fettuccine

Mix ingredients in ½-quart microwavable bowl. Microwave uncovered 2 minutes on high. Stir, and microwave 1 to 2 minutes longer on high, stirring after 1 minute until thick.

Serves 6

NUTRITIONAL DATA

PER SERVING		EXCHANGES	
calories	344	milk	0.0
% calories from fat	20	vegetable	0.0
fat (gm)	7.3	fruit	0.0
sat. fat (gm)	2.3	bread	3.5
cholesterol (mg)	6.3	meat	0.5
sodium (mg)	326	fat	1.5
protein (gm)	13.8		
carbohydrate (gm)	54		

FETTUCCINE WITH PESTO AND ROASTED PEPPERS

J ust add a salad and some bread for an easy, complete meal. If you don't have pesto, you can buy some in the refrigerator section of your supermarket.

- 8 oz. fettuccine
- 1 tablespoon olive oil
- 1 7-oz. jar roasted bell peppers, drained, rinsed, and sliced
- ½ cup prepared Pesto Sauce (see index) or purchased sauce

  Spike, to taste

  Black pepper, freshly ground, to taste

  Romano or Parmesan cheese, freshly grated

Boil fettuccine in large pot until just tender but still firm to bite, stirring occasionally.

Meanwhile, heat oil in heavy small skillet over medium-low heat. Add peppers, and stir until heated through.

Drain fettuccine well. Return to pot. Mix in peppers and pesto. Season with Spike and pepper. Serve, passing cheese.

Serves 2

NUTRITIONAL DATA

PER SERVING		EXCHANGES	
calories	517	milk	0.0
% calories from fat	21	vegetable	1.0
fat (gm)	12.1	fruit	0.0
sat. fat (gm)	3.2	bread	5.0
cholesterol (mg)	8.5	meat	0.5
sodium (mg)	173	fat	2.5
protein (gm)	20.6		
carbohydrate (gm)	79.7		

FETTUCCINE WITH RED BELL PEPPER SAUCE

T his sauce is also good on fish or sliced veal.

- 2 tablespoons unsalted butter
- 2 tablespoons olive oil
- 2¼ cups red onion, chopped
- 2 large cloves garlic, minced
- 3 large red bell peppers, roasted, peeled, seeded, and chopped
- 2 cups chicken stock
- ¼ teaspoon black pepper, freshly ground
  Spike, to taste
- 2 tablespoons fresh oregano, chopped
- 1 lb. fettuccine
- ⅓ cup Parmesan cheese, freshly grated

In large skillet over medium heat, melt butter and oil. Add onions, and sauté until slightly brown, about 4 minutes. Add garlic, and sauté another minute. Add peppers, and cook 3 minutes. Add stock and black pepper. Cook 10 minutes.

Transfer pepper mixture to bowl of food processor and puree. Season with Spike to taste. Cook pasta in salted water according to package directions. Toss drained pasta with sauce, and place in a heated bowl. Sprinkle with Parmesan cheese, and serve.

Serves 6

NUTRITIONAL DATA

PER SERVING		EXCHANGES	
calories	407	milk	0.0
% calories from fat	28	vegetable	1.5
fat (gm)	12.7	fruit	0.0
sat. fat (gm)	5.8	bread	3.5
cholesterol (mg)	21.4	meat	0.5
sodium (mg)	442	fat	2.0
protein (gm)	14.4		
carbohydrate (gm)	58.6		

FETTUCCINE WITH MUSSELS AND GREENS

      2 tablespoons olive oil
     ¼ cup onion, minced
      2 tablespoons garlic, minced
     ½ cup dry white wine
      1 tablespoon lemon rind, grated
      1 sweet red pepper, diced
    2½ lbs. fresh mussels, scrubbed clean and debearded
      1 lb. fresh spinach, stems removed, leaves washed
         and dried
    2¼ cups loosely packed arugula or other bitter greens
         (watercress, dandelion greens, collard greens,
         turnip greens)
      1 lb. homemade Fettuccine (see p. 111)
         Black pepper, freshly ground

Heat olive oil in large saucepan over medium heat. Add onion and garlic, and sauté slowly until soft, about 3 to 5 minutes. Add wine, lemon rind, and red pepper; raise heat to high, and add mussels.

Cover and steam mussels until they open, about 3 minutes. Lift lid and check them occasionally, removing mussels that have opened. Discard any that refuse to open. Remove all mussels to warm bowl.

Add spinach and greens to skillet, and cook about 10 seconds, until they are just wilted. Remove from heat.

Bring large pot of water to a boil. Add pasta, and cook until just done. Drain noodles well, and transfer to pan with sauce. Return pan to low heat, and toss noodles to coat well with sauce.

Add mussels, and toss again, then divide pasta among warm serving plates. Top each portion with freshly ground black pepper, and serve immediately.

Serves 4

NUTRITIONAL DATA

PER SERVING		EXCHANGES	
calories	702	milk	0.0
% calories from fat	24	vegetable	2.0
fat (gm)	18.3	fruit	0.0
sat. fat (gm)	2.5	bread	4.0
cholesterol (mg)	334.7	meat	5.5
sodium (mg)	1157	fat	1.5
protein (gm)	56.1		
carbohydrate (gm)	71.1		

LINGUINE WITH ARTICHOKES

12 fresh cooked artichoke hearts, cut in sixths*
 1 package (1 lb.) linguine, uncooked
 5 tablespoons olive oil, divided
½ cup fresh mushrooms, sliced
 4 large cloves garlic, minced
   Spike and pepper, to taste
⅔ cup dry white wine
 1 cup green onion, chopped
⅓ cup grated Parmesan cheese
 2 tablespoons fresh oregano, chopped
 2 tablespoons fresh parsley, chopped

Cook pasta according to package directions; drain.

Meanwhile, in large skillet, heat 2 tablespoons of oil. Add mushrooms; cook over medium heat about 5 minutes or until tender. Add artichoke hearts, garlic, and seasoning; cook 2 minutes, stirring frequently. Add wine and green onion; cook until about 3 tablespoons liquid remains.

Toss hot pasta with remaining oil, Parmesan cheese, parsley, and sauce; serve immediately.

*Note: Or substitute 2¼ cups canned artichoke hearts, drained, or frozen artichoke hearts, thawed.

Serves 4

NUTRITIONAL DATA

PER SERVING		EXCHANGES	
calories	674	milk	0.0
% calories from fat	29	vegetable	3.0
fat (gm)	22.2	fruit	0.0
sat. fat (gm)	4.5	bread	5.0
cholesterol (mg)	6.6	meat	1.0
sodium (mg)	268	fat	4.0
protein (gm)	23.7		
carbohydrate (gm)	90.3		

LINGUINE WITH PESTO AND POTATOES

This dish may seem strange to Americans because we don't usually mix starch upon starch, but this Ligurian dish is memorable.

1 lb. new potatoes, scrubbed

2 tablespoons olive oil plus 1 tablespoon if using dried pasta

1 recipe homemade Fettuccine (see p. 111) or 1 lb. purchased dried broad noodles

1 recipe Pesto Sauce (see p. 292), room temperature

2 tablespoons fresh oregano, minced

2 tablespoons fresh basil, minced

2 tablespoons parsley, minced

Parmesan cheese, freshly grated

In vegetable steamer, steam potatoes until just tender. Dry well, slice ¼-inch thick, then toss in bowl with 2 tablespoons olive oil.

Boil large pot of water. If you are using dried pasta, add 1 tablespoon of oil. Add pasta, and cook until just done. Drain well, and transfer to warm serving bowl.

Add potatoes, pesto, oregano, and basil. Toss thoroughly, making sure that potatoes are coated with pesto. Garnish with parsley.

Divide pasta among warm serving plates, and pass Parmesan separately.

Serves 4

NUTRITIONAL DATA

PER SERVING		EXCHANGES	
calories	472	milk	0.0
% calories from fat	30	vegetable	1.0
fat (gm)	15.9	fruit	0.0
sat. fat (gm)	5.4	bread	4.0
cholesterol (mg)	123.6	meat	0.5
sodium (mg)	502	fat	3.0
protein (gm)	18.7		
carbohydrate (gm)	64.1		

LINGUINE WITH SUN-DRIED TOMATOES

1 tablespoon olive oil

2 large shallots, chopped

½ cup evaporated skim milk

½ pt. Sun-Dried Tomatoes (see index), sliced and drained

½ lb. linguine

1 oz. Romano or Parmesan cheese, freshly grated
Spike, to taste
Pepper, freshly ground, to taste

2 tablespoons pine nuts, toasted
Fresh Italian parsley, minced
Additional Romano or Parmesan cheese, freshly grated

Heat oil in large skillet over medium heat. Add shallots, and stir 1 minute. Add milk, and bring to boil. Turn off heat, and add sun-dried tomatoes.

Meanwhile, boil linguine in large pot until just tender but still firm to bite, stirring occasionally. Drain well. Return linguine to pot. Add sauce and cheese, and stir to coat. Season with Spike and pepper.

Divide between plates. Sprinkle with nuts and parsley. Serve, passing additional cheese.

Serves 2

NUTRITIONAL DATA

PER SERVING		EXCHANGES	
calories	626	milk	1.0
% calories from fat	26	vegetable	0.0
fat (gm)	18.4	fruit	0.0
sat. fat (gm)	4	bread	5.0
cholesterol (mg)	17	meat	0.5
sodium (mg)	257	fat	3.4
protein (gm)	27.8		
carbohydrate (gm)	87.6		

RIGATONI WITH WHITE BEANS, GREEN BEANS, AND PINE NUTS

These beans with or without the pine nuts make a good side dish for meat.

1 cup dried cannellini beans, soaked overnight
6 cups chicken stock
1 teaspoon dried oregano
  Pinch cayenne pepper
2 large cloves garlic, crushed
1½ cups green beans, trimmed
1 lb. rigatoni
2 tablespoons olive oil
2 tablespoons unsalted butter
  Spike, to taste
  Black pepper, freshly ground, to taste
⅓ cup pine nuts
⅓ cup Parmesan cheese, freshly grated

Drain soaked cannellini beans, and place in saucepan. Cover beans with 4 cups of chicken stock. Add oregano, cayenne, and garlic. Bring to medium boil, then reduce heat to low. Simmer until very tender, about 1 hour and 15 minutes. Cool beans in liquid.

In saucepan over medium heat, cover green beans with remaining stock, and simmer until barely tender, about 10 minutes. Set aside to cool in liquid.

To serve, cook rigatoni in salted water until tender, according to package directions.

In skillet heat oil and butter. Drain both beans, add to skillet, and heat in oil and butter mixture.

Drain pasta and place in heated bowl. Add bean mixture, Spike, and pepper; toss. Sprinkle with pine nuts and Parmesan cheese.

Serves 4

NUTRITIONAL DATA

PER SERVING		EXCHANGES	
calories	846	milk	0.0
% calories from fat	30	vegetable	1.0
fat (gm)	28.5	fruit	0.0
sat. fat (gm)	12.6	bread	8.0
cholesterol (mg)	50.3	meat	0.5
sodium (mg)	1658	fat	5.0
protein (gm)	37.8		
carbohydrate (gm)	114.1		

RIGATONI WITH SPICY TOMATO AND CHEESE SAUCE

A blend of Cheddar and Romano cheese makes this dish a real crowd pleaser.

¼ cup butter substitute
3 tablespoons all-purpose flour
¾ cup evaporated skim milk
½ cup chicken broth
1 14½ oz. can tomatoes, drained and diced
1½ teaspoons dried red pepper flakes
1 teaspoon black pepper, freshly ground
2 teaspoons oregano
8 fresh basil leaves, chopped
1 cup sharp Cheddar cheese, shredded
½ cup Romano cheese, grated
1 lb. rigatoni pasta, freshly cooked
Additional grated Romano

Melt butter substitute in large skillet over medium-low heat. Add flour, and stir 3 minutes. Gradually whisk in milk and chicken broth. Bring to boil, stirring frequently. Add tomatoes, red pepper flakes, pepper, oregano, and basil; simmer 5 minutes, stirring occasionally.

Reduce heat to low. Add Cheddar and Romano, and stir until melted and well blended. Pour sauce over rigatoni. Toss thoroughly. Serve, passing additional Romano (not included in Nutritional Data) in a bowl.

Serves 4

NUTRITIONAL DATA

PER SERVING		EXCHANGES	
calories	708	milk	0.5
% calories from fat	26	vegetable	1.0
fat (gm)	20.1	fruit	0.0
sat. fat (gm)	11.9	bread	5.5
cholesterol (mg)	62.9	meat	2.0
sodium (mg)	1046	fat	3.0
protein (gm)	37		
carbohydrate (gm)	91.6		

SHELLS WITH PEPPER AND PECORINO

2 tablespoons olive oil

1 lb. medium shells

1 tablespoon Italian seasoning

1 cup hard pecorino cheese, grated, or Parmesan, grated

1 tablespoon black pepper, freshly ground

1 cup fresh seasoned Italian bread crumbs

In saucepan heat oil. Cook pasta until tender in salted water following package directions. Drain pasta, and place in heated serving bowl.

Pour oil over and toss quickly. Add Italian seasoning, cheese, and black pepper. Toss to coat.

Serve in individual heated bowls, and top with a sprinkle of bread crumbs.

Serves 4

NUTRITIONAL DATA

PER SERVING		EXCHANGES	
calories	600	milk	0.0
% calories from fat	26	vegetable	0.0
fat (gm)	17.1	fruit	0.0
sat. fat (gm)	6.3	bread	5.5
cholesterol (mg)	19.6	meat	1.5
sodium (mg)	532	fat	2.5
protein (gm)	26.9		
carbohydrate (gm)	82.1		

SPAGHETTI WITH ANCHOVIES

2 tablespoons olive oil

4 large cloves garlic, minced

1 1¾-oz. canned anchovy fillets, drained and chopped

8 oz. spaghetti

1 teaspoon fresh lemon juice

  Pepper, freshly ground, to taste

  Fresh Italian parsley, chopped

  Parmesan cheese, freshly grated

Heat oil in heavy small skillet over low heat. Add garlic, and cook 2 minutes. Add anchovies, and cook until garlic just begins to color, 3 minutes.

Meanwhile, boil spaghetti in large pot until just tender but still firm to bite, stirring occasionally. Drain well. Return spaghetti to pot.

Add oil mixture and lemon juice, and toss to coat. Season with pepper.

Divide between plates. Sprinkle generously with parsley. Serve, passing Parmesan.

Serves 2

NUTRITIONAL DATA

PER SERVING		EXCHANGES	
calories	632	milk	0.0
% calories from fat	26	vegetable	0.5
fat (gm)	18.1	fruit	0.0
sat. fat (gm)	2.8	bread	6.0
cholesterol (mg)	21.1	meat	0.5
sodium (mg)	916	fat	3.5
protein (gm)	22.8		
carbohydrate (gm)	92.9		

SPAGHETTI WITH GARLIC AND ROSEMARY

2 tablespoons olive oil
4 3-inch pieces fresh rosemary
4 large cloves garlic, coarsely chopped
1 cup beef broth, reduced to 1 tablespoon
1 lb. spaghetti
¼ cup black olives, sliced
⅓ cup Parmesan cheese, freshly grated

In saucepan over medium heat, combine oil, rosemary and garlic. Cook until garlic begins to soften, and brown lightly, about 5 minutes. Stir in reduced broth, and set aside.

Cook pasta until al dente in salted water according to package directions. Place drained pasta in large serving bowl.

Using fine-mesh sieve, strain infused oil over pasta. Add olives, and toss well. Sprinkle with Parmesan cheese, and serve.

Serves 4

NUTRITIONAL DATA

PER SERVING		EXCHANGES	
calories	585	milk	0.0
% calories from fat	23	vegetable	0.5
fat (gm)	14.6	fruit	0.0
sat. fat (gm)	3.3	bread	6.0
cholesterol (mg)	6.6	meat	0.5
sodium (mg)	632	fat	1.5
protein (gm)	19.8		
carbohydrate (gm)	92.7		

PASTA PUTTANESCA

T he legend of this dish is that Rome's ladies of the night favored it because it was so quick to make.

   2 tablespoons olive oil
  ½ cup onion, minced
   2 tablespoons garlic, minced
 2½ cups tomatoes, peeled, seeded, and chopped
   2 oz. canned anchovies, minced
   1 teaspoon hot red pepper flakes
   1 tablespoon capers
   1 cup unpitted Kalamata olives
   1 lb. dried spaghetti
   2 tablespoons parsley, minced

Heat olive oil in large skillet over low heat. Add onion and garlic; sauté slowly until very soft, about 10 minutes. Add tomatoes; simmer 10 minutes. Add anchovies and pepper flakes; cook 1 minute. Stir in capers and olives.

Bring large pot of salted water to a boil. Add spaghetti, and cook until pasta is just tender. Drain thoroughly, and add to sauce in skillet. Toss together well, and serve immediately, garnished with minced parsley.

Serves 4

NUTRITIONAL DATA

PER SERVING		EXCHANGES	
calories	659	milk	0.0
% calories from fat	29	vegetable	2.5
fat (gm)	22.9	fruit	0.0
sat. fat (gm)	3	bread	6.0
cholesterol (mg)	12	meat	0.5
sodium (mg)	1647	fat	4.0
protein (gm)	21.7		
carbohydrate (gm)	102.6		

CHEESY MANICOTTI

1 cup packaged manicotti shells or 16 packaged conchiglioni (jumbo shells)
2 egg whites
6 oz. skim mozzarella cheese, shredded
1½ cups non-fat ricotta cheese
2 tablespoons parsley, minced
2 teaspoons basil, chopped
2 teaspoons oregano, chopped
⅓ cup grated Parmesan cheese
2 cups Classic Spaghetti Sauce (see index)
¼ cup grated Parmesan or Romano cheese

Cook manicotti. Immediately drain. Rinse with cold water, then drain well.

Meanwhile, for filling, in medium mixing bowl, stir together the egg whites, mozzarella cheese, ricotta cheese, parsley, basil, oregano, and Parmesan cheese. Stuff filling into each cooked shell.

Arrange filled shells in a 12 x 7 ½ x 2-inch baking dish. Pour sauce over top. Sprinkle with Parmesan or Romano cheese. Bake, covered, in a 350-degree oven 35 to 40 minutes or until heated through.

Serves 4

NUTRITIONAL DATA

PER SERVING		EXCHANGES	
calories	566	milk	0.0
% calories from fat	26	vegetable	3.5
fat (gm)	17	fruit	0.0
sat. fat (gm)	8.9	bread	2.5
cholesterol (mg)	62.8	meat	5.0
sodium (mg)	981	fat	0.5
protein (gm)	47.2		
carbohydrate (gm)	64.6		

SPINACH LASAGNA ROLLS

1 10-oz. package leaf spinach, thawed, drained, and
   chopped
1 15-oz. container non-fat ricotta cheese
½ cup grated Parmesan cheese
1 egg, beaten to blend
1 tablespoon fresh Italian parsley, chopped
   Spike, to taste
   Pepper, to taste
2 cups Classic Spaghetti Sauce (see index) or
   purchased sauce
8 lasagna noodles, freshly cooked
½ cup skim mozzarella cheese, grated

Preheat oven to 350 degrees. Heat heavy medium skillet sprayed
with vegetable cooking spray over medium-high heat. Add spinach,
and cook until tender, about 4 minutes. Cool.

Combine spinach, ricotta, Parmesan, egg, and parsley in large
bowl. Season with Spike and pepper. Spread 1 cup spaghetti sauce
over bottom of 8-inch square baking dish.

Pat 1 lasagna noodle dry with paper towel. Set on waxed paper
sheet. Spread about ⅓ cup ricotta mixture over noodle. Carefully
roll up noodle, starting at 1 short end, to enclose filling. Arrange
seam side down in prepared dish. Repeat with remaining noodles.
Top with remaining 1 cup sauce. Sprinkle with mozzarella. Bake
until cheese melts, about 45 minutes.

Serves 6

NUTRITIONAL DATA

PER SERVING		EXCHANGES	
calories	321	milk	0.0
% calories from fat	27	vegetable	2.0
fat (gm)	10.9	fruit	0.0
sat. fat (gm)	4.8	bread	1.5
cholesterol (mg)	72.4	meat	3.0
sodium (mg)	625	fat	0.0
protein (gm)	29.3		
carbohydrate (gm)	35.8		

LASAGNA WITH DRIED MUSHROOM SAUCE

T his dish from Piedmont is rich and woodsy because of the porcini mushrooms. You can substitute water for the chicken stock if you prefer a vegetarian version.

1½ recipes Basic Pasta, lasagna (see pp. 110–112) or purchased

FILLING

1 cup ricotta cheese

½ cup parsley, minced, plus 3 tablespoons for garnish

¼ cup dried red pepper flakes

MUSHROOM SAUCE

1 cup chicken stock, canned

2 oz. dried porcini mushrooms

3 tablespoons olive oil

1 tablespoon butter

1 onion, minced

2 tablespoons garlic, finely minced

2¾ cups Basic Tomato-Basil Sauce (see index) or purchased tomato sauce

½ cup fresh basil leaves, loosely packed

4 sprigs fresh oregano

¼ cup fresh chives, chopped

1 bay leaf

1¼ cups dry red wine

Spike, to taste

Black pepper, freshly ground, to taste

6 tablespoons basil leaves, shredded

¼ cup Parmesan cheese, grated

Bring large pot of water to boil. Add lasagna noodles, and cook until almost tender. Drain and refresh under cold water. Drain thoroughly and dry. Moisten noodles with vegetable cooking spray, and spread out on clean kitchen towels.

Preheat oven to 350 degrees. Coat bottom and sides of pan (approximately 13x11x2 inches) with vegetable cooking spray.

To make Filling: Combine ricotta, parsley, and red pepper flakes. Set aside.

To make Mushroom Sauce: In small saucepan, bring chicken stock to boil. Add dried mushrooms and simmer 20 minutes. Carefully lift mushrooms out with slotted spoon. Strain liquid through cheesecloth and reserve.

Pick through porcini carefully to remove any grit. Chop coarsely. Set aside.

Heat oil and butter in large skillet over moderate heat. When butter foams, add onion and sauté 3 minutes. Add garlic and sauté until onion softens and begins to color—an additional 5-7 minutes.

Add tomato sauce, basil leaves, oregano, chives, and bay leaf. Stir well, then add strained stock, mushrooms, wine, Spike, and pepper. Simmer until liquid is reduced to a rich dark sauce, about 45-50 minutes.

Remove bay leaf and herb sprigs. Taste and adjust seasoning. Stir in shredded basil and remove from heat.

Spread 1 cup Mushroom Sauce over bottom of pan. Top with one-third of lasagna noodles. Spread Filling over noodle layer. Top with another one-third of noodles, then 1½ cups Mushroom Sauce. Add remaining layer of noodles and remaining Mushroom Sauce. Dust top with Parmesan.

Cover pan with foil and bake 15 minutes. Uncover and bake until lasagna bubbles around edges. Do not overcook. Let rest 10 minutes before serving.

Serves 6

VEGETABLE LASAGNA

    4 cups Basic Tomato-Basil Sauce (see index) or
      purchased
    1 recipe Basic Pasta, lasagna (see pp. 110–112), or
      purchased lasagna noodles
    1 teaspoon olive oil, divided
    2 cups fresh mushrooms, thinly sliced
    ½ cup onion, finely chopped
    2 cups fresh broccoli, finely chopped
    ½ cup carrots, finely chopped
    1 clove garlic, minced
    1 cup light ricotta cheese
    ¼ cup grated Parmesan cheese, divided
    2 tablespoons fresh parsley, finely chopped
    6 oz. skim mozzarella cheese, divided

Prepare tomato sauce and set aside. Prepare basic pasta (lasagna) and set aside.

Heat ½ teaspoon oil in medium skillet over medium-low heat; add sliced mushrooms and chopped onion. Cover, and cook 5 minutes, stirring occasionally.

Cook, uncovered, an additional 3 minutes or until liquid evaporates. Spoon into bowl, and set aside. Add remaining ½ teaspoon oil to skillet, and place over medium-high heat. Add broccoli, carrots, and garlic; sauté 2 minutes. Set aside.

Position knife blade in food processor bowl; add light ricotta cheese, and process until smooth. Add 2 tablespoons grated Parmesan cheese and finely chopped fresh parsley. Process 10 seconds or until blended, and set aside.

Spread 1 cup tomato sauce in bottom of a 13 × 9 × 2-inch baking dish. Arrange 4 lasagna noodles lengthwise in a single layer on top of tomato sauce. Spoon broccoli mixture evenly over noodles. Top with ¼ cup shredded mozzarella cheese and 1 teaspoon grated Parmesan cheese.

Layer 4 noodles over cheese. Spread light ricotta cheese mixture evenly over noodles; top with ¼ cup mozzarella cheese.

Arrange 4 noodles on top of cheese. Spread remaining 3 cups tomato sauce over noodles. Sprinkle with remaining ¾ cup mozzarella cheese and remaining 2 teaspoons Parmesan cheese.

Cover and bake at 350 degrees for 30 minutes. Bake, uncovered, an additional 20 minutes. Let stand 10 minutes before serving.

Serves 8

NUTRITIONAL DATA

PER SERVING		EXCHANGES	
calories	270	milk	0.0
% calories from fat	29	vegetable	3.5
fat (gm)	9	fruit	0.0
sat. fat (gm)	3.5	bread	1.0
cholesterol (mg)	71.7	meat	1.0
sodium (mg)	597	fat	1.0
protein (gm)	16.2		
carbohydrate (gm)	32.9		

BAKED ZITI

1 lb. lean ground turkey
½ cup onion, finely chopped
¼ cup plain dry bread crumbs
2 teaspoons parsley, finely chopped
1 teaspoon oregano
1 teaspoon garlic, minced
¾ teaspoon Worcestershire sauce
1 teaspoon Spike
½ teaspoon pepper, freshly ground
1 teaspoon dried thyme leaves
1 teaspoon dried basil leaves
⅛ teaspoon crushed red pepper
1 can (28 oz.) crushed tomatoes in puree
1 can (8 oz.) tomato sauce
½ cup water
8 oz. ziti, freshly cooked, drained, and returned to pot
4 oz. skim mozzarella cheese, shredded
2 tablespoons grated Parmesan cheese

Mix first 12 ingredients in medium-size bowl until well blended.

Heat oven to 400 degrees. Spray 13 × 9 × 2-inch baking pan with vegetable cooking spray.

Heat large skillet sprayed with vegetable cooking spray and place over high heat. When skillet is hot, crumble in meat mixture. Cook 5 minutes or until it loses its pink color, stirring often to break up meat.

Add crushed tomatoes, tomato sauce, and water; bring to a boil. Reduce heat to low, cover, and simmer 15 minutes, stirring several times. Add to drained ziti in pot, and stir to mix.

Scrape all into ungreased baking pan; sprinkle cheese over top. Cover with foil, and bake 10 minutes. Remove foil, and bake uncovered 5 minutes or until lightly browned.

Serves 6

NUTRITIONAL DATA

PER SERVING		EXCHANGES	
calories	349	milk	0.0
% calories from fat	28	vegetable	2.0
fat (gm)	10.6	fruit	0.0
sat. fat (gm)	4.1	bread	2.0
cholesterol (mg)	40.4	meat	2.0
sodium (mg)	866	fat	1.0
protein (gm)	23.2		
carbohydrate (gm)	39.7		

PENNE WITH SAUSAGE, PEAS, GOAT'S CHEESE, AND TOMATO CONFIT

- ¾ lb. Italian turkey sausage
- 1 lb. penne
- 2 cups petite peas, cooked or thawed if frozen
- 4 tablespoons goat's cheese

Crumble sausage, and sauté in a nonstick pan for about 20 minutes. Set aside. Cook penne according to package directions. Drain, and place in large pasta bowl. Add peas and tomato confit (recipe follows). Top each portion with goat's cheese.

TOMATO CONFIT

- 4 ripe red tomatoes
- 1 tablespoon shallots or scallions, finely minced
- ½ teaspoon red wine vinegar
- 1 tablespoon olive oil
  - Spike, to taste
  - Pepper, freshly ground, to taste
- 8 fresh basil leaves, chopped
- 2 tablespoons parsley, minced

Peel, seed, and juice the tomatoes, then fold them gently in bowl with shallots or scallions, vinegar, oil and Spike and pepper to taste. Fold in basil leaves. Let steep for 10 minutes to blend flavors. Turn into sieve to drain. Return to bowl, correct seasoning, and fold in parsley. Set aside.

Serves 4

NUTRITIONAL DATA

PER SERVING		EXCHANGES	
calories	741	milk	0.0
% calories from fat	29	vegetable	1.0
fat (gm)	23.9	fruit	0.0
sat. fat (gm)	5.7	bread	6.0
cholesterol (mg)	82.3	meat	2.0
sodium (mg)	658	fat	4.0
protein (gm)	35.9		
carbohydrate (gm)	94.4		

SAUSAGE AND BELL PEPPER PASTA

3 cloves garlic, minced
1 lb. Italian turkey sausage (hot or sweet), cut into 1-inch pieces
1 large green or yellow bell pepper, cut into strips
1 large red bell pepper, cut into strips
1 large onion, sliced
1 14½-oz. can tomatoes, diced, juices reserved
1 tablespoon dried basil, crumbled
2 tablespoons fresh basil, chopped
1 teaspoon dried oregano, crumbled
1 tablespoon fresh oregano, chopped
  Spike, to taste
  Black pepper, freshly ground, to taste
1 lb. penne pasta, freshly cooked
  Grated Parmesan

Heat large skillet sprayed with vegetable cooking spray over medium heat. Add garlic, and sauté until golden, about 1 minute. Mix in sausage, and cook until brown, about 8 minutes.

Mix in bell peppers, onion, tomatoes with juices, basil, and oregano. Season with Spike and pepper. Cover, and simmer 8 minutes. Uncover, and cook 2 minutes.

Pour over pasta, and toss. Serve, passing Parmesan (not included in Nutritional Data).

Serves 6

NUTRITIONAL DATA

PER SERVING		EXCHANGES	
calories	468	milk	0.0
% calories from fat	29	vegetable	1.5
fat (gm)	15.2	fruit	0.0
sat. fat (gm)	2.4	bread	3.5
cholesterol (mg)	61.1	meat	1.5
sodium (mg)	638	fat	2.0
protein (gm)	23.6		
carbohydrate (gm)	58.5		

RIGATONI WITH ESCAROLE AND SAUSAGE

1 lb. Italian turkey sausage
1 head escarole, leaves cut into 1-inch long strips
2 cloves garlic, minced
1 lb. rigatoni
1 oz. Romano cheese, freshly grated
  Spike, to taste
1½ cups fresh bread crumbs

Cook sausage in heavy, large skillet over medium heat until brown and cooked through, about 10 minutes. Cool sausage slightly. Cut into ¼-inch slices. Set aside.

Cook escarole in large pot of boiling water until just tender, about 5 minutes. Drain well.

Heat heavy, large skillet sprayed with vegetable cooking spray over high heat. Add sausage, escarole, and garlic, and sauté mixture for 3 minutes.

Meanwhile, boil rigatoni in large pot until just tender but still firm to bite. Drain well. Transfer to large broiler-proof dish. Turn on broiler.

Add sausage mixture and Romano to rigatoni, and toss. Season with Spike. Sprinkle with bread crumbs. Broil until bread crumbs are golden brown, about 1 minute.

Serves 4

NUTRITIONAL DATA

PER SERVING		EXCHANGES	
calories	740	milk	0.0
% calories from fat	30	vegetable	1.0
fat (gm)	24.9	fruit	0.0
sat. fat (gm)	5	bread	5.5
cholesterol (mg)	98.8	meat	3.0
sodium (mg)	982	fat	3.5
protein (gm)	38.2		
carbohydrate (gm)	88.3		

7
PIZZA

When pizza came to America, it put on weight. A simple, earthy dish that began thousands of years ago in the Mediterranean region as flat dough baked on stones in an open fire evolved, on its way to becoming America's favorite meal, into a cheese and meat-laden giant among fast foods.

Pockets of thin-crust, tomato-brushed, Italian-style pizza survived, but until recently, when most Americans reached for the phone during the football game, they expected to measure their money's worth in pizza weight. When pizza became fashionable, it began to lose weight again. The crust took on new significance, and the plain, strong flavors of scant toppings were emphasized.

These recipes are only beginnings. The beauty of pizza is that the crust is a blank canvas and the choice of toppings is up to you. The healthful pizza is in your hands.

Pizza How-To

The key to a great pizza is the crust, and for the home baker many will agree that the key to a great crust is a very hot oven and a pizza stone or pizza tiles. (Unglazed stones or tiles imitate the lining of a pizza oven; they absorb moisture from the dough, making it crisp, and distribute heat evenly.)

If you don't have pizza stones or tiles, you can still make a good pizza crust by baking it on an upside-down cookie sheet. Once you have a good crust, toppings are a matter of taste. Low-fat pizzas use imaginative toppings and little cheese.

BASIC PIZZA DOUGH

C hewy and flavorful, this basic dough makes an excellent crust. It makes one 14-inch or two 9-inch-round pizzas.

    2 cups all-purpose flour
    1 package rapid-rising dry yeast
    ½ teaspoon salt
    ⅔ cup very warm water (120-130 degrees)
    1 tablespoon olive oil
    1 tablespoon honey

In large bowl, combine 2 cups flour, yeast, and salt. In 1-cup measuring cup, combine water, oil, and honey; stir into flour mixture until soft dough forms. Turn dough out onto floured surface.

Knead dough, adding some of remaining flour, if necessary, until dough is very elastic, 10 to 15 minutes (dough should be soft, do not add too much flour).

Wash, dry, and lightly oil mixing bowl. Place dough in oiled bowl, turning to bring oiled side up. Cover with clean cloth; let dough rise in warm place, away from drafts, until double in size, 30 to 45 minutes. Shape, and bake in following pizza recipes.

Using Active Dry Yeast: Replace 1 package rapid-rising dry yeast with 1 package active dry yeast. In large bowl, sprinkle yeast over warm water (110-115 degrees) and let stand 5 minutes. Add remaining ingredients, knead, and set aside as above. Rising time should change from 30 minutes to 50 to 60 minutes or until double in size. (Nutritional Data is same as for Basic Pizza Dough, above.)

Overnight: Prepare Basic Pizza Dough but do not allow to rise. Loosely wrap, and refrigerate dough immediately. Next day, un-wrap dough, and cover with clean cloth. Let warm to room temperature and shape following recipe directions. This method is best using active dry yeast rather than the rapid-rising variety.

NUTRITIONAL DATA

PER CRUST		EXCHANGES	
calories	1114	milk	0.0
% calories from fat	13	vegetable	0.0
fat (gm)	15.9	fruit	0.0
sat. fat (gm)	2.3	bread	13.5
cholesterol (mg)	0	meat	0.0
sodium (mg)	1072	fat	3.0
protein (gm)	28.8		
carbohydrate (gm)	210.8		

♥

BASIC PIZZA DOUGH VARIATIONS

(Nutritional Data below is based on 14-inch crust
(see preceding recipe) cut into 8 servings)

Whole Wheat

Prepare Basic Pizza Dough (preceding recipe) but reduce all-purpose flour to 1 cup and add 1 cup whole wheat flour.

NUTRITIONAL DATA

PER SERVING		EXCHANGES	
calories	197	milk	0.0
% calories from fat	18	vegetable	0.0
fat (gm)	4	fruit	0.0
sat. fat (gm)	0.6	bread	2.5
cholesterol (mg)	0	meat	0.0
sodium (mg)	201	fat	0.5
protein (gm)	5.7		
carbohydrate (gm)	35.1		

Cornmeal

Prepare Basic Pizza Dough (preceding recipe) but reduce all-purpose flour to 1½ cups and add ½ cup cornmeal.

NUTRITIONAL DATA

PER SERVING		EXCHANGES	
calories	206	milk	0.0
% calories from fat	17	vegetable	0.0
fat (gm)	3.9	fruit	0.0
sat. fat (gm)	0.6	bread	2.5
cholesterol (mg)	0	meat	0.0
sodium (mg)	201	fat	0.5
protein (gm)	5.1		
carbohydrate (gm)	36.9		

Parmesan

Prepare Basic Pizza Dough (preceding recipe) but add ¼ cup grated Parmesan cheese.

NUTRITIONAL DATA

PER SERVING		EXCHANGES	
calories	232	milk	0.0
% calories from fat	23	vegetable	0.0
fat (gm)	5.7	fruit	0.0
sat. fat (gm)	1.7	bread	2.5
cholesterol (mg)	4.9	meat	0.5
sodium (mg)	317	fat	0.5
protein (gm)	7.8		
carbohydrate (gm)	36.4		

BIG BATCH PIZZA DOUGH

T his recipe for pizza dough is my favorite for parties. It makes 4 thin-crust, 12-inch pizzas.

- 1 envelope (2 teaspoons) active dry yeast
- 1 teaspoon granulated sugar
- 1¼ cups warm water (105-115 degrees)
- 5 cups all-purpose or bread flour
- 2 large eggs
- 2 teaspoons salt
- Topping of choice

Stir yeast and sugar into water. Let stand about 10 minutes until foamy.

In food processor, put flour, eggs, and salt in work bowl fitted with metal blade. Turn processor on, and pour yeast mixture through feed tube in a steady stream. Process until dough cleans sides of bowl, then process 45 seconds longer (this replaces much kneading) or until dough is smooth and elastic.

By hand or with electric mixer, mix yeast mixture and eggs in large bowl. Add flour, and stir or beat until dough pulls away from sides of bowl. Turn dough out on lightly floured surface, and knead 5 minutes or until smooth and elastic.

Put dough into large oiled bowl, and turn dough to oil top. Cover bowl with plastic wrap. Let dough rise in a warm, draft-free place 1 hour or until doubled.

Punch down dough, and divide into 4 equal pieces. Shape pieces into smooth balls. (Dough can be made ahead up to this point and refrigerated or frozen.) Let rest 30 minutes so dough will be easier to handle. Dough will rise but not double in volume.

For each pizza, spray 12-inch round pizza pan or large cookie sheet with nonstick cooking spray. Place dough on lightly floured surface.

With floured hands, pat into 6-inch round. Stretch or roll out dough with rolling pin into 11-inch circle. Lift onto prepared pan, and press dough with knuckles or fingers out to edges of pizza pan or into 12-inch circle on inverted cookie sheet.

Add toppings (not included in Nutritional Data below) and bake on lowest rack at 500 degrees for 10 to 12 minutes or until edges of crust are browned and crisp. Cut in wedges with pizza wheel or knife.

Makes 4 pizzas
Each Pizza Serves 8

NUTRITIONAL DATA

PER SERVING		EXCHANGES	
calories	77	milk	0.0
% calories from fat	6	vegetable	0.0
fat (gm)	0.5	fruit	0.0
sat. fat (gm)	0.1	bread	1.0
cholesterol (mg)	13.3	meat	0.0
sodium (mg)	137	fat	0.0
protein (gm)	2.5		
carbohydrate (gm)	15.2		

RAPID RISE PIZZA DOUGH

This recipe will let you make a pizza in less than an hour. The recipe makes one 14-inch pizza or two 12-inch pizzas.

    3 cups all-purpose flour
    1 package rapid-rising dry yeast
    ¾ teaspoon salt
    1 cup very warm water (125-130 degrees)
    2 tablespoons olive oil
      Cornmeal

In large bowl, combine 2 cups flour, undissolved yeast, and salt. Stir very warm water and oil into dry ingredients. Stir in enough remaining flour to make soft dough.

Knead dough on lightly floured surface until smooth and elastic, about 4 to 6 minutes. Cover, let rest on floured surface for 10 minutes.

Lightly oil one 14-inch or two 12-inch round pizza pans. Sprinkle with cornmeal.

Form dough into smooth ball. Roll dough to fit pan or pans.

Try the Basic Tomato-Basil Sauce recipe (see index), or use your favorite homemade or prepared sauce. Add your favorite toppings and grated cheese. Slice raw vegetables thinly to prevent a soggy pizza.

Bake in preheated 400-degree oven for 20 to 30 minutes or until done. Time depends on size and thickness of crust and selected toppings.

Note: Sauce and toppings not included in Nutritional Data below.
Serves 8

NUTRITIONAL DATA

PER SERVING		EXCHANGES	
calories	203	milk	0.0
% calories from fat	17	vegetable	0.0
fat (gm)	3.8	fruit	0.0
sat. fat (gm)	0.6	bread	2.5
cholesterol (mg)	0	meat	0.0
sodium (mg)	201	fat	0.5
protein (gm)	5.2		
carbohydrate (gm)	36.2		

RAPID RISE PIZZA DOUGH VARIATIONS

(Nutritional Data below is based on 14-inch crust
(see preceding recipe) cut into 8 servings)

Garlic & Herb Dough

Add 2 teaspoons basil, oregano, or rosemary leaves and 1 clove finely minced garlic along with dry ingredients.

NUTRITIONAL DATA

PER SERVING		EXCHANGES	
calories	204	milk	0.0
% calories from fat	17	vegetable	0.0
fat (gm)	3.8	fruit	0.0
sat. fat (gm)	0.6	bread	2.5
cholesterol (mg)	0	meat	0.0
sodium (mg)	201	fat	0.5
protein (gm)	5.3		
carbohydrate (gm)	36.5		

Cornmeal Dough

Replace ½ cup of all-purpose flour with ½ cup cornmeal as you combine dry ingredients.

NUTRITIONAL DATA

PER SERVING		EXCHANGES	
calories	142	milk	0.0
% calories from fat	13	vegetable	0.0
fat (gm)	2.1	fruit	0.0
sat. fat (gm)	0.3	bread	1.5
cholesterol (mg)	0	meat	0.0
sodium (mg)	134	fat	0.5
protein (gm)	3.5		
carbohydrate (gm)	27.1		

Cheese Dough

Add ½ cup grated Parmesan cheese along with other dry ingredients.

NUTRITIONAL DATA

PER SERVING		EXCHANGES	
calories	153	milk	0.0
% calories from fat	17	vegetable	0.0
fat (gm)	2.9	fruit	0.0
sat. fat (gm)	0.8	bread	1.5
cholesterol (mg)	2.5	meat	0.5
sodium (mg)	192	fat	0.5
protein (gm)	4.9		
carbohydrate (gm)	26.5		

Whole Wheat Dough

Replace 1 cup of all-purpose flour with 1 cup whole wheat flour as you combine dry ingredients.

NUTRITIONAL DATA

PER SERVING		EXCHANGES	
calories	133	milk	0.0
% calories from fat	14	vegetable	0.0
fat (gm)	2.1	fruit	0.0
sat. fat (gm)	0.3	bread	1.5
cholesterol (mg)	0	meat	0.0
sodium (mg)	134	fat	0.5
protein (gm)	4		
carbohydrate (gm)	25.3		

VEGETABLE PIZZA

A rainbow of vegetables tops a whole wheat crust in this delicious pizza.

- 1 recipe Whole Wheat variation of Basic Pizza Dough (see p. 141)
- 1 tablespoon cornmeal
- 1 7-oz. jar roasted red peppers, drained
- 1 tablespoon white wine
- 1 teaspoon Spike, divided
- ½ teaspoon black pepper, freshly ground, divided
- 1 small (½ lb.) eggplant, cut crosswise into ½-inch thick slices and each slice quartered
- 2 cloves garlic, minced
- 1 small zucchini, coarsely grated
- 1 small yellow squash, cut crosswise into ¼-inch thick slices
- 1 large tomato, cut into chunks
- 1 tablespoon fresh oregano leaves (1 teaspoon dried)
- 1 tablespoon fresh sage leaves, crumbled (1 teaspoon dried)
- ¼ lb. skim mozzarella cheese, shredded
  Fresh parsley leaves, chopped

Prepare Whole Wheat variation of Basic Pizza Dough. Set aside to rise. Lightly dust large baking sheet with cornmeal. On baking sheet, shape dough into 14-inch round. Pinch edges to form rim. Prick surface of dough with fork.

In food processor, with chopping blade, process roasted red peppers, white wine, Spike, and pepper until smooth. Spread pepper mixture over whole wheat round inside border.

Press zucchini into sieve to remove excess liquid, and spread it over pepper mixture.

In large skillet sprayed with vegetable cooking spray, add eggplant and garlic; sauté 3 minutes or until eggplant is slightly tender and lightly browned. In medium-size bowl, combine eggplant mixture, yellow squash, tomato, oregano, and sage and season with Spike and pepper. Spoon mixture onto whole wheat round over the zucchini. Sprinkle all with shredded cheese.

Bake pizza at 450 degrees (preheated) on lower oven rack 10 to 15 minutes or until crust is lightly browned and cheese is melted. Sprinkle with chopped parsley. Serve immediately.

Serves 8

NUTRITIONAL DATA

PER SERVING		EXCHANGES	
calories	200	milk	0.0
% calories from fat	20	vegetable	2.0
fat (gm)	4.7	fruit	0.0
sat. fat (gm)	1.8	bread	1.5
cholesterol (mg)	8	meat	0.5
sodium (mg)	204	fat	0.5
protein (gm)	8.6		
carbohydrate (gm)	32.3		

WILD MUSHROOM PIZZA

This sophisticated pizza is a meal on a crust.

- 1 recipe Basic Pizza Dough (see p. 140)
- 1 oz. dried porcini or other dried wild mushrooms, chopped
- 1¼ cups boiling water
- 2 teaspoons olive oil
- 2 oz. oyster mushrooms, hard stem ends removed
- 1 medium onion, chopped
- 1 clove garlic, minced
- 2 tablespoons red wine (Marsala preferred)
- 3 oz. shiitake mushrooms, stems discarded and caps thinly sliced
- ⅓ cup evaporated skim milk
- 1 large tomato, seeded and chopped
- ½ cup thawed frozen green peas
  Spike, to taste
- ⅛ teaspoon black pepper, freshly ground

Prepare Basic Pizza Dough. Set aside to rise. Meanwhile, soak dried mushrooms in boiling water.

In large skillet, heat oil. Sauté oyster mushrooms 1 minute or until lightly browned. Remove oyster mushrooms to small bowl, and set aside.

Add to skillet, onion and garlic; cook until onion is lightly browned. Add wine, dried mushrooms, 1 cup soaking water, shiitake mushrooms, and milk. Cook until mixture thickens to sauce. Remove from heat, and stir in tomato, peas, Spike, and pepper.

Divide pizza dough in half. Lightly grease two 9-inch round pizza pans or large baking sheet. Shape dough halves into 9-inch rounds, and place in pizza pans or baking sheet. Pinch edges to form rim. Prick surface of dough with fork.

Fill pizza rounds with mushroom mixture. Bake pizzas at 475 degrees (preheated) on lower oven rack 8 minutes. Top pizzas with reserved oyster mushrooms and bake 2 to 4 minutes longer or until crust is golden brown. Serve hot.

Serves 8

NUTRITIONAL DATA

PER SERVING		EXCHANGES	
calories	197	milk	0.0
% calories from fat	15	vegetable	3.0
fat (gm)	3.4	fruit	0.0
sat. fat (gm)	0.5	bread	1.5
cholesterol (mg)	0.4	meat	0.0
sodium (mg)	161	fat	0.5
protein (gm)	6.2		
carbohydrate (gm)	35.1		

SALAD PIZZA

½ recipe Basic Pizza Dough (see p. 140)
1 cup radicchio, thinly sliced
1 cup arugula, thinly sliced
1½ cups red onions, thinly sliced and separated into rings
2 large plum tomatoes, coarsely chopped
1 tablespoon balsamic vinegar
1 teaspoon Spike
¼ teaspoon black pepper
3 oz. skim mozzarella cheese, shredded

Prepare ½ recipe Basic Pizza Dough. Set aside to rise.

Spray 14-inch pizza pan with nonstick cooking spray. Press dough into pan; pinch edges to form a rim. Prick surface of dough with fork; bake at 475 degrees (preheated) 10 to 15 minutes, until golden. Remove from oven.

Meanwhile in large bowl, combine radicchio, arugula, onion, and tomatoes. Add vinegar, Spike, and pepper; toss to mix well. Set aside for 15 minutes.

With slotted spoon, place radicchio mixture onto baked dough; spread to within 1 inch of edge. Sprinkle with cheese. Bake 5 to 10 minutes longer, until cheese melts.

Serves 8

NUTRITIONAL DATA

PER SERVING		EXCHANGES	
calories	124	milk	0.0
% calories from fat	21	vegetable	1.0
fat (gm)	2.9	fruit	0.0
sat. fat (gm)	1.2	bread	1.0
cholesterol (mg)	6	meat	0.5
sodium (mg)	126	fat	0.0
protein (gm)	6		
carbohydrate (gm)	19		

♥

WHOLE WHEAT PIZZA FESTIVO

½ recipe Whole Wheat variation of Basic Pizza Dough (see p. 141)

½ cup salsa

12 oz. cooked black beans, drained

1½ cups green bell pepper, chopped

1 medium red onion, chopped

2 tablespoons canned green chilies, chopped

2¼ oz. Monterey Jack cheese, shredded

2¼ oz. cheddar cheese, shredded

Prepare Whole Wheat Pizza Dough. Set aside to rise.

Spray 14-inch pizza pan with nonstick cooking spray. Roll dough into 14-inch round. Place dough on prepared pan; pinch edges to form rim. Prick surface with fork.

Spread salsa to within 1 inch of edge. Top evenly with beans, bell pepper, onion, and chilies. Sprinkle with both cheeses. Bake at 475 degrees (preheated) 20-30 minutes, until crust is golden.

Serves 8

NUTRITIONAL DATA

PER SERVING		EXCHANGES	
calories	205	milk	0.0
% calories from fat	28	vegetable	1.0
fat (gm)	6.4	fruit	0.0
sat. fat (gm)	3.8	bread	1.5
cholesterol (mg)	15.9	meat	0.5
sodium (mg)	298	fat	1.0
protein (gm)	10.4		
carbohydrate (gm)	27.5		

PESTO PIZZA

*S ince nonfat yogurt replaces some of the oil in
the pesto topping, this version is much lower
in fat than traditional recipes.*

1½ cups packed fresh basil leaves
1½ tablespoons Parmesan cheese (¼ oz.), freshly
     grated
1½ tablespoons olive oil
 1 clove garlic, minced
 3 tablespoons nonfat yogurt
 2 large tomatoes, sliced, optional
    Lemon pepper
 1 recipe Basic Pizza Dough (see p. 140)

In food processor or blender, combine basil, cheese, olive oil, and garlic. Process until well blended. Add yogurt, and process until smooth. Season with lemon pepper. (Pesto topping can be prepared ahead and stored, covered, in refrigerator for up to 2 days).

Place pizza stone, baking tiles, or inverted baking sheet on lowest rack of oven.

Divide pizza dough into 8 pieces. Using your fists, stretch one piece into 6-inch round. Alternatively, with a rolling pin, roll out on lightly floured surface. (Keep remaining dough covered with towel or plastic wrap as you work.)

Place round on a cornmeal-dusted pizza peel or inverted baking sheet, using enough cornmeal so dough slides easily. Stretch or roll second round of dough and place beside first. Spread 1 tablespoon pesto on each round of dough. If desired, arrange ½ cup sliced tomatoes (not included in Nutritional Data) over top of each one. Season lightly with lemon pepper.

Carefully slide pizzas from peel or baking sheet onto heated pizza stone, baking tiles, or baking sheet. Bake at 500 degrees or highest setting (preheated) for 10 to 14 minutes, or until the bottoms are crisp and browned. Working with 2 pizzas at once, repeat with remaining dough and toppings.

Makes 8, 6-inch pizzas
Serves 8

NUTRITIONAL DATA

PER SERVING		EXCHANGES	
calories	174	milk	0.0
% calories from fat	26	vegetable	1.0
fat (gm)	5	fruit	0.0
sat. fat (gm)	0.9	bread	1.5
cholesterol (mg)	1	meat	0.0
sodium (mg)	165	fat	1.0
protein (gm)	4.7		
carbohydrate (gm)	27.8		

FRENCH ONION PIZZA

*R*osemary and black olives added to the dough give these pizzas an earthy flavor, while the onion adds sweetness. Cut into small wedges, they make delicious appetizers.

- 2 cups onions (2 medium), sliced
- 1 recipe Basic Pizza Dough (see p. 140)
  Cornmeal
- ½ cup Kalamata or Baeta olives, pitted and chopped
- 1 tablespoon fresh rosemary or 1 teaspoon dried rosemary, crumbled
- 4 oz. skim mozzarella cheese, grated
  Black pepper, freshly ground, to taste

Heat nonstick skillet, sprayed with vegetable cooking spray, over medium heat. Add onions, and sauté about 10 minutes, or until lightly browned and very tender. Let cool.

Place pizza stone, baking tiles or inverted baking sheet on lowest rack of oven.

Add olives and rosemary to pizza dough, and knead on a lightly floured surface until they are mixed. Divide dough into 8 pieces. Working with 2 pieces at once, form dough into rounds, and place on cornmeal-dusted pizza peel or an inverted baking sheet.

Sprinkle ⅛ of cheese over each pizza round, and arrange 2 slices of onions over top. Season with pepper.

Carefully slide pizzas onto heated pizza stone, baking tiles or baking sheet, and bake at 500 degrees or highest setting (preheated) for 10-14 minutes, or until bottoms are crisp and browned. Repeat with remaining dough and toppings.

Makes 8, 6-inch pizzas

Serves 8

NUTRITIONAL DATA

PER SERVING		EXCHANGES	
calories	219	milk	0.0
% calories from fat	30	vegetable	2.0
fat (gm)	7.3	fruit	0.0
sat. fat (gm)	2.1	bread	1.5
cholesterol (mg)	8	meat	0.5
sodium (mg)	478	fat	1.0
protein (gm)	7.7		
carbohydrate (gm)	31		

MIXED SEAFOOD PIZZA

M ountains of fresh scallops and shrimp marinated in garlic and herbs complement a spicy tomato sauce in this feast from the sea.

  2 tablespoons olive oil
  2 cloves garlic, finely chopped
 ½ teaspoon dried oregano leaves
 ½ teaspoon marjoram leaves
 ⅛ teaspoon crushed red pepper
 ½ lb. bay scallops
 ½ lb. medium shrimp, shelled and deveined
  1 tablespoon lemon juice
  1 tablespoon red-wine vinegar
 ¼ teaspoon black pepper, freshly ground
    Basic Pizza Dough (see p. 140)
    Basic Tomato-Basil Sauce (see index)
  1 tablespoon capers
  8 ripe olives, pitted and sliced
  1 tablespoon fresh parsley, chopped

To prepare seafood filling, heat 1 tablespoon olive oil in large skillet over medium heat. Add garlic, oregano, marjoram, and crushed red pepper. Sauté 2 minutes. Add scallops and shrimp, and cook, stirring occasionally, 3 to 4 minutes, or until shrimp are pink and firm and scallops are opaque.

Transfer scallop and shrimp mixture, including pan juices, to bowl. Add remaining tablespoon of olive oil, lemon juice, vinegar, and toss to combine. Refrigerate seafood mixture to marinate while preparing pizza dough and tomato sauce.

Prepare Basic Pizza Dough. Set aside to rise. Meanwhile, prepare Tomato Sauce.

To assemble and bake pizza, lightly oil a 13x9-inch baking pan. Roll out pizza dough to 15x11-inch rectangle. Line pan with dough, leaving a 1-inch rim of dough on all sides. Let dough rest 10 minutes. Reserve 3 tablespoons tomato sauce; spread remaining sauce on top of dough. Bake pizza at 450 degrees (preheated) on lower oven rack 12 minutes.

Meanwhile, drain liquid from seafood into large skillet. Cook until liquid is reduced to syrup that barely coats skillet. Pour over seafood mixture; toss to coat.

Top pizza with seafood mixture; brush reserved tomato sauce onto seafood. Sprinkle top of pizza with capers and olives, and bake 5 to 7 minutes longer or until pizza crust is well browned. Garnish with parsley, and serve immediately.

Serves 8

NUTRITIONAL DATA

PER SERVING		EXCHANGES	
calories	285	milk	0.0
% calories from fat	35	vegetable	2.0
fat (gm)	8	fruit	0.0
sat. fat (gm)	1.7	bread	1.5
cholesterol (mg)	52.9	meat	1.5
sodium (mg)	592	fat	1.0
protein (gm)	15.4		
carbohydrate (gm)	39.2		

CLAM PIZZA WITH THYME

- 1 recipe Basic Pizza Dough (see p. 140)
- 36 littleneck clams, scrubbed
- 2 tablespoons olive oil
- 6 cloves garlic, minced
- ¼ cup Parmesan cheese, freshly grated
- 1⅓ teaspoon ground thyme
  Black pepper, freshly ground, to taste
  Crushed red pepper (optional)

Prepare Basic Pizza Dough. Set aside to rise.

Preheat oven to 500 degrees, and place a pizza stone, if using, on bottom of oven.

Shuck clams over bowl in sink, allowing clams and their juice to fall into bowl. When all clams have been shucked, swish each in the juice to rinse off any sand and shell bits. Coarsely chop any clams that are not very small, and put all in clean bowl.

Let clam juice sit for 5 minutes so that sand and the grit settle to bottom. Pour clear liquor into cup, leaving grit behind. Stir ¼ cup of liquor into shucked clams along with olive oil and garlic. Generously sprinkle cornmeal over a large flat cookie sheet.

On cookie sheet, shape dough into 14-inch round. Pinch edges to form rim. Prick surface of dough with fork. Spoon clam mixture evenly over dough to within ½-inch of rim. Sprinkle pizza with Parmesan cheese. Shake pan to see if pizza is sticking; if it is, carefully lift dough where trouble spot is and add cornmeal underneath.

With quick jerk, slide pizza off sheet and onto hot stone; if not using stone, simply set cookie sheet on bottom rack of the oven.

Bake pizza about 5 minutes, until crusty brown on bottom. Remove from oven, season with thyme, black pepper, and crushed red pepper. Serve immediately.

Serves 8

NUTRITIONAL DATA

PER SERVING		EXCHANGES	
calories	219	milk	0.0
% calories from fat	28	vegetable	0.0
fat (gm)	6.7	fruit	0.0
sat. fat (gm)	1.4	bread	1.5
cholesterol (mg)	16.9	meat	1.0
sodium (mg)	216	fat	1.0
protein (gm)	10.5		
carbohydrate (gm)	28.5		

SHRIMP AND FETA PIZZA

½ recipe Whole Wheat variation of Basic Pizza
   Dough (see p. 141)
½ teaspoon dried basil
½ teaspoon dried oregano
36 medium shrimp, shelled and deveined
2 cups snow peas, thinly sliced
1 cup scallions, chopped
2 cloves garlic, minced
4½ oz. feta cheese, crumbled

Prepare ½ recipe Whole Wheat Pizza Dough. Set aside to rise.

Spray 14-inch pizza pan with nonstick cooking spray. Roll dough on prepared pan; pinch edges to form rim. Prick surface of dough with fork; spray with olive oil-flavored vegetable cooking spray. Sprinkle with half of the basil and oregano.

Bake dough at 475 degrees (preheated) 10-12 minutes, until golden.

Meanwhile, in large, nonstick, sprayed skillet, sauté shrimp, peas, scallions, and garlic. Sprinkle with remaining basil and oregano, and cook, stirring frequently, for 5-6 minutes.

Spread shrimp mixture evenly over pre-baked crust. Sprinkle with feta cheese. Bake 5-8 minutes more or until cheese softens.

Serves 8

NUTRITIONAL DATA

PER SERVING		EXCHANGES	
calories	162	milk	0.0
% calories from fat	28	vegetable	0.5
fat (gm)	5.1	fruit	0.0
sat. fat (gm)	2.7	bread	1.0
cholesterol (mg)	62.6	meat	1.0
sodium (mg)	294	fat	0.5
protein (gm)	11.9		
carbohydrate (gm)	17.2		

SPICY SHRIMP AND GARLIC PIZZA

2 cloves garlic, minced

½ lb. uncooked medium shrimp, peeled and deveined

1 recipe Whole Wheat variation of Basic Pizza Dough (see p. 141)

4 oz. skim mozzarella cheese, shredded

1 tablespoon fresh oregano, chopped, or 1 teaspoon dried, crumbled

3 green onions, sliced

½ teaspoon dried red pepper flakes

Put large skillet sprayed with nonstick vegetable spray on medium-high heat. Add garlic, and stir. Add shrimp, and cook until just pink, about 3 minutes. Cool.

Shape dough into 14-inch round. Pinch edges to form rim. Prick surface of dough with fork. Distribute cheese over pizza crust. Sprinkle oregano over cheese. Top with shrimp. Sprinkle with green onions and pepper flakes. Bake on rack in lowest third of 500-degree preheated oven until crust is golden brown, about 20 minutes.

Serves 8

NUTRITIONAL DATA

PER SERVING		EXCHANGES	
calories	194	milk	0.0
% calories from fat	21	vegetable	0.0
fat (gm)	4.7	fruit	0.0
sat. fat (gm)	1.8	bread	1.5
cholesterol (mg)	51.5	meat	1.5
sodium (mg)	250	fat	0.0
protein (gm)	12.3		
carbohydrate (gm)	26.2		

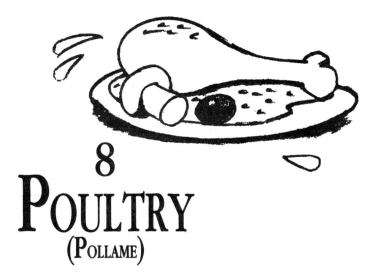

8
POULTRY
(POLLAME)

In Italy chicken is more popular than red meat. Italians love the versatility of chicken; you can grill, boil, bake, sauté, roast, stuff, and braise chicken. Chicken can be used in salads or mixed with pasta, rice, or couscous.

Every region in Italy has its own special chicken dishes. In the north, porcini mushrooms and red wine sauces are popular. In the south, chicken is served with tomato sauces, vegetables, or herbs.

Many of these recipes include vegetable cooking spray, and since it is now available flavored with olive oil or butter, you may consider using these to improve flavor.

ROAST CAPON

R *oast capon is a wonderful holiday meal.*
You can stuff it with a savory filling or with
a fruit filling.

    4 cups day-old bread, shredded
    3 tablespoons skim milk
    ¼ cup onion, finely chopped
    ½ cup fresh parsley, chopped
    1 oz. grated Romano cheese
    1 large egg, beaten
    ⅔ cup dry white wine
       Spike, to taste
       Black pepper, freshly ground, to taste
       5-lb. capon
    2 tablespoons fresh rosemary
    ½ cup dry white wine

To make stuffing, put bread in small bowl, and add milk. Crumble bread in milk, and set aside.

In large frying pan sprayed with vegetable cooking spray, brown onion, and sauté for about 5 minutes or until browned. Transfer to large bowl, add soaked bread, parsley, cheese, egg, ⅔ cup wine, Spike, and pepper. Mix well.

Wash and dry capon inside and out. Stuff filling loosely into body cavity. Sew or skewer the opening closed and truss capon. Put capon on rack in roasting pan, spray with vegetable cooking spray, and rub breast with Spike, if desired. Sprinkle the rosemary over capon.

In preheated 350-degree oven, roast capon 2½ hours, or until meat is tender and internal temperature registers 180 degrees, basting occasionally with wine. Carve capon into serving pieces, and serve with stuffing.

Serves 8

NUTRITIONAL DATA

PER SERVING		EXCHANGES	
calories	242	milk	0.0
% calories from fat	37	vegetable	0.0
fat (gm)	9.8	fruit	0.0
sat. fat (gm)	3	bread	0.5
cholesterol (mg)	86.3	meat	3.0
sodium (mg)	166	fat	0.5
protein (gm)	22.4		
carbohydrate (gm)	9		

ANISETTE CHICKEN BREASTS

4 skinless, boneless chicken breast halves (6 oz. each)
1 teaspoon Spike
½ teaspoon pepper, freshly ground
2 cups fresh mushrooms, sliced
¼ cup skim milk
2 tablespoons all-purpose flour
2 tablespoons evaporated skim milk
¼ cup licorice-flavored liqueur

Flatten each chicken breast half to ¼-inch thickness between plastic wrap. Heat 12-inch skillet sprayed with vegetable cooking spray over medium-high heat. Cook chicken, turning occasionally, until brown. Sprinkle with Spike and pepper.

Add mushrooms. Cover, and cook over medium heat 15 minutes. Remove chicken and mushrooms with slotted spoon onto warm platter, and keep warm.

Mix milk, flour, and evaporated milk until smooth. Heat in skillet to boiling. Add liqueur; heat to boiling, stirring constantly. Boil and stir 4 minutes. Pour sauce over chicken.

Serves 4

NUTRITIONAL DATA

PER SERVING		EXCHANGES	
calories	217	milk	0.0
% calories from fat	13	vegetable	2.0
fat (gm)	3.1	fruit	0.0
sat. fat (gm)	0.8	bread	0.0
cholesterol (mg)	69.2	meat	3.0
sodium (mg)	78	fat	0.0
protein (gm)	27.4		
carbohydrate (gm)	12.2		

CHICKEN DIAVOLO

Diavolo *means "devilish" or, in this case, spicy. The "heat" can be controlled by varying the amount of crushed red pepper flakes. You can barbecue this chicken on the grill.*

¼ cup white wine
½ teaspoon crushed red pepper flakes
1 teaspoon dried rosemary, crumbled
1 teaspoon dried oregano, crumbled
2½-lb. broiling chicken, quartered
3 tablespoons Italian parsley, minced

Combine wine, red pepper flakes, rosemary, and oregano in small bowl. Set aside for up to 1 hour.

Preheat broiler or prepare barbecue. Brush both sides of chicken lavishly with pepper-infused wine, and broil about 5 inches from heat for about 15 minutes on each side or until cooked through.

If you would like chicken to be spicier, baste once or twice with wine while it is cooking. Sprinkle with parsley before serving.

Serves 4

NUTRITIONAL DATA

PER SERVING		EXCHANGES	
calories	163	milk	0.0
% calories from fat	44	vegetable	0.0
fat (gm)	7.7	fruit	0.0
sat. fat (gm)	2.1	bread	0.0
cholesterol (mg)	56	meat	3.0
sodium (mg)	34	fat	0.0
protein (gm)	19		
carbohydrate (gm)	0.9		

CHICKEN GUBBIAN STYLE

I n the quiet hill town of Gubbio in the region of Umbria, you will find simple peasant food that reflects old traditions. The people here still make time for the pleasure of another's company, and dining together is one of their great pleasures.

    3-lb. chicken, quartered
1 large white onion, coarsely chopped
¼ cup red wine
4 fresh sage leaves or 1 teaspoon dried sage
8 fresh basil leaves or 1 teaspoon dried basil
2 sprigs fresh rosemary or 1 teaspoon dried rosemary
1 cup dry white wine
1½ cups fresh plum tomatoes (3 tomatoes), seeded and pureed
    Spike, to taste
    Black pepper, freshly ground, to taste

Wash and dry chicken pieces. Set aside.

Heat large skillet sprayed with vegetable cooking oil over medium heat. Add onion, and sauté slowly for 5 minutes or until tender. Raise heat to medium-high, add chicken pieces, and brown on all sides. Add vinegar, and boil until it evaporates. Lower heat, add sage, basil, and rosemary; cook for 20 minutes.

Raise heat, add wine, and boil until it evaporates. Add tomato puree, Spike, and pepper, reduce heat to medium-low, and cook 25 minutes or until sauce has thickened and chicken is easily pierced with fork.

Transfer chicken to platter, and spoon some of the sauce over top. Serve immediately.

Serves 4

NUTRITIONAL DATA

PER SERVING		EXCHANGES	
calories	267	milk	0.0
% calories from fat	32	vegetable	1.5
fat (gm)	9.5	fruit	0.0
sat. fat (gm)	2.6	bread	0.0
cholesterol (mg)	67.4	meat	3.0
sodium (mg)	61	fat	1.5
protein (gm)	24.1		
carbohydrate (gm)	9		

CHICKEN WITH LAUREL

*I*n much of central Italy, native bay laurel trees *scent the air, making it heavenly. In Rome laurel leaves often flavor an elaborate roast chicken that's sauced with flaming liqueur and wreathed with a laurel garland. This version is garnished with orange slices, fresh bay leaves, and green peas.*

    5-lb. roasting chicken
    4 large oranges
    1 medium onion, sliced
    6 fresh bay leaves or 3 or 4 dry bay leaves
    ¼ cup orange juice
    2 cups peas, cooked and drained
    Small cluster fresh bay leaves

Reserve chicken neck and giblets for other uses. Pull off and discard lumps of fat from chicken. Rinse chicken inside and out; pat dry. Cut one unpeeled orange into chunks; fill neck and body cavities of chicken with orange chunks, onion, and bay leaves. Tie chicken legs together with a piece of kitchen string; also tie a length of string around breast portion of chicken to secure wings.

Place chicken, breast down, on rack in large roasting pan. Roast, uncovered, in 350-degree oven for 30 minutes. Turn chicken breast up. Spray skin with olive oil-flavored cooking spray, and roast 30 more minutes. Continue to roast until meat near thighbone is no longer pink (about 30 more minutes); cut to test.

Meanwhile grate 1 teaspoon peel (colored part only) from one of remaining oranges. Squeeze enough juice from same orange to make ¼ cup; set peel and juice aside. Cut off and discard peel and white membrane from remaining 2 oranges. Slice fruit crosswise, and set aside. Reserve small strip of peel for garnish.

When chicken is done, discard orange chunks, onion, and bay leaves from cavities. Tip chicken to drain juices from body into roasting pan; transfer chicken to platter, and cover with foil to keep warm.

Skim and discard fat from pan drippings. Add grated orange peel and orange juice; bring to a boil over high heat, stirring to incorporate browned bits. Reduce heat to medium. Pour liqueur into small pan. Warm over medium heat until bubbly, then carefully ignite with a match; stir into sauce. Poor sauce into serving bowl.

Arrange peas on platter around chicken; garnish with strip of orange peel. Surround chicken with orange slices, and garnish with cluster of bay leaves. Offer sauce to spoon over meat.

Note: I sometimes use lemon balm instead of bay leaves in this recipe.

Serves 4

NUTRITIONAL DATA

PER SERVING		EXCHANGES	
calories	432	milk	0.0
% calories from fat	33	vegetable	0.0
fat (gm)	15.6	fruit	1.0
sat. fat (gm)	4.3	bread	1.0
cholesterol (mg)	112	meat	5.5
sodium (mg)	68	fat	0.0
protein (gm)	43.4		
carbohydrate (gm)	28.9		

CHICKEN AND LEMON

T his is an ideal recipe for a busy day because it is so quick to make.

2 lbs. chicken pieces

3 large cloves garlic, chopped

2 sprigs rosemary

2 fresh sage leaves

8 fresh basil leaves

Spike, to taste

Black pepper, freshly ground, to taste

Juice of 1 large lemon

8 lemon slices

2 tablespoons Italian parsley, chopped

Wash and dry chicken pieces; set aside.

Heat large deep skillet sprayed with vegetable cooking spray over medium heat. Add garlic, rosemary, sage, and basil. Sauté until garlic is soft and herbs are wilted. Remove and discard garlic and herbs.

Add chicken pieces to skillet, and brown on all sides. Sprinkle chicken with Spike and pepper, and pour lemon juice over it. Cover pan, and simmer over medium-low heat for 45 minutes or until chicken is tender.

Place lemon slices over chicken pieces and sprinkle with parsley. Simmer 5 more minutes. Using a slotted spoon, transfer chicken to serving platter, and serve immediately, with pan juices spooned over.

Serves 8

NUTRITIONAL DATA

PER SERVING		EXCHANGES	
calories	114	milk	0.0
% calories from fat	38	vegetable	0.0
fat (gm)	4.8	fruit	0.0
sat. fat (gm)	1.3	bread	0.0
cholesterol (mg)	48.6	meat	2.0
sodium (mg)	45	fat	0.0
protein (gm)	15.8		
carbohydrate (gm)	1.5		

CHICKEN BREASTS IN LEMON SAUCE

4 skinless, boneless chicken breast halves (about 6 oz. each)
½ cup all-purpose flour
3 cloves garlic, minced
2 tablespoons lemon juice
½ teaspoon black pepper, freshly ground
1 tablespoon large capers, drained
  Raspberries
  Strawberries
  Parsley sprigs

Cut each chicken breast horizontally to make 2 thin slices. Coat with flour. Heat 12-inch skillet sprayed with vegetable cooking spray over medium-high heat.

Cook chicken and garlic 4 to 6 minutes, turning once, until chicken is brown. Add lemon juice; sprinkle with pepper. Heat. Sprinkle with capers.

Garnish with raspberries, strawberries, and parsley (not included in Nutritional Data).

Serves 4

NUTRITIONAL DATA

PER SERVING		EXCHANGES	
calories	196	milk	0.0
% calories from fat	15	vegetable	0.0
fat (gm)	3.1	fruit	0.0
sat. fat (gm)	0.8	bread	0.5
cholesterol (mg)	68.6	meat	3.0
sodium (mg)	60	fat	0.0
protein (gm)	26.9		
carbohydrate (gm)	13.5		

BREAST OF CHICKEN IN MUSHROOM SAUCE

T *his delicate sauce, combining domestic mushrooms with stronger porcini and tomatoes,
has a fresh taste that enhances the flavor of the
chicken.*

- ¼ oz. dried porcini mushrooms
- ¼ cup onion, chopped
- ¼ lb. fresh mushrooms (about ½ cup), cleaned and sliced
- ⅓ cup dry white wine
- ½ lb. plum tomatoes (4-5), peeled, seeded, and chopped
  Spike, to taste
  Black pepper, freshly ground, to taste
- 1 tablespoon fresh basil, chopped, or 1 teaspoon dried
- 1 tablespoon fresh oregano, chopped, or 1 teaspoon dried
- 4 skinless, boneless chicken breast halves (about 1½ lbs.)
- ½ cup chicken broth or salt-free canned chicken broth

Soak dried porcini in warm water for 10 minutes.

In small skillet sprayed with vegetable cooking spray, over medium heat, add onion and sliced mushrooms, and sauté for about 2 minutes, until onions are soft and mushrooms give off their moisture. Add wine, and cook until alcohol evaporates, about 1 minute. Add tomatoes, and crush them with back of large spoon.

Add reserved porcini, including strained soaking liquid. Simmer sauce over medium-high heat to reduce slightly, about 3 minutes. Season with Spike, pepper, basil, and oregano.

In large skillet sprayed with vegetable cooking spray, over medium-high heat, cook chicken breasts for 5 minutes, turning once, until nicely browned on both sides. Drain off excess pan drippings.

Add chicken broth, and cook 2 to 3 minutes longer or until chicken is cooked through.

Add mushroom sauce to chicken. Stir well, and cook for 1 minute. Serve immediately.

Serves 4

NUTRITIONAL DATA

PER SERVING		EXCHANGES	
calories	181	milk	0.0
% calories from fat	18	vegetable	1.0
fat (gm)	3.6	fruit	0.0
sat. fat (gm)	1.3	bread	0.0
cholesterol (mg)	70.9	meat	3.0
sodium (mg)	191	fat	0.0
protein (gm)	26.9		
carbohydrate (gm)	6.7		

CHICKEN PICCATA

1 lb. boneless chicken breasts (4), thinly sliced
¼ cup flour
½ teaspoon salt
¼ teaspoon pepper
   Butter Buds equivalent to 6 tablespoons butter
3 tablespoons lemon juice
½ cup white wine
2 tablespoons fresh parsley, chopped

Coat chicken with flour, and sauté quickly in large nonstick skillet, turning once. Season with salt and pepper.

Combine Butter Buds, lemon juice, and white wine, and add to skillet. Tilt skillet to distribute liquid evenly. Turn chicken once again, then cover, and simmer until tender.

Add a small amount of water, if necessary, to prevent juices from becoming too thick. Sprinkle with chopped parsley during last minute of cooking time.

Serves 4

NUTRITIONAL DATA

PER SERVING		EXCHANGES	
calories	150	milk	0.0
% calories from fat	13	vegetable	0.0
fat (gm)	2	fruit	0.0
sat. fat (gm)	0.6	bread	0.5
cholesterol (mg)	45.7	meat	2.0
sodium (mg)	575	fat	0.0
protein (gm)	17.7		
carbohydrate (gm)	8.2		

CHICKEN, ROMAN STYLE

T his is a popular dish in Rome, where in the summer it is served barely warm instead of hot from the pan.

- 1 large red bell pepper, cored, seeded, and cut into strips about ⅛ inch wide
- 1 large yellow bell pepper, cored, seeded, and cut into strips about ⅛ inch wide
- 1 large clove garlic, minced
- 3½-lb. chicken, cut up
- ¼ cup dry white wine
- 2 28-oz. cans plum tomatoes, drained
- 2 tablespoons fresh oregano or 1 tablespoon dried oregano

  Spike, to taste

  Black pepper, freshly ground, to taste

Heat large skillet sprayed with vegetable cooking spray over medium heat for 1 minute. Add peppers, cover pan, and sauté peppers, stirring once or twice, until they are soft, about 4 minutes. Transfer peppers to plate, and reserve.

Add garlic to pan, and sauté over medium heat for 1 minute. Add chicken, and sauté, turning once, until golden brown, about 10 minutes.

Increase heat to high; add wine, and cook, shaking pan, until alcohol evaporates, about 1 minute. Crush tomatoes, and add them to pan along with oregano.

Reduce heat to medium-low; simmer, covered, for 15 minutes. Add reserved peppers to pan and simmer, covered, 5 minutes more or until chicken is cooked through. Season with Spike and pepper. Cool slightly before serving.

Serves 6

NUTRITIONAL DATA

PER SERVING		EXCHANGES	
calories	208	milk	0.0
% calories from fat	33	vegetable	2.5
fat (gm)	7.8	fruit	0.0
sat. fat (gm)	2.1	bread	0.0
cholesterol (mg)	52.3	meat	2.5
sodium (mg)	462	fat	0.0
protein (gm)	20.4		
carbohydrate (gm)	13.6		

SAUTÉED CHICKEN BREASTS WITH SAGE

In this simple dish from Florence, a marinade of lemon juice, oil, and sage infuses the chicken with wonderful flavor.

4 skinless, boneless chicken breast halves (6 oz. each)
3 tablespoons fresh lemon juice
28 fresh whole sage leaves
1 teaspoon Spike
    Black pepper, freshly ground, to taste
4 slices lemon

Place chicken in 8-inch-square glass baking dish sprayed with vegetable cooking spray. Add lemon juice, and sage leaves. Cover, and set aside at room temperature for 30 minutes. Remove chicken from marinade, and pat dry. Strain marinade into small bowl; reserve sage leaves separately.

In skillet sprayed with vegetable cooking spray, place chicken breasts, smooth side down, and cook until nicely browned on bottom, about 5 minutes. Turn breasts, and season them with Spike and pepper. Tuck reserved sage leaves around chicken, and cook until chicken is browned on bottom and just white throughout, about 5 minutes longer.

Remove skillet from heat. Transfer chicken to cutting board. Slice chicken breasts diagonally, ½ inch thick, and arrange on warm platter. Place sage leaves over chicken. Cover loosely with foil.

Pour off grease, then heat skillet over moderately high heat until hot. Pour in reserved marinade, and stir with wooden spoon, scraping up brown bits from bottom of pan. Sauce will boil almost immediately. As soon as it becomes brown glaze (in less than 1 minute), pour sauce over chicken, and garnish with lemon halves.

Serves 4

NUTRITIONAL DATA

PER SERVING		EXCHANGES	
calories	147	milk	0.0
% calories from fat	21	vegetable	0.0
fat (gm)	3.4	fruit	0.0
sat. fat (gm)	1	bread	0.0
cholesterol (mg)	68.6	meat	3.0
sodium (mg)	60	fat	0.0
protein (gm)	25.5		
carbohydrate (gm)	3.2		

♥

CHICKEN WITH SPINACH AND BEAN SALAD

T his is a great one-dish meal. Both the bean salad and spinach can be prepared ahead and then the spinach can be reheated.

BEAN SALAD

- 1 15-oz. can Great Northern beans, drained, rinsed, and patted dry
- ½ cup celery, chopped
- ½ cup tomato, chopped
- ¼ cup red onion, chopped
- 3 tablespoons white wine
- 1 teaspoon balsamic vinegar
- ½ teaspoon dried oregano
- ½ teaspoon dried tarragon
  Spike, to taste
  Black pepper, freshly ground, to taste

CHICKEN WITH SPINACH

- 1 10-oz. package fresh spinach, washed and stems removed
- 2 cloves garlic, minced
- 2 tablespoons pine nuts
  Black pepper, freshly ground, to taste
- 2 10-oz. whole boneless, skinless chicken breasts, split and pounded to flatten

To make Bean Salad: In small bowl, combine beans, celery, tomato, and red onion. In separate bowl, whisk together wine, vinegar, oregano, and tarragon. Season with Spike and pepper. Add dressing to bean mixture, and toss gently.

To make Chicken with Spinach: In large skillet sprayed with vegetable cooking spray, over medium heat, cook spinach with water clinging to its leaves until wilted and soft, 4 to 5 minutes. Drain excess water.

Add garlic and pine nuts. Cook and stir 3 minutes. Season with pepper and set aside.

Place chicken breasts on broiler pan and set pan about 5 inches from heat. Broil breasts, turning once, until they are cooked through, 3 to 4 minutes on each side.

Reheat spinach if necessary. Distribute spinach evenly among four heated serving plates. Place chicken breast on top of each spinach portion. Place bean salad on each plate. Serve at once.

Serves 4

NUTRITIONAL DATA

PER SERVING		EXCHANGES	
calories	298	milk	0.0
% calories from fat	17	vegetable	1.0
fat (gm)	5.8	fruit	0.0
sat. fat (gm)	0.8	bread	1.5
cholesterol (mg)	57.2	meat	2.8
sodium (mg)	127	fat	0.0
protein (gm)	32.6		
carbohydrate (gm)	29.3		

BRAISED CHICKEN WITH TOMATOES

T*his is a very fragrant dish because of the rosemary, garlic, and balsamic vinegar mingled together. The addition of tomatoes makes it complete.*

4-lb. chicken, cut into pieces
Black pepper, freshly ground, to taste
3 cloves garlic, minced
½ cup dry white wine
¼ cup balsamic vinegar
5 plum tomatoes, seeded and chopped
2 tablespoons black olives, sliced
1 tablespoon dried rosemary
2 tablespoons fresh oregano or 1 tablespoon dried

Grind some pepper over chicken. Heat large skillet sprayed with vegetable cooking spray over medium-high heat. Add chicken, and sear on all sides, turning occasionally, for about 10 minutes. Transfer chicken to platter; cover with aluminum foil to keep warm.

Drain off all but about 3 tablespoons of pan drippings. Over medium heat, sauté garlic in pan drippings for about 1 minute. Turn up heat to medium-high, add wine, and simmer vigorously until wine is reduced by half. Add vinegar, chopped tomatoes, olives, and rosemary.

Return chicken to pan, cover, and simmer gently for 10 to 12 minutes or until the juices run clear when a chicken thigh is pierced with tip of paring knife. Serve immediately.

Serves 6

NUTRITIONAL DATA

PER SERVING		EXCHANGES	
calories	220	milk	0.0
% calories from fat	39	vegetable	1.5
fat (gm)	9.6	fruit	0.0
sat. fat (gm)	2.4	bread	0.0
cholesterol (mg)	59.7	meat	3.0
sodium (mg)	139	fat	0.5
protein (gm)	21.2		
carbohydrate (gm)	8.9		

CHICKEN BREASTS WITH VERMOUTH

The quintessential Italian aperitif adds a special touch to this chicken.

- 4 boneless, skinless chicken breasts
- 2 tablespoons all-purpose flour
  Pinch of salt
  Pinch of pepper
- 2 tablespoons margarine
- 2 cups dry white vermouth
- 2 tablespoons Italian parsley, chopped

Remove excess fat from chicken and discard. Place chicken between 2 layers of waxed paper. Pound chicken with kitchen mallet 5 times on each side.

In flat dish, combine flour, salt, and pepper. Remove waxed paper from chicken. Roll chicken in flour mixture until well coated.

In large nonstick skillet over medium heat, melt margarine. Add chicken, and cook 3 to 5 minutes on each side or until golden and meat is white all the way through. Remove chicken from pan and keep warm on ovenproof serving plate in 275-degree preheated oven.

To same pan over medium heat, add vermouth. Stir well, scraping bottom of pan lightly so that margarine and chicken particles mix with vermouth. Cook 5 to 10 minutes or until vermouth is reduced to about 2 tablespoons. Pour over chicken, sprinkle with parsley, and serve.

Serves 4

NUTRITIONAL DATA

PER SERVING		EXCHANGES	
calories	468	milk	0.0
% calories from fat	23	vegetable	0.0
fat (gm)	11.8	fruit	0.0
sat. fat (gm)	2.9	bread	0.0
cholesterol (mg)	146	meat	8.5
sodium (mg)	197	fat	0.0
protein (gm)	53.9		
carbohydrate (gm)	4.3		

CHICKEN VESUVIO

C hicken Vesuvio is a wonderful one-dish meal. It starts off in a large skillet on top of the stove and finishes in a roasting pan in the oven.

3½-lb. frying chicken, cut into pieces

4 medium-size baking potatoes (about 1 lb.), each quartered lengthwise

4 cloves garlic, minced

2 teaspoons dried oregano, crumbled

1 tablespoon dried basil, crumbled

2 tablespoons fresh parsley, minced

Black pepper, freshly ground, to taste

½ cup dry white wine

1 cup frozen peas, thawed

Heat large skillet sprayed with vegetable cooking spray over medium-high heat. Add half of chicken pieces, skin side down, and cook until slightly brown, about 5 minutes. Transfer chicken to large roasting pan. Brown remaining chicken, and transfer it to roasting pan.

Drain off all but about 3 tablespoons of liquid in pan. Add potato wedges in single layer, and sauté, turning once or twice, until outside begins to crisp and turn light brown, about 4 minutes. Transfer potatoes to pan with chicken.

Sprinkle garlic, oregano, basil, and parsley evenly over chicken and potatoes. Add pepper. Drizzle with wine.

Bake 30 to 35 minutes in preheated 450-degree oven. Turn chicken and potatoes twice, until juice runs clear when chicken thigh is pierced with knife. About 5 minutes before chicken is done, add peas to pan.

Arrange chicken pieces and potato wedges on a plate. Serve at once.

Serves 6

NUTRITIONAL DATA

PER SERVING		EXCHANGES	
calories	264	milk	0.0
% calories from fat	25	vegetable	1.0
fat (gm)	7.3	fruit	0.0
sat. fat (gm)	2	bread	1.5
cholesterol (mg)	52.3	meat	2.5
sodium (mg)	39	fat	0.0
protein (gm)	21.1		
carbohydrate (gm)	24.9		

CHICKEN IN WINE

*T*his dish must be started two days in advance, but the work is well worth it.

3 lbs. chicken pieces

MARINADE

1 large onion, thinly sliced
2 tablespoons fresh rosemary
2 tablespoons fresh parsley, minced
2 tablespoons fresh sage, minced
2 tablespoons fresh basil, minced
1 bay leaf
1 rib celery, diced
1 large carrot, diced
2 cloves garlic, minced
2 cups dry red wine
Spike, to taste
Black pepper, freshly ground, to taste

CHICKEN

3 tablespoons all-purpose flour
2 cups red wine
8 slices Italian bread

Wash and dry chicken pieces. Set aside.

To make Marinade: In deep rectangular dish large enough to hold chicken pieces in single layer, combine all marinade ingredients. Add chicken pieces to marinade, cover dish, and refrigerate for 2 days, occasionally turning chicken in marinade.

Remove chicken pieces from marinade, and set aside. Strain marinade through strainer lined with cheesecloth into bowl, pressing on solids with spoon to extract all juice; reserve. Discard solids.

To make Chicken: In large skillet sprayed with vegetable cooking spray over medium-high heat, brown chicken on all sides. Sprinkle chicken with flour and add reserved marinade. Add red wine to cover chicken. Cover skillet, and simmer over low heat 35 minutes.

Meanwhile, in skillet sprayed with vegetable cooking spray, sauté bread a few slices at a time until browned on both sides. Drain bread on brown paper.

Uncover skillet, and cook chicken, turning pieces occasionally until liquid is reduced by half and sauce is thickened. To serve, put 2 slices of bread on each plate, arrange chicken on top, and spoon sauce over.

Serves 6

NUTRITIONAL DATA

PER SERVING		EXCHANGES	
calories	300	milk	0.0
% calories from fat	19	vegetable	0.0
fat (gm)	6.1	fruit	0.0
sat. fat (gm)	1.7	bread	2.0
cholesterol (mg)	44.9	meat	3.0
sodium (mg)	232	fat	0.0
protein (gm)	19.6		
carbohydrate (gm)	26.3		

ITALIAN TURKEY BURGERS

I talians caught burger fever long ago. But like most things, they've made them their own with a few Italian touches.

- ½ lb. ground turkey
- ¼ cup egg substitute
- ¾ cup Italian-flavored bread crumbs
- 1 cup white mushrooms, thinly sliced
- ½ cup red wine
- ½ cup Italian Tofuto (see index)

With your hands, combine turkey with egg substitute. Separate mixture into 4 balls, then flatten into patties. Pour bread crumbs onto plate. Coat turkey burgers with bread crumbs.

Spray large nonstick skillet with cooking spray. Add turkey burgers, and cook over medium heat 3 to 5 minutes on each side or until golden brown and center is no longer pink. Remove from heat.

Transfer turkey burgers to shallow baking dish and place in 275-degree oven to keep warm.

In same pan, sauté mushrooms 5 minutes or until softened. Stir wine and Tofuto into pan, and bring liquid to a boil.

Remove turkey from oven and place on individual dinner plates or serving platter. Serve turkey burgers with sauce.

Variations: Whole wheat bread crumbs and sour-dough crumbs can be used instead of Italian-flavored bread crumbs. You can also use ½ cup plain nonfat yogurt instead of Tofuto, and 2 egg whites can be used instead of liquid egg substitute. (Not covered in Nutritional Data.)

Serves 4

NUTRITIONAL DATA

PER SERVING		EXCHANGES	
calories	191	milk	0.0
% calories from fat	28	vegetable	0.0
fat (gm)	5.9	fruit	0.0
sat. fat (gm)	1.5	bread	1.0
cholesterol (mg)	21.4	meat	1.5
sodium (mg)	218	fat	1.0
protein (gm)	13.3		
carbohydrate (gm)	16.3		

TURKEY MEATBALLS

Instead of beef or pork meatballs, try this on pasta, or make smaller versions for soup. I am confident you will love it.

- 1 lb. ground turkey
- ¾ cup Italian-seasoned bread crumbs
- 1 medium onion, chopped
- 2 egg whites
- ½ teaspoon dried leaf marjoram
- 1 teaspoon dried oregano
- 1 teaspoon dried basil
- 1 teaspoon Spike
- ¼ teaspoon black pepper, freshly ground
- ½ cup white wine or water
- 2 cups Basic Tomato-Basil Sauce (see index) or purchased tomato sauce

In large bowl, combine turkey, bread crumbs, onion, egg whites, marjoram, oregano, basil, Spike, and pepper. This is best mixed with your hands. Slowly pour wine into turkey mixture. Mix with hands 1 minute or until mixture forms large ball.

Shape into small uniform meatballs, and place in shallow un-greased nonstick baking pan. Place dish under broiler until meatballs are browned.

Cover meatballs with tomato sauce. Bake at 350 degrees 30-35 minutes or until meatballs are firm and no longer pink in center and sauce is bubbly. Spoon meatballs and sauce over cooked pasta, rice, or polenta.

Serves 4

NUTRITIONAL DATA

PER SERVING		EXCHANGES	
calories	318	milk	0.0
% calories from fat	31	vegetable	2.5
fat (gm)	11.2	fruit	0.0
sat. fat (gm)	2.7	bread	1.0
cholesterol (mg)	42.2	meat	2.0
sodium (mg)	543	fat	1.5
protein (gm)	21.9		
carbohydrate (gm)	28.5		

9
MEAT
(CARNE)

While meat may be high in calories, it is also high in vitamins and other valuable nutrients. While it is a good idea to reduce meat consumption to lose weight, it is also important to trim off all visible fat.

Italians prefer the white-fleshed meats, veal and pork. Americans are primarily beef eaters. Since most meats have about the same calories you should choose those you like best.

In the recipes that follow, broth, herbs, and various seasonings substitute for the fat to produce good Italian taste and low-calorie, low-fat meals. In Italy beef is usually served in small pieces in stews, ragouts, and on skewers. Still smaller pieces are served as meatballs in pasta sauces.

BEEF RAGOUT

2 lbs. lean beef, cut into 1-inch cubes
3 cups beef broth
1 clove garlic, chopped
½ teaspoon pepper, freshly ground
1 teaspoon oregano
1 teaspoon thyme
2 cups carrots, sliced
2 cups celery, sliced
½ lb. small white onions
   Flour (optional)

Place beef on cookie sheet under broiler, turning to brown evenly. Put into pot with broth, garlic, pepper, oregano, and thyme. Cover, and simmer for 1 to 1½ hours until the meat is almost tender. Add carrots and celery and cook for 20 minutes. Add onions and cook for 15 minutes more. Remove garlic, taste for seasoning, and thicken, if you wish, with flour-and-water paste (not included in Nutritional Data).

Serves 8

NUTRITIONAL DATA

PER SERVING		EXCHANGES	
calories	215	milk	0.0
% calories from fat	35	vegetable	1.0
fat (gm)	8.4	fruit	0.0
sat. fat (gm)	2.9	bread	0.0
cholesterol (mg)	77.2	meat	3.5
sodium (mg)	386	fat	0.0
protein (gm)	27.1		
carbohydrate (gm)	7.2		

BEEF WITH MUSHROOMS

1   piece lean eye round or eye rib of beef, about 1½ lbs.
1   teaspoon Spike
¼   teaspoon black pepper, freshly ground
1   large onion or 2 shallots, sliced
¾   lbs. mushrooms, sliced
1   teaspoon tarragon, crushed
1   teaspoon oregano, crushed
½   cup sherry wine

Trim fat from meat. Spray it with vegetable cooking spray. Brown it on both sides in large skillet or shallow baking pan. Sprinkle with Spike and pepper, and bake at 375 degrees (preheated) for 30 to 40 minutes. Test for doneness by making small slit with small pointed knife. Beef should be rare.

Meanwhile sauté onions or shallots in same skillet for 2 minutes or until transparent. Add mushrooms, herbs, and sherry, and cook for about 3 minutes more. Carve beef, and pass hot mushroom sauce.

Serves 6

NUTRITIONAL DATA

PER SERVING		EXCHANGES	
calories	324	milk	0.0
% calories from fat	41	vegetable	1.0
fat (gm)	14.5	fruit	0.0
sat. fat (gm)	5.8	bread	0.0
cholesterol (mg).	96.8	meat	5.5
sodium (mg)	88	fat	0.0
protein (gm)	35.5		
carbohydrate (gm)	6.8		

BEEF STEW

2 lbs. lean beef, cut into 1- to 1½-inch cubes

2 onions, chopped

2 cloves garlic, minced

½ cup beef broth

½ cup red wine

¼ teaspoon black pepper, freshly ground

1 teaspoon oregano

1 teaspoon thyme

1 can (14 oz.) Italian tomatoes

Sauté meat in heavy pot sprayed with vegetable cooking spray, turning frequently to brown evenly. Be careful not to burn. Add onions and garlic, and cook until brown. Add remaining ingredients, cover, and simmer until beef is tender, about 40 minutes.

Serves 6

NUTRITIONAL DATA

PER SERVING		EXCHANGES	
calories	290	milk	0.0
% calories from fat	34	vegetable	1.5
fat (gm)	10.7	fruit	0.0
sat. fat (gm)	3.8	bread	0.0
cholesterol (mg)	103	meat	5.0
sodium (mg)	246	fat	0.0
protein (gm)	35.4		
carbohydrate (gm)	8.6		

STEAK FLORENTINE

3-lb. porterhouse or sirloin steak
2 teaspoons lemon juice
1 teaspoon Spike
½ teaspoon cracked pepper

Spray steak with vegetable cooking spray. Broil over charcoal or in broiler for 3 or 4 minutes on each side, depending on thickness of steak. It should be served medium-rare or medium. Sprinkle with lemon juice, Spike, and pepper before you turn it and again afterwards.

Serves 6

NUTRITIONAL DATA

PER SERVING		EXCHANGES	
calories	461	milk	0.0
% calories from fat	46	vegetable	0.0
fat (gm)	22.9	fruit	0.0
sat. fat (gm)	9.1	bread	0.0
cholesterol (mg)	169.3	meat	8.5
sodium (mg)	139	fat	0.0
protein (gm)	59.6		
carbohydrate (gm)	0.3		

MEATBALLS IN WINE

2 slices white bread
1 lb. ground lean turkey or beef
1 teaspoon Spike
¼ teaspoon black pepper, freshly ground
1 teaspoon oregano
1 teaspoon thyme
   Flour
½ cup red wine

Soak bread a few minutes in warm water to cover, and squeeze dry. Put into bowl with turkey and seasonings, and mix thoroughly with your hands. Form into balls about 1 inch in diameter.

Roll lightly in flour, and sauté in a skillet sprayed with vegetable cooking spray until browned on all sides, 2 or 3 minutes. Add wine; cover, and cook for 10 minutes. Pour juices over top, and serve.

Serves 4

NUTRITIONAL DATA

PER SERVING		EXCHANGES	
calories	194	milk	0.0
% calories from fat	42	vegetable	0.0
fat (gm)	9	fruit	0.0
sat. fat (gm)	2.4	bread	0.5
cholesterol (mg)	42.2	meat	2.0
sodium (mg)	129	fat	1.0
protein (gm)	16.1		
carbohydrate (gm)	6.7		

PEPPER STEAK

1⅓ lbs. sirloin steak

4 tablespoons mignonette pepper (broken into small bits)

¼ cup Armagnac

2 tablespoons Dijon mustard

2 tablespoons evaporated skim milk

Heat skillet sprayed with vegetable cooking spray. Sprinkle meat with pepper, and place into hot pan. Cook on both sides. Flambé with Armagnac.

Remove meat from skillet, and place it on plate. Add mustard and evaporated skim milk to skillet, and stir well. Simmer to desired consistency. Taste, and add more pepper if desired. Pour sauce over meat, and serve.

Serves 4

NUTRITIONAL DATA

PER SERVING		EXCHANGES	
calories	294	milk	0.0
% calories from fat	27	vegetable	0.0
fat (gm)	8.7	fruit	0.0
sat. fat (gm)	3.3	bread	0.0
cholesterol (mg)	108.2	meat	5.5
sodium (mg)	189	fat	0.0
protein (gm)	37.8		
carbohydrate (gm)	7.7		

STEAK ON A SKEWER

1⅔ lbs. lean beef steaks, sirloin or fillet
2 tablespoon beef broth
2 tablespoons red wine
1 clove garlic, crushed
1 teaspoon Spike
¼ teaspoon black pepper, freshly ground
¼ teaspoon sugar
1 teaspoon rosemary, crushed
1 ripe large tomato, cut in eighths

Cut steak into ½-inch cubes. Combine other ingredients except tomato, and marinate steak for 3 or 4 hours in mixture.

String on 6 long skewers, putting each tomato wedge after 2 or 3 steak cubes. Broil for 3 minutes near heat, brush with marinade, turn, brush again, and broil for 2 minutes more. Brush with marinade again before serving.

Serves 6

NUTRITIONAL DATA

PER SERVING		EXCHANGES	
calories	251	milk	0.0
% calories from fat	36	vegetable	0.0
fat (gm)	9.8	fruit	0.0
sat. fat (gm)	3.8	bread	0.0
cholesterol (mg)	108.2	meat	4.5
sodium (mg)	88	fat	0.0
protein (gm)	36.9		
carbohydrate (gm)	1.2		

STEW WITH 3 MEATS

1 large onion, minced
1 lb. lean beef, cut into 1-inch cubes
½ lb. pork cut into 1-inch cubes
½ lb. veal, cut into 1-inch cubes
1 cup water
1 cup beef broth
1 teaspoon paprika
1 teaspoon Spike
¼ teaspoon pepper, freshly ground
1 can (8 oz.) Italian peeled tomatoes
Flour (optional)

Sauté onion in skillet sprayed with vegetable cooking spray. Remove, and drain on paper towels. In same skillet, brown pork; add veal and brown; add beef and brown. Return onions to pan, and add water, broth, paprika, Spike, and pepper.

Cover, and simmer for 1 hour. Add tomatoes, and simmer for 30 minutes, until beef is tender. If you want a thicker sauce, thicken with flour-and-water paste, (not included in Nutritional Data), stirring in just before serving. Heat, but do not boil.

Serves 6

NUTRITIONAL DATA

PER SERVING		EXCHANGES	
calories	221	milk	0.0
% calories from fat	38	vegetable	1.0
fat (gm)	9.2	fruit	0.0
sat. fat (gm)	3.2	bread	0.0
cholesterol (mg)	92	meat	4.0
sodium (mg)	259	fat	0.0
protein (gm)	29		
carbohydrate (gm)	4.4		

VEAL CUTLETS

1⅓ lbs. veal cutlets, cut very thin
  2 tablespoons flour
  ¼ teaspoon Spike
  ¼ teaspoon pepper, freshly ground
  ¼ cup liquid Butter Buds
  ¼ cup white wine

Pound veal flat, and dust with mixture of flour, Spike, and pepper. Brown in Butter Buds for 3 minutes on each side. Add wine, cover, and cook for 2 minutes.
    Serves 4

NUTRITIONAL DATA

PER SERVING		EXCHANGES	
calories	172	milk	0.0
% calories from fat	28	vegetable	0.0
fat (gm)	5.1	fruit	0.0
sat. fat (gm)	2	bread	0.0
cholesterol (mg)	94.4	meat	3.0
sodium (mg)	256	fat	0.0
protein (gm)	22.9		
carbohydrate (gm)	3.7		

VEAL CHOPS WITH GREEN BEANS

6 small lean veal chops
1 teaspoon sugar
2 medium onions, sliced thin
1 teaspoon Spike
¼ teaspoon black pepper, freshly ground
½ teaspoon oregano
½ teaspoon marjoram
1 cup chicken broth
1 jar (4 oz.) pimientos, chopped
1 package (10 oz.) frozen green beans

Sprinkle chops with sugar, and brown in very hot skillet, turning once. Add onions and seasonings, and stir in broth. Cover, and simmer for 25 minutes. Add pimientos and beans, and simmer 15-20 minutes.

Serves 6

NUTRITIONAL DATA

PER SERVING		EXCHANGES	
calories	207	milk	0.0
% calories from fat	27	vegetable	1.5
fat (gm)	6.2	fruit	0.0
sat. fat (gm)	2.2	bread	0.0
cholesterol (mg)	103.1	meat	3.0
sodium (mg)	254	fat	0.0
protein (gm)	28.8		
carbohydrate (gm)	8.6		

HERBED VEAL CHOPS

6 small veal chops, trimmed
1 teaspoon Spike
¼ teaspoon pepper
2 tablespoons parsley, minced
½ teaspoon basil
½ teaspoon sage
⅓ cup white wine

Sauté veal chops in skillet sprayed with vegetable cooking spray over high heat, turning to brown evenly. Sprinkle with remaining ingredients except wine, and continue to cook over low heat for 10 minutes, turning several times. Add wine, and cook for 10 minutes more.

Remove chops to heated platter. Adjust seasoning of liquid. Stir, bring to boil, and pour over chops.

Serves 6

NUTRITIONAL DATA

PER SERVING		EXCHANGES	
calories	176	milk	0.0
% calories from fat	30	vegetable	0.0
fat (gm)	5.6	fruit	0.0
sat. fat (gm)	1.6	bread	0.0
cholesterol (mg)	100.1	meat	3.0
sodium (mg)	77	fat	0.0
protein (gm)	27.2		
carbohydrate (gm)	0.4		

VEAL ROLLS WITH HAM

1 lb. veal cutlets, cut thin
1 teaspoon Spike
½ teaspoon or 8 small leaves sage
¼ lb. lean prosciutto or other ham, sliced very thin
   Flour
⅓ cup white wine

Pound veal thin, and cut into 8 pieces. Sprinkle with Spike and sage. Trim fat from ham, cut into 8 pieces, and place it over veal. Roll and fasten with toothpicks. Dust with flour, and brown in skillet sprayed with vegetable cooking spray until golden on all sides. Place on hot platter and remove toothpicks.

Pour wine into pan, and stir with wooden spoon to loosen any brown bits. Bring to boil, and pour over veal rolls.

Serves 4

NUTRITIONAL DATA

PER SERVING		EXCHANGES	
calories	164	milk	0.0
% calories from fat	30	vegetable	0.0
fat (gm)	5.3	fruit	0.0
sat. fat (gm)	2	bread	0.0
cholesterol (mg)	86.4	meat	3.0
sodium (mg)	436	fat	0.0
protein (gm)	24		
carbohydrate (gm)	0.2		

VEAL SCALOPPINE WITH LEMON

1½ lbs. thin veal cutlets

1 teaspoon Spike

¼ teaspoon pepper

Flour

2 tablespoons lemon juice

2 tablespoons lemon thyme, chopped (optional)

Lemon slices

Pound veal thin, sprinkle with Spike and pepper, and dust thoroughly with flour. Heat skillet sprayed with vegetable cooking spray, and brown cutlets, turning once. Add lemon juice and thyme, and simmer for 4 minutes. Serve garnished with lemon slices.

Serves 4

NUTRITIONAL DATA

PER SERVING		EXCHANGES	
calories	161	milk	0.0
% calories from fat	33	vegetable	0.0
fat (gm)	5.6	fruit	0.0
sat. fat (gm)	2.2	bread	0.0
cholesterol (mg)	106.2	meat	3.0
sodium (mg)	88	fat	0.0
protein (gm)	25.4		
carbohydrate (gm)	0.7		

VEAL CHOPS WITH MUSHROOMS

6 small veal loin chops
1 teaspoon Spike
¼ teaspoon black pepper, freshly ground
  Flour
2 medium onions, sliced
½ lb. mushrooms, sliced
1 red bell pepper, chopped, or 1 jar (4 oz.) pimientos, chopped
1 cup chicken broth

Sprinkle chops with Spike and pepper, and dust with flour. Sauté in skillet sprayed with vegetable cooking spray, turning to brown evenly, for 3 minutes on each side. Add onions, and sauté until lightly browned.

Add mushrooms and pepper or pimientos, and cook 2 minutes. Add broth, cover, and simmer until chops are tender, about 15 minutes. Serve chops with onion-mushroom mixture and liquid poured over.

Serves 6

NUTRITIONAL DATA

PER SERVING		EXCHANGES	
calories	183	milk	0.0
% calories from fat	32	vegetable	1.0
fat (gm)	6.6	fruit	0.0
sat. fat (gm)	2.9	bread	0.0
cholesterol (mg)	93.1	meat	3.0
sodium (mg)	250	fat	0.0
protein (gm)	24.2		
carbohydrate (gm)	6.4		

VEAL CHOPS WITH PEPPERS

6 small veal chops, trimmed
3 red onions, sliced thin
3 bell peppers, green or red, cut into thin strips
2 cups fresh or canned tomatoes, chopped
1 teaspoon Spike
1 teaspoon oregano
1 teaspoon thyme
¼ teaspoon black pepper, freshly ground

Sauté chops in skillet sprayed with vegetable cooking spray, turning to brown evenly. Sauté onions and peppers in separate pan sprayed with vegetable spray until the onions are transparent and light brown. Combine with chops, and add tomatoes, Spike, oregano, thyme, and pepper. Stir, and cook 10 minutes.
Serves 6

NUTRITIONAL DATA

PER SERVING		EXCHANGES	
calories	224	milk	0.0
% calories from fat	25	vegetable	2.5
fat (gm)	6.1	fruit	0.0
sat. fat (gm)	1.6	bread	0.0
cholesterol (mg)	100.1	meat	3.0
sodium (mg)	86	fat	0.0
protein (gm)	29.0		
carbohydrate (gm)	13.1		

SALTIMBOCCA

12 small (1 oz.) scallops taken from fillet of veal
12 small (½ oz.) slices parma ham
   Spike, to taste
   Pepper, freshly ground, to taste
   Flour
½ cup Marsala wine
4 parsley sprigs

Place slice of parma ham on each veal scallop. Hold each scallop together with toothpick. Add Spike and pepper to each scallop. Dip each scallop in flour; shake off excess.

Heat skillet sprayed with vegetable cooking spray over medium high heat. Brown scallops on both sides for about 3 minutes. Add Marsala wine, and cook about 3 minutes. Remove veal, and cook until sauce is reduced by about half. Pour sauce over veal, and serve garnished with parsley.

Serves 4

NUTRITIONAL DATA

PER SERVING		EXCHANGES	
calories	327	milk	0.0
% calories from fat	33	vegetable	0.0
fat (gm)	8.2	fruit	0.0
sat. fat (gm)	2.9	bread	0.0
cholesterol (mg)	113.4	meat	4.5
sodium (mg)	665	fat	0.0
protein (gm)	13.2		
carbohydrate (gm)	0.5		

VEAL STEW WITH WINE

1 large onion, chopped
1 large clove garlic, minced
1½ lbs. lean veal, sliced
¼ cup water
½ cup tomato sauce
1 cup white wine
1 teaspoon Spike
¼ teaspoon black pepper, freshly ground
Flour

In large saucepan sprayed with vegetable cooking spray, brown onion and garlic for 2 minutes. Add veal, and turn to brown evenly. Add remaining ingredients except flour, cover, and simmer until veal is tender, about 45 minutes. Add more wine or water if needed. Thicken juices with flour-and-water paste, and adjust seasoning.
Serves 6

NUTRITIONAL DATA

PER SERVING		EXCHANGES	
calories	256	milk	0.0
% calories from fat	31	vegetable	1.0
fat (gm)	8.5	fruit	0.0
sat. fat (gm)	3.1	bread	0.0
cholesterol (mg)	128.1	meat	4.0
sodium (mg)	243	fat	0.0
protein (gm)	32.5		
carbohydrate (gm)	4.3		

ROAST LEG OF LAMB

Leg of lamb (about 4 lbs.)
3 cloves garlic, slivered
1 tablespoon rosemary
2 teaspoons Spike
½ teaspoon black pepper, freshly ground

Wipe lamb, trim off fat, and make small slits in number of places with sharp knife. Insert garlic slivers, and rub with mixture of rosemary, Spike, and pepper. Roast at 375 degrees (preheated) about 1¼ hours for rare lamb, 1½ hours for pink, and up to 2 hours for well done. Do not cover.
Serves 8

NUTRITIONAL DATA

PER SERVING		EXCHANGES	
calories	255	milk	0.0
% calories from fat	38	vegetable	0.0
fat (gm)	10.3	fruit	0.0
sat. fat (gm)	3.6	bread	0.0
cholesterol (mg)	117	meat	4.5
sodium (mg)	90	fat	0.0
protein (gm)	37.3		
carbohydrate (gm)	0.7		

LAMB WITH MUSHROOMS

6 slices cooked lean lamb

½ cup chicken broth

½ lb. mushrooms, sliced

2 tablespoons flour

1 teaspoon Spike

½ teaspoon pepper

2 tablespoons parsley, minced

½ teaspoon dried oregano

1 teaspoon fresh mint, chopped

Moisten lamb with ¼ cup of broth. Sauté mushrooms in small skillet sprayed with vegetable cooking spray. Dust lamb lightly with flour and Spike, and add to mushrooms.

In separate pan sprayed with vegetable cooking spray, blend in remaining flour, stir in remaining ¼ cup of broth, and add pepper, parsley, oregano, and mint. Simmer until thickened. Pour over lamb, and reheat.

Serves 6

NUTRITIONAL DATA

PER SERVING		EXCHANGES	
calories	159	milk	0.0
% calories from fat	34	vegetable	1.0
fat (gm)	5.9	fruit	0.0
sat. fat (gm)	2.3	bread	0.0
cholesterol (mg)	64.7	meat	2.5
sodium (mg)	133	fat	0.0
protein (gm)	21.4		
carbohydrate (gm)	4.2		

PORK SCALOPPINE

1⅓ lbs. pork tenderloin
1 clove garlic, crushed
1 teaspoon salt
¼ teaspoon black pepper, freshly ground
½ teaspoon rosemary
½ teaspoon sage
2 teaspoons lemon juice

Trim off fat, and cut pork into ⅓-inch slices. Brown in skillet sprayed with vegetable cooking spray, turning once. Add remaining ingredients, reduce heat, and cook for about 20 minutes. If pork sticks, add 1-2 tablespoons of water.
Serves 4

NUTRITIONAL DATA

PER SERVING		EXCHANGES	
calories	195	milk	0.0
% calories from fat	27	vegetable	0.0
fat (gm)	5.6	fruit	0.0
sat. fat (gm)	1.9	bread	0.0
cholesterol (mg)	107.5	meat	4.0
sodium (mg)	611	fat	0.0
protein (gm)	33.5		
carbohydrate (gm)	0.7		

PORK COOKED IN MILK

2 lbs. lean loin of pork, boned
1 clove garlic, split
2 cups skim milk
1 teaspoon Spike
¼ teaspoon pepper
2 to 3 teaspoons warm water

Trim fat from pork. If necessary, roll it and tie with string so it will keep its shape. Brown lightly, with garlic, on all sides in skillet sprayed with vegetable cooking spray. Remove garlic, and add milk slowly; add Spike and pepper.

Cover, and simmer gently for about 1½ hours, until meat is tender. Most of milk will be absorbed. Skim off excess fat. Add water if needed, and scrape up all the brown bits. Slice pork thin, and pour sauce over it.

Serves 6

NUTRITIONAL DATA

PER SERVING		EXCHANGES	
calories	210	milk	0.5
% calories from fat	44	vegetable	0.0
fat (gm)	10	fruit	0.0
sat. fat (gm)	3.5	bread	0.0
cholesterol (mg)	69.4	meat	3.0
sodium (mg)	94	fat	0.0
protein (gm)	24.3		
carbohydrate (gm)	4.2		

PORK TENDERLOIN IN WINE

- 2 lbs. pork tenderloin
- 1 clove garlic, crushed
- 1 teaspoon Spike
- 2 teaspoons olive oil
- ½ cup chicken broth
- ½ cup white wine

Pork tenderloin has almost no fat, but if it has any, trim it off. Cut into 6 pieces, and flatten slightly. Rub with garlic and Spike. Sauté in oil for 2 to 3 minutes to brown on both sides. Add broth and wine. Cook uncovered for about 15 minutes, until pork is tender and most of liquid is absorbed.

Serves 6

NUTRITIONAL DATA

PER SERVING		EXCHANGES	
calories	249	milk	0.0
% calories from fat	38	vegetable	0.0
fat (gm)	10.3	fruit	0.0
sat. fat (gm)	2.9	bread	0.0
cholesterol (mg)	109.1	meat	4.5
sodium (mg)	161	fat	0.0
protein (gm)	33.6		
carbohydrate (gm)	0.5		

RABBIT, FARMER STYLE

In Sorrento, country-style rabbit dishes are very popular. Americans do not use rabbit as frequently as in Italy, but if you can find it fresh, rather than frozen, you will be surprised at how good it is.

    1½ lbs. rabbit pieces, boneless and skinless
        Juice of 1 large lemon
     ½ cup all-purpose flour
        Spike
        Black pepper, freshly ground
    1½ cups onions, coarsely chopped
     1 tablespoon fresh rosemary or 1 teaspoon dried
        rosemary
     1 cup dry white wine
     1 cup shelled fresh peas, boiled, or frozen peas,
        thawed

Place rabbit pieces in bowl, and cover with cold water. Add lemon juice, cover, and refrigerate overnight.

Remove rabbit pieces from water, and dry well. Combine flour, 1 teaspoon Spike, and 1 teaspoon pepper, and lightly flour the rabbit pieces.

Heat large skillet sprayed with vegetable cooking spray to medium-high heat. Add rabbit pieces, and brown them on all sides. Sprinkle with rosemary, and remove from heat.

Spread onions in bottom of baking dish. Top with rabbit pieces, wine, peas, Spike, and pepper to taste. Cover dish with foil, and bake in preheated 375-degree oven for 35 minutes or until the rabbit pieces are tender.

Serve in baking dish

Serves 6

NUTRITIONAL DATA

PER SERVING		EXCHANGES	
calories	266	milk	0.0
% calories from fat	24	vegetable	0.0
fat (gm)	6.9	fruit	0.0
sat. fat (gm)	2	bread	1.0
cholesterol (mg)	67.7	meat	3.5
sodium (mg)	33	fat	0.0
protein (gm)	26.9		
carbohydrate (gm)	16.5		

10
SEAFOOD
(FRUTTI DI MARE)

Italians adore fish and shellfish, and it's no wonder since Italy is surrounded by water on 3 sides. The Adriatic and Mediterranean offer a treasure of sea fare. Italian fish soup is a dish of great pride, and each region claims to have the best, most authentic version.

The fish market at Rialto is a sight to behold. Everyone is there in the early morning: restaurant owners, private cooks, gourmets, housewives, and workmen. Everyone is looking for a bargain and the best catch of the day.

The following Italian recipes call for fish available in the United States. These include bass, red snapper, salmon, swordfish, sea trout, scrod, sole, and others, in addition to shellfish.

One rule applies to cooking all fish: do not overcook. Fish is delicate, and it should be cooked slowly and for a short time.

GRILLED FISH STEAKS WITH GARLIC-LEMON SAUCE

4 fish steaks (any fish), about 1½ lbs. total
2 tablespoons bread crumbs
2 cloves garlic, minced
2 tablespoons lemon juice
1 teaspoon Spike
½ teaspoon paprika
2 tablespoons white wine

Broil steaks about 5 minutes on each side. Meanwhile, make the sauce by combining crumbs, garlic, lemon juice, Spike, and paprika and mix well. Add wine gradually while stirring to make a thick creamy mixture. Serve fish topped with sauce.

Serves 4

NUTRITIONAL DATA

PER SERVING		EXCHANGES	
calories	159	milk	0.0
% calories from fat	12	vegetable	0.0
fat (gm)	2	fruit	0.0
sat. fat (gm)	0.5	bread	0.0
cholesterol (mg)	79.8	meat	3.0
sodium (mg)	147	fat	0.0
protein (gm)	28.9		
carbohydrate (gm)	3.6		

FISH FILLETS WITH ORANGE

M*ake this dish in a casserole that goes from oven to table.*

- ¼ lb. mushrooms, sliced
- 2 scallions, minced
- 2 tablespoons olive oil
- 3 tablespoons frozen orange juice concentrate or 6 tablespoons orange juice
- 1 tablespoon orange zest
- ½ cup white wine
- ½ teaspoon Spike
- ¼ teaspoon black pepper, freshly ground
- 2 lbs. fish fillets, sole or flounder
- 6 thin orange slices

Sauté mushrooms and scallions in oil for 3 minutes. Add thawed orange juice concentrate or orange juice, orange zest, wine, Spike, and pepper, and stir.

Place fillets in greased shallow baking dish, and pour mixture over them. Liquid should cover fish; if it doesn't, add more wine or juice. Bake for 30 minutes at 350 degrees (preheated).

Place orange slices on each fillet, and serve.

Serves 6

NUTRITIONAL DATA

PER SERVING		EXCHANGES	
calories	193	milk	0.0
% calories from fat	30	vegetable	0.0
fat (gm)	6.2	fruit	0.5
sat. fat (gm)	1	bread	0.0
cholesterol (mg)	70.9	meat	3.0
sodium (mg)	112	fat	0.0
protein (gm)	25.8		
carbohydrate (gm)	4.1		

FISH FILLETS WITH PICANTE SAUCE

1½ lbs. fresh or frozen fish fillets
Paprika
1 cup yogurt
½ teaspoon prepared mustard
½ teaspoon dried dill
½ teaspoon dried thyme
1 tablespoon lemon juice
1 teaspoon Spike
½ teaspoon pepper, freshly ground
2 tablespoons parsley, minced

If using frozen fish, thaw. Cut into 2 pieces, and dust with paprika. Spray small baking dish with vegetable spray, and lay fish in it.

Combine yogurt, mustard, dill, thyme, lemon juice, Spike, and pepper. Blend well, and spread over fish. Bake 20 minutes at 350 degrees (preheated). Sprinkle with parsley, and serve.

Serves 4

NUTRITIONAL DATA

PER SERVING		EXCHANGES	
calories	177	milk	0.5
% calories from fat	15	vegetable	0.0
fat (gm)	2.7	fruit	0.0
sat. fat (gm)	1	bread	0.0
cholesterol (mg)	83.3	meat	3.5
sodium (mg)	173	fat	0.0
protein (gm)	31.5		
carbohydrate (gm)	4.9		

♥

FISH FILLETS WITH TOMATO SAUCE

2 lbs. fish fillets: sole, flounder, haddock, or halibut

3 tablespoons onion, chopped

1 tablespoon butter

¼ lb. mushrooms, sliced

6 oz. Basic Tomato-Basil Sauce (see index) or use canned

8 fresh basil leaves, chopped

¼ cup fresh oregano leaves, chopped

Put fillets in greased, flat, shallow baking dish. Sauté onion in butter for 3 or 4 minutes; add mushrooms and sauté for 2 minutes more. Add tomato sauce, basil, and oregano; stir, and pour over fillets. Bake at 350 degrees (preheated) about 30 minutes.

Serves 6

NUTRITIONAL DATA

PER SERVING		EXCHANGES	
calories	159	milk	0.0
% calories from fat	23	vegetable	0.5
fat (gm)	3.9	fruit	0.0
sat. fat (gm)	1.6	bread	0.0
cholesterol (mg)	76	meat	3.0
sodium (mg)	172	fat	0.0
protein (gm)	26.2		
carbohydrate (gm)	4		

STUFFED FILLETS POACHED IN WINE

2 tablespoons scallions or shallots, minced
⅓ lb. mushrooms, sliced thin
2 teaspoons fresh parsley, minced
2 teaspoons fresh chives, minced
2 teaspoons fresh oregano, minced
½ teaspoon black pepper, freshly ground
1 teaspoon Spike, divided
6 fillets (2½ lbs.) sole or flounder
½ cup dry white wine

Sauté scallions or shallots until limp in pan sprayed with vegetable cooking spray. Add mushrooms, simmer, and stir for 2 minutes. Then add parsley, chives, oregano, pepper, and ½ teaspoon Spike.

Place fillets flat on board, and spread with mushroom mixture to about ¼ inch from edge of fillet. Roll fillets, and fasten with toothpicks. Sprinkle with remaining Spike. Place in greased skillet, and pour wine over fillets. Cover, and simmer for about 15 minutes (wine should not boil).

When ready to serve, remove toothpicks, and transfer fillets to hot platter, and pour liquid over them.

Serves 6

NUTRITIONAL DATA

PER SERVING		EXCHANGES	
calories	160	milk	0.0
% calories from fat	11	vegetable	0.0
fat (gm)	1.9	fruit	0.0
sat. fat (gm)	0.4	bread	0.0
cholesterol (mg)	79.8	meat	3.0
sodium (mg)	126	fat	0.0
protein (gm)	29		
carbohydrate (gm)	2.2		

FLOUNDER WITH PESTO

This is a nice company dish because inside each fish bundle is a surprise. Pesto fills each one for a taste sensation.

- 4 4-oz. fresh or frozen sole or flounder fillets (about ½ inch thick)
- 2 tablespoons lemon juice
- 2 tablespoons shallots, finely chopped
- 1 clove garlic, minced
- ½ teaspoon black pepper, freshly ground
- ¼ cup Pesto Sauce (see index)

Thaw fish, if frozen. Place each fish fillet on a 9 × 9-inch piece of heavy foil or parchment paper. Fold each fillet crosswise in half.

In small bowl stir together lemon juice, shallots, garlic, and pepper. Spoon evenly over fish. Spoon pesto evenly over fish.

Seal each square of foil or paper by folding the edges together. Place in 15 × 10 × 1-inch baking pan. Bake in 400-degree oven about 15 minutes or till fish puffs slightly and flakes easily with fork (carefully open to check doneness).

Serves 4

NUTRITIONAL DATA

PER SERVING		EXCHANGES	
calories	112	milk	0.0
% calories from fat	16	vegetable	0.5
fat (gm)	2	fruit	0.0
sat. fat (gm)	0.7	bread	0.0
cholesterol (mg)	55.3	meat	2.0
sodium (mg)	124	fat	0.0
protein (gm)	20.2		
carbohydrate (gm)	2.6		

HADDOCK BAKED IN MILK SAUCE

1 lb. fresh or frozen haddock (½- to ¾-inch thick)
½ cup evaporated skim milk
¼ cup green onion, sliced
¼ cup parsley, snipped
¼ cup fresh oregano, snipped
2 tablespoons grated Parmesan cheese
2 tablespoons dry white wine
1 clove garlic, minced
1 teaspoon Spike
¼ teaspoon black pepper, freshly ground

Thaw fish if frozen; remove any skin. Cut into 4 serving-size portions. Place fish in an 11 × 7 × 1½-inch baking pan.

In small bowl, stir together evaporated skim milk, onion, parsley, oregano, Parmesan cheese, wine, garlic, Spike, and pepper. Pour milk mixture over fish.

Bake, uncovered, in 350-degree oven 20 to 25 minutes or till fish flakes easily with fork.

Serves 4

NUTRITIONAL DATA

PER SERVING		EXCHANGES	
calories	155	milk	0.5
% calories from fat	12	vegetable	0.0
fat (gm)	2	fruit	0.0
sat. fat (gm)	0.8	bread	0.0
cholesterol (mg)	70.9	meat	2.0
sodium (mg)	176	fat	0.0
protein (gm)	26.1		
carbohydrate (gm)	5.6		

BALSAMIC-GLAZED SALMON FILLETS

- 4 cloves garlic, minced
- 1 tablespoon white wine
- 1 tablespoon honey
- ⅓ cup balsamic vinegar
- 4 teaspoons Dijon mustard
- ¼ teaspoon Spike
  Pepper, freshly ground, to taste
- 6 salmon fillets, each about 5 oz., rinsed and patted dry
- 1 tablespoon fresh oregano, chopped
- 12 fresh basil leaves, cut in julienne strips

Cook garlic in small skillet sprayed with vegetable cooking spray over medium heat until garlic is soft, about 3 minutes. Do not brown.

Add wine, honey, vinegar, mustard, Spike, and pepper. Stir well to combine. Simmer, uncovered, until slightly thickened, about 3 minutes. If not using right away, refrigerate. Gently reheat before using.

Arrange fillets in single layer on baking pan lined with foil and sprayed with vegetable cooking spray. Brush with warm glaze. Sprinkle on oregano. Bake in preheated 475-degree oven on upper rack until sizzling and glazed, 10 to 14 minutes, depending on thickness of fillets. To be sure that it's cooked as desired, use paring knife to cut through thickest part. Do not overcook. Brush with remaining glaze. Sprinkle very lightly with Spike and pepper.

Use spatula to transfer to warm serving platter. Garnish fillets with julienne basil.

Serves 6

NUTRITIONAL DATA

PER SERVING		EXCHANGES	
calories	163	milk	0.0
% calories from fat	29	vegetable	0.0
fat (gm)	5	fruit	0.0
sat. fat (gm)	1	bread	0.0
cholesterol (mg)	25.4	meat	3.0
sodium (mg)	914	fat	0.0
protein (gm)	20.6		
carbohydrate (gm)	7.2		

COLD SALMON

2 lbs. salmon steaks
2 tablespoons lemon juice
1 tablespoon parsley, minced
1 teaspoon Spike
  Lemon wedges
  Boston lettuce leaves
1 cup Dijonaise Sauce (see index)

Wrap fish in cheesecloth, and cover with water. Add lemon juice, parsley, and Spike. Simmer for 15 minutes. Place on cold platter, and remove the cheesecloth.

Chill in refrigerator for several hours. Garnish with lettuce leaves and lemon wedges, and pass the Dijonaise Sauce.

Serves 6

NUTRITIONAL DATA

PER SERVING		EXCHANGES	
calories	168	milk	0.0
% calories from fat	29	vegetable	0.0
fat (gm)	5.6	fruit	0.0
sat. fat (gm)	1.2	bread	0.0
cholesterol (mg)	27.1	meat	3.0
sodium (mg)	1357	fat	0.0
protein (gm)	22		
carbohydrate (gm)	8.9		

FILLETS OF SOLE IN PARCHMENT

- 2 cups assorted lettuce (Boston, romaine, leaf, etc.), torn
- 1½ lbs. fillet of sole or flounder
- 2 scallions, chopped
- 2 tomatoes, peeled and chopped
- 4 teaspoons butter, melted
- 1 teaspoon Spike
- ½ teaspoon black pepper, freshly ground
- 1 teaspoon dill weed
- 1 teaspoon basil
- 1 teaspoon oregano
- 4 teaspoons white wine

Cut parchment (or foil) into 4 large squares. Put small amount of lettuce on each, and cover with fish, dividing fillets evenly. Combine remaining ingredients, and divide among fish squares. Wrap fish envelope-fashion so no moisture will escape.

Bake on baking sheet at 350 degrees (preheated) for about 35 minutes. Serve in the packages so each person may empty fish and all juices onto his or her plate.

Serves 4

NUTRITIONAL DATA

PER SERVING		EXCHANGES	
calories	196	milk	0.0
% calories from fat	28	vegetable	1.0
fat (gm)	5.9	fruit	0.0
sat. fat (gm)	2.8	bread	0.0
cholesterol (mg)	90	meat	3.0
sodium (mg)	171	fat	0.0
protein (gm)	29.5		
carbohydrate (gm)	4.6		

FILLETS OF SOLE WITH PARMESAN

1½ lbs. fillets of sole
½ teaspoon Spike
  Flour
2 tablespoons grated Parmesan cheese
¼ cup chicken broth
¼ cup fresh oregano, minced
  Chives, minced

Sprinkle sole with Spike, dust with flour, and sauté in pan sprayed with vegetable spray for 5 minutes, turning once to brown evenly. Sprinkle with cheese, and add broth. Cover, and simmer for 5 minutes. Top with oregano, and sprinkle with chives.
Serves 4

NUTRITIONAL DATA

PER SERVING		EXCHANGES	
calories	158	milk	0.0
% calories from fat	18	vegetable	0.0
fat (gm)	3	fruit	0.0
sat. fat (gm)	1.3	bread	0.0
cholesterol (mg)	83.4	meat	3.0
sodium (mg)	243	fat	0.0
protein (gm)	29.9		
carbohydrate (gm)	1.2		

BAKED SWORDFISH WITH FENNEL

1 lb. fresh or frozen swordfish, shark, or tuna steaks, cut 1 inch thick

1 fennel or anise bulb (about 1 lb.)*

¼ cup dry white wine

2 tablespoons chives, snipped

⅛ teaspoon crushed red pepper

1½ cups Chunky Vegetable Sauce (see index) or purchased garden-style spaghetti sauce

Spike, to taste

Pepper, to taste

1 tablespoon lemon juice

1 tablespoon lemon rind, grated

4 oz. packaged orzo, rosamarina, or other pasta, cooked and drained

Thaw fish if frozen. Cut into 4 serving-size portions. Set aside.

For sauce, cut fennel into thin wedges. In medium saucepan combine fennel, wine, chives, and red pepper. Bring to boiling. Reduce heat. Cover, and simmer about 10 minutes or till fennel is almost tender. Stir in Chunky Vegetable Sauce or spaghetti sauce. Pour mixture into a 10 × 6 × 2-inch baking dish.

Lightly sprinkle fish with Spike and pepper. Arrange fish on top of sauce in baking dish. Drizzle fish with lemon juice, and add lemon rind.

Bake covered in 350-degree oven for 40 to 45 minutes or until fish flakes easily with fork. Transfer fish to platter. Spoon sauce over fish. Serve with hot orzo.

*Note: If fresh fennel isn't available, substitute about 1½ cups chopped celery.

Serves 4

NUTRITIONAL DATA

PER SERVING		EXCHANGES	
calories	378	milk	0.0
% calories from fat	26	vegetable	3.0
fat (gm)	10.8	fruit	0.0
sat. fat (gm)	2.1	bread	1.5
cholesterol (mg)	44.7	meat	3.0
sodium (mg)	220	fat	0.5
protein (gm)	29.4		
carbohydrate (gm)	39.1		

GRILLED SWORDFISH

1 lb. fresh or frozen swordfish, salmon, or halibut steaks or fillets
½ cup dry white wine
½ teaspoon lemon peel, finely shredded
2 tablespoons lemon juice
1 tablespoon parsley, snipped
1 tablespoon fresh basil or oregano, snipped
Lemon wedges for garnish

Thaw fish, if frozen. Cut fish into 4 serving-size portions. Place in shallow baking dish.

For marinade, in small bowl, stir together wine, lemon peel, lemon juice, parsley, and basil or oregano. Pour marinade over fish. Cover, and marinate in refrigerator for 1 to 2 hours, turning fish over occasionally.

Drain fish, reserving marinade. Measure thickness of fish. Bring coals in barbecue grill to medium hot. Place fish in greased grill basket or on grill topper. Grill on uncovered grill directly over coals for 4 to 6 minutes per ½ inch thickness or till fish flakes easily, turning once and brushing with marinade 2 or 3 times. Serve with lemon.

Serves 4

NUTRITIONAL DATA

PER SERVING		EXCHANGES	
calories	161	milk	0.0
% calories from fat	26	vegetable	0.0
fat (gm)	4.6	fruit	0.0
sat. fat (gm)	1.2	bread	0.0
cholesterol (mg)	44.7	meat	3.0
sodium (mg)	104	fat	0.0
protein (gm)	22.6		
carbohydrate (gm)	1.2		

MARINATED TROUT

4   8-oz. fresh or frozen pan-dressed rainbow trout or lake perch
    Spike, to taste
    Pepper, to taste
½ cup white wine
1   tablespoon lemon juice
½ teaspoon dried thyme, crushed
½ teaspoon dried oregano, crushed
1   cup fresh mushrooms, sliced
1   medium carrot, chopped (½ cup)
1   small onion, chopped (⅓ cup)
1   clove garlic, minced
¼ cup chicken broth

Thaw fish, if frozen. Place fish in shallow baking dish. Sprinkle with Spike and pepper.

For marinade, stir together Marsala, lemon juice, thyme, and oregano; pour over fish. Cover, and marinate in refrigerator for 2 hours. Drain fish, reserving marinade. Pat fish dry.

In 12-inch skillet sprayed with vegetable cooking spray, cook mushrooms, carrot, onion, and garlic till tender but not brown. Push to edges of skillet. Add fish, and cook 4 minutes on each side. Add marinade and broth.

Cover, and simmer about 4 minutes or till fish flakes easily with fork. Transfer fish and vegetables to platter; cover. Simmer marinade mixture till reduced to ¼ cup; spoon over fish.

Serves 4

NUTRITIONAL DATA

PER SERVING		EXCHANGES	
calories	311	milk	0.0
% calories from fat	6	vegetable	1.0
fat (gm)	7.9	fruit	0.0
sat. fat (gm)	1.7	bread	0.0
cholesterol (mg)	130.9	meat	5.0
sodium (mg)	130	fat	0.0
protein (gm)	47.7		
carbohydrate (gm)	4.5		

HERB-TOPPED LOBSTER TAILS

1½ lbs. lobster tails

¼ cup dry bread crumbs

2 tablespoons grated Parmesan or Romano cheese

1 tablespoon parsley, snipped

1 tablespoon basil, snipped

1 tablespoon oregano, snipped

1 tablespoon lemon balm, snipped

¼ teaspoon garlic powder

¼ teaspoon cayenne pepper

¼ cup liquid Butter Buds

Partially thaw lobster tails. Rinse and pat dry. To butterfly tails, use kitchen shears or sharp, heavy knife to cut lengthwise through centers of hard top shells and meat, cutting to, but not through, bottom shells. Using fingers, press shell halves apart.

Place lobster tails, shell side down, on unheated rack of broiler pan. Broil 4 to 6 inches from heat for 10 to 11 minutes or till meat is just opaque.

Meanwhile, stir together bread crumbs, cheese, herbs, garlic powder, and cayenne pepper. Add Butter Buds, and toss together. Sprinkle crumb mixture over lobster meat.

Broil 1 to 2 minutes more or till crumbs are golden.

Serves 4

NUTRITIONAL DATA

PER SERVING		EXCHANGES	
calories	201	milk	0.0
% calories from fat	14	vegetable	0.0
fat (gm)	2.8	fruit	0.0
sat. fat (gm)	1	bread	0.5
cholesterol (mg)	163.6	meat	3.0
sodium (mg)	785	fat	0.0
protein (gm)	34.2		
carbohydrate (gm)	6.7		

GRILLED OYSTERS, TREVISO STYLE

A warm grilled oyster salad is a wonderful way to start an Italian meal. I like to use colorful lettuces with a slightly bitter edge, like curly endive and red radicchio.

 2 tablespoons lemon juice
 ½ cup white wine
 1 teaspoon capers, chopped
 1 teaspoon lemon rind, grated
 2 tablespoons parsley, minced
 2 tablespoons green onion, minced
 ½ teaspoon Spike
 ½ teaspoon black pepper, freshly ground
 1 small head curly endive
 1 small head radicchio
 30 fresh oysters

To make dressing, combine lemon juice, wine, capers, lemon rind, parsley, green onion, Spike, and pepper. Whisk well, and set aside.

Separate lettuces into individual leaves. Wash well, and dry thoroughly. Tear large leaves into small pieces. Arrange on serving platter.

Over medium-hot charcoal fire, position rack above coals and set oysters directly on rack. After about 2½ minutes, they will begin to open. They should be fully open and hot after about 3½ minutes. Remove oysters as they open. Be careful not to overcook. Discard any that don't open.

Pour oyster liquor into small bowl. Remove oysters from shells, and arrange them atop lettuce. Add reserved oyster liquor to dressing and whisk well. Taste, and adjust Spike if necessary; pour dressing over oysters. Grind some black pepper over top, and serve immediately.

Serves 6 (as an appetizer)

NUTRITIONAL DATA

PER SERVING		EXCHANGES	
calories	67	milk	0.0
% calories from fat	19	vegetable	0.5
fat (gm)	1.5	fruit	0.0
sat. fat (gm)	0	bread	0.0
cholesterol (mg)	0	meat	1.0
sodium (mg)	23	fat	0.0
protein (gm)	7.2		
carbohydrate (gm)	3.5		

GRILLED SCALLOP KEBABS

If rain dampens your barbecue, broil the scallop and vegetable kebabs 4 to 5 inches from the heat for the times given.

⅝ lb. fresh or frozen scallops

¼ cup white wine

2 tablespoons lime juice or lemon juice

1 tablespoon parsley, snipped

1 clove garlic, minced

½ teaspoon dried basil, crushed

½ teaspoon dried oregano, crushed

½ teaspoon Spike

Pepper, dash

1 medium zucchini, cut into ½-inch slices

1 medium green or red bell pepper, cut into 1-inch squares

8 fresh mushrooms

8 cherry tomatoes

Thaw scallops if frozen. Halve any large ones. Place in plastic bag, and refrigerate.

For marinade, in small bowl stir together wine, lime or lemon juice, parsley, garlic, basil, oregano, ½ teaspoon Spike, and dash of pepper. Pour marinade over scallops. Seal bag. Marinate in refrigerator for 3 to 4 hours, turning bag occasionally.

Meanwhile, cook zucchini, pepper, and mushrooms, covered, in small amount of boiling water for 2 minutes. Drain.

Drain scallops, reserving marinade. Alternately thread scallops, zucchini, pepper, and mushrooms onto 8 12-inch skewers.

Place skewers on greased grill rack. Grill uncovered directly over medium-hot coals for 10 to 12 minutes or till scallops are opaque, brushing with marinade and turning occasionally. Add tomatoes to ends of skewers the last minute of cooking.

Serves 4

NUTRITIONAL DATA

PER SERVING		EXCHANGES	
calories	94	milk	0.0
% calories from fat	9	vegetable	1.0
fat (gm)	0.9	fruit	0.0
sat. fat (gm)	0.1	bread	0.0
cholesterol (mg)	22.5	meat	1.5
sodium (mg)	117	fat	0.0
protein (gm)	13.1		
carbohydrate (gm)	2.3		

LEMON-MARINATED SHRIMP

*S*erve with a large green salad and Italian bread.

    1 lb. fresh or frozen large shrimp in shells
    ¼ cup white wine
    1 teaspoon lemon peel, finely shredded
    2 tablespoons lemon juice
    2 cloves garlic, minced
    ½ teaspoon dried oregano, crushed
    ½ teaspoon dried basil, crushed
    ½ teaspoon dried lemon balm, crushed

Thaw shrimp if frozen. Peel shrimp, leaving tails intact. Devein shrimp. Rinse, and pat dry.

In large bowl combine wine, lemon peel, lemon juice, garlic, oregano, basil, and lemon balm. Add shrimp; stir well. Cover, and marinate in refrigerator for 2 hours. Drain, reserving marinade.

Place shrimp on unheated rack of broiler pan. Broil 4 to 5 inches from heat about 4 minutes for large or about 6 minutes for jumbo or till shrimp turn pink, turning and brushing with marinade once.

Serves 4

NUTRITIONAL DATA

PER SERVING		EXCHANGES	
calories	93	milk	0.0
% calories from fat	10	vegetable	0.0
fat (gm)	1	fruit	0.0
sat. fat (gm)	0.3	bread	0.0
cholesterol (mg)	174.2	meat	2.0
sodium (mg)	199	fat	0.0
protein (gm)	18.7		
carbohydrate (gm)	0.5		

SHRIMP MARCO

20 large shrimp (12 per lb.), peeled, deveined, and butterflied
2 cups very dry bread crumbs, seasoned
4 teaspoons garlic, finely minced
4 teaspoons shallots, finely minced
4 teaspoons thyme, minced
4 teaspoons fresh parsley, chopped
   Spike, to taste
   Black pepper, freshly ground, to taste
½ cup liquid Butter Buds
4 tablespoons white wine

Lightly pound butterflied shrimp. Mix bread crumbs with garlic, shallots, thyme, and parsley. Add Spike and pepper to taste.

Combine Butter Buds and wine. Brush shrimp with Butter Buds mixture, and dust them with seasoned bread crumbs.

Bake shrimp in large baking dish at 350 degrees (preheated) for about 5 minutes, until shrimp lose their transparency. Do not overcook. Finish shrimp under broiler until bread crumbs are lightly browned.

Serves 4

NUTRITIONAL DATA

PER SERVING		EXCHANGES	
calories	375	milk	0.0
% calories from fat	11	vegetable	0.0
fat (gm)	4.2	fruit	0.0
sat. fat (gm)	1	bread	2.5
cholesterol (mg)	290.8	meat	3.5
sodium (mg)	1058	fat	0.0
protein (gm)	38.1		
carbohydrate (gm)	40.2		

SHRIMP WITH PEPPERS

1½ cups green, red, or yellow bell peppers, chopped
 1 cup onion, chopped
 1 teaspoon dried basil, crushed
 1 teaspoon dried oregano, crushed
 1 tablespoon olive oil
 2 oz. prosciutto or fully cooked ham, finely chopped
 1 lb. fresh shrimp, peeled and deveined
 2 tablespoons Marsala or other white wine
 1 tablespoon white wine vinegar
 1 teaspoon lemon peel, finely shredded
 ½ teaspoon crushed red pepper
   Lemon slices

In large skillet cook peppers, onion, basil, and oregano in hot oil till tender but not brown. Stir in ham, and cook for 1 minute more.

Stir shrimp, Marsala, vinegar, lemon peel, and red pepper into skillet. Cover, and cook over medium heat 4 to 6 minutes or till shrimp turn pink. Serve with lemon.

Serves 4

NUTRITIONAL DATA

PER SERVING		EXCHANGES	
calories	187	milk	0.0
% calories from fat	26	vegetable	2.0
fat (gm)	5.4	fruit	0.0
sat. fat (gm)	1.1	bread	0.0
cholesterol (mg)	181.9	meat	2.5
sodium (mg)	391	fat	0.0
protein (gm)	23.6		
carbohydrate (gm)	9.8		

11
VEGETABLES
(VERDURE)

Italy produces an enormous variety of vegetables, and vegetable cooking is one of the glories of Italian cuisine. Italian cooks have developed an impressive number of vegetable dishes. In Italy, vegetables are considered an important part of a meal, not just an add-on or afterthought.

Every section of an Italian city has its own market, offering a dazzling array of fresh vegetables. In Italy, it is the custom to shop daily for vegetables to be eaten the same day.

Herbs play an important part in preparing vegetables, as do sauces. You will find here a large selection of vegetables, some commonplace like cabbage, cauliflower, and broccoli, others, such as fennel and artichokes, less common but easy to prepare and delicious.

A word about onions, which come in a variety of colors and flavors. The red Italian and large yellow Spanish are mild and sweet; the cooking yellow and white are sharp and pungent. If you want to dull the sharpness of an onion, soak it in cold water for 15 to 30 minutes. In the recipes that follow, I recommend red onions.

ARTICHOKES, FORESTER'S STYLE

Artichokes and mushrooms make a wonder-ful combination of textures and flavors. You can cook this dish ahead and reheat before serving.

8 artichokes (about 2 lbs.)
Juice of 1 lemon
3 cloves garlic, minced
½ cup Basic Tomato-Basil Sauce (see index) or 1 cup canned Italian plum tomatoes, drained
½ lb. fresh mushrooms, cleaned and sliced
⅓ cup water
⅓ cup dry white wine
Pinch of oregano
Pepper, freshly ground, to taste
2 tablespoons fresh basil, chopped
2 tablespoons fresh parsley, chopped

Trim, clean, and quarter artichokes, and remove chokes. Place them in water with juice of 1 lemon until ready to use.

Heat saucepan sprayed with vegetable cooking spray, add garlic, and sauté 1 minute.

Drain artichokes, add to garlic, and sauté for 3 to 4 minutes. Add tomato sauce or tomatoes, mushrooms, water, wine, oregano, and pepper.

Combine thoroughly and simmer, partly covered, stirring occasionally, for 20 to 25 minutes, until artichokes are cooked but still firm. Add basil and parsley, adjust for seasoning, and serve.

Serves 6

NUTRITIONAL DATA

PER SERVING		EXCHANGES	
calories	102	milk	0.0
% calories from fat	5	vegetable	1.0
fat (gm)	0.7	fruit	0.0
sat. fat (gm)	0.1	bread	1.0
cholesterol (mg)	0	meat	0.0
sodium (mg)	192	fat	0.0
protein (gm)	6.2		
carbohydrate (gm)	20.2		

ASPARAGUS WITH LEMON

*T his is one of the best recipes for asparagus—
and nothing could be simpler.*

2 lbs. asparagus
2 tablespoons lemon juice, fresh
  Lemon pepper
3 tablespoons Parmesan cheese, freshly grated

Trim asparagus, and cook spears by steaming them for about 8 minutes. Place them on heated serving platter. Pour lemon juice over them, add lemon pepper, and sprinkle with Parmesan. Serve hot.
  Serves 6

NUTRITIONAL DATA

PER SERVING		EXCHANGES	
calories	50	milk	0.0
% calories from fat	21	vegetable	1.0
fat (gm)	1.4	fruit	0.0
sat. fat (gm)	0.7	bread	0.0
cholesterol (mg)	2.5	meat	0.5
sodium (mg)	64	fat	0.0
protein (gm)	4.9		
carbohydrate (gm)	6.8		

ASPARAGUS WITH MUSHROOM SAUCE

C hopped yellow bell peppers add a flash of color to the excellent flavor.

½ oz. dried wild mushrooms *(Boletus edulis)*
2 tablespoons butter
3 tablespoons parsley, finely chopped
½ cup onion, finely chopped
1 cup evaporated skim milk
  Pinch of nutmeg
2 tablespoons plain low-fat yogurt
  Pepper, freshly ground, to taste
2 tablespoons lemon juice
2 lbs. asparagus
½ cup yellow bell pepper, finely chopped

Soak wild mushrooms in 1 cup warm water for 20 minutes. Rinse well to remove grit. Drain, finely chop, and set aside.

Make sauce. Heat butter in saucepan, add parsley and onion, and sauté over medium heat for 1 minute. Add dried mushrooms, and sauté another minute. Stir in evaporated skim milk, nutmeg, and yogurt. Continue cooking, stirring constantly, until sauce thickens, about 3 minutes. Add pepper and lemon juice, and set aside.

Cook asparagus by steaming spears about 8 minutes. Warm sauce through, and pour over asparagus. Garnish with yellow peppers.

Serves 6

NUTRITIONAL DATA

PER SERVING		EXCHANGES	
calories	124	milk	0.5
% calories from fat	30	vegetable	1.5
fat (gm)	4.5	fruit	0.0
sat. fat (gm)	2.6	bread	0.0
cholesterol (mg)	12.2	meat	0.0
sodium (mg)	98	fat	1.0
protein (gm)	7.9		
carbohydrate (gm)	15.7		

BROCCOLI IN WINE

1½ lbs. broccoli
1 cup onions, thinly sliced
2 tablespoons capers
1 teaspoon rosemary
1 teaspoon oregano
¼ lb. skim mozzarella cheese, shredded
½ cup dry red wine
1 tablespoon lemon juice, fresh

Wash broccoli in cold water. Trim away dark green inedible outer skin of stems, exposing tender, pale green inner flesh. If stems are very thick, cut them into ½-inch slices. Otherwise cut the broccoli lengthwise into ½-inch strips, keeping florets intact.

In large saucepan sprayed with vegetable cooking spray, sauté onions; cover with half the broccoli and half the capers. Sprinkle with herbs and distribute, on top, half the cheese. Repeat layering process, ending with cheese. Pour in red wine, cover, and simmer over low heat until the broccoli is cooked but still firm, about 20 minutes. Do not stir broccoli while it cooks. Add lemon juice just before serving.

Serves 6

NUTRITIONAL DATA

PER SERVING		EXCHANGES	
calories	106	milk	0.0
% calories from fat	27	vegetable	2.0
fat (gm)	3.5	fruit	0.0
sat. fat (gm)	2	bread	0.0
cholesterol (mg)	10.7	meat	0.5
sodium (mg)	131	fat	0.5
protein (gm)	8.4		
carbohydrate (gm)	9.4		

BRAISED CABBAGE IN WINE

1 large onion, thinly sliced

1 teaspoon dried rosemary or 1 tablespoon fresh rosemary

1 medium head cabbage, coarsely shredded

1 tablespoon Classic Spaghetti Sauce (see index) or canned tomato sauce

1 cup dry white wine

Spike, to taste

Pepper, freshly ground, to taste

In large saucepan sprayed with vegetable oil, add onion and rosemary, and sauté over medium heat until onion becomes translucent. Add cabbage, and cook, stirring, for 5 minutes until cabbage begins to wilt. Add sauce, white wine, and Spike and pepper to taste. Cover, and cook slowly over low heat for about 25 minutes until cabbage is tender. Serve hot.

Serves 8

NUTRITIONAL DATA

PER SERVING		EXCHANGES	
calories	46	milk	0.0
% calories from fat	4	vegetable	1.5
fat (gm)	0.2	fruit	0.0
sat. fat (gm)	0	bread	0.0
cholesterol (mg)	0.3	meat	0.0
sodium (mg)	21	fat	0.0
protein (gm)	1.2		
carbohydrate (gm)	5.9		

CAULIFLOWER SICILIAN STYLE

½ cup leeks (white parts only) or onions, thinly sliced

3 cloves garlic, minced

1 medium cauliflower, washed, trimmed, and cut into small florets

1 medium tomato, thinly sliced

1 green bell pepper, seeded and thinly sliced

½ cup dry white wine

Pepper, freshly ground, to taste

½ teaspoon ground oregano

2 tablespoons parsley, chopped

2 tablespoons basil, chopped

2 tablespoons capers

2 tablespoons Italian black olives, pitted and chopped

1 lemon, cut into 6 wedges

In large skillet sprayed with vegetable cooking spray, sauté leeks or onions until they begin to color, about 5 minutes. Add garlic, and sauté another minute. Stir in cauliflower, and cook over medium heat, stirring constantly, 3 minutes to combine ingredients. Reduce heat, and cook covered for 5 minutes.

Remove cover, add tomato, bell pepper, white wine, and pepper. Combine, and simmer covered for another 5 minutes. Blend in oregano, parsley, basil, and 1 tablespoon each of capers and olives. Heat through, and place cauliflower in heated serving bowl. Sprinkle remaining capers and olives on top, surround with lemon wedges, and serve.

Serves 6

NUTRITIONAL DATA

PER SERVING		EXCHANGES	
calories	68	milk	0.0
% calories from fat	17	vegetable	2.5
fat (gm)	1.6	fruit	0.0
sat. fat (gm)	0.1	bread	0.0
cholesterol (mg)	0	meat	0.0
sodium (mg)	146	fat	0.0
protein (gm)	4.3		
carbohydrate (gm)	9.7		

CHICKPEAS, ROMAN STYLE

C hickpeas are a nourishing legume that is very popular in the Mediterranean and Middle East. You can use canned chickpeas in this recipe.

1½ cups dried chickpeas or 2½ to 3 cups canned chickpeas

1 tablespoon flour if dried chickpeas are used

1 teaspoon salt for cooking dried chickpeas

2 tablespoons olive oil

2 teaspoons fresh rosemary or 1 teaspoon dried rosemary

3 cloves garlic, minced

½ hot pepper, seeded and chopped

2 tablespoons parsley, chopped

3 medium tomatoes, peeled, seeded, and chopped or 1 cup canned Italian plum tomatoes, drained and chopped

1 teaspoon Spike

1 teaspoon oregano

2 tablespoons chives, minced

Soak dried chickpeas for 8 hours in 4 cups water with 1 tablespoon flour. Rinse, place chickpeas in large saucepan with 6 cups water and 1 teaspoon salt, and cook until tender, about 1½ hours. When cooked, drain, and set aside. The cooking liquid can be reserved and used for soup.

While chickpeas are cooking, prepare sauce. Heat olive oil in saucepan, add rosemary, garlic, and hot pepper, and sauté for 1 to 2 minutes over medium heat, until garlic begins to color. Add parsley, tomatoes, Spike, and oregano, and simmer over low heat for 15 to 20 minutes, until you have a fairly thick tomato sauce.

Add chickpeas and cook for 10 minutes, stirring occasionally to blend flavors. Sprinkle with chives, and serve.

Serves 6

NUTRITIONAL DATA

PER SERVING		EXCHANGES	
calories	269	milk	0.0
% calories from fat	25	vegetable	0.5
fat (gm)	7.7	fruit	0.0
sat. fat (gm)	2.2	bread	2.5
cholesterol (mg)	3.9	meat	0.0
sodium (mg)	369	fat	1.5
protein (gm)	12.4		
carbohydrate (gm)	38.6		

BAKED EGGPLANT

*T his dish is outstanding. Tomato sauce, ore-
gano, and garlic enhance the eggplant's
naturally good taste.*

> 6 small young eggplants (about 3 lbs.), washed and
> cut in half lengthwise
> 2 cloves garlic, finely chopped
> ½ cup Classic Spaghetti Sauce (see index) or use
> canned tomato sauce
> 1 tablespoon oregano
> 1 teaspoon Spike
> Pepper, freshly ground, to taste

Cut cross hatches ½-inch apart and ¼-inch deep on skin of
eggplants. Place eggplants, skin side up, in sprayed baking dish
large enough to accommodate them side by side. Rub garlic into
slits. Spread about 1 tablespoon sauce on each eggplant half, and
sprinkle with oregano, Spike, and pepper.

Spray eggplants lightly with vegetable cooking spray. Bake in
375-degree preheated oven 35 to 40 minutes, until eggplants are
tender and cooked through. To test, use cake tester inserted in
center of eggplant. If cooked, tester will go in easily. Remove from
oven, and serve hot.

Serves 6

NUTRITIONAL DATA

PER SERVING		EXCHANGES	
calories	76	milk	0.0
% calories from fat	14	vegetable	3.0
fat (gm)	1.3	fruit	0.0
sat. fat (gm)	0.4	bread	0.0
cholesterol (mg)	3.1	meat	0.0
sodium (mg)	78	fat	0.0
protein (gm)	3.2		
carbohydrate (gm)	15.1		

FENNEL WITH TOMATO SAUCE

1 leek, green leaves included, washed well and sliced in thin rounds
3 cloves garlic, minced
4 fennel bulbs (about 4 oz.), trimmed and cut into wedges 1 inch thick
3 tablespoons Classic Spaghetti Sauce (see index) or use canned tomato sauce
¾ cup water
½ teaspoon salt
  Pepper, freshly ground, to taste
1 tablespoon parsley, finely chopped

Spray large saucepan with vegetable cooking spray, add leek, and sauté over medium heat, stirring frequently, until lightly browned, about 3 minutes. Add garlic, cook 1 minute more, then add fennel wedges, and sauté for 2 minutes, turning to coat.

Combine sauce with ¾ cup water, and pour mixture over fennel. Add salt and pepper, cover, reduce heat to low, and simmer, stirring occasionally, for 10 to 12 minutes, until fennel is cooked through but still firm. Transfer to heated serving platter, sprinkle with parsley, and serve hot.

Serves 6

NUTRITIONAL DATA

PER SERVING		EXCHANGES	
calories	25	milk	0.0
% calories from fat	13	vegetable	1.0
fat (gm)	0.4	fruit	0.0
sat. fat (gm)	0.1	bread	0.0
cholesterol (mg)	1.1	meat	0.0
sodium (mg)	227	fat	0.0
protein (gm)	1.2		
carbohydrate (gm)	4.7		

GARDEN PESTO PIE

CRUST

- 3 cups unsifted all-purpose flour
- 2 packages fast-rising yeast
- 2 teaspoons sugar
- 1 teaspoon salt
- 1 cup very warm water (120–130 degrees)
- ½ teaspoon olive oil

FILLING

- ½ teaspoon olive oil
- 1 cup onion, finely chopped
- 15 oz. light ricotta cheese
- 8 oz. egg substitute
- ⅛ teaspoon salt
- ½ teaspoon white pepper
- ⅛ teaspoon nutmeg, grated
- 2 cups Pesto Sauce (see index) or purchased pesto

To make Crust: Combine 1½ cups flour, yeast, sugar, and salt in large bowl. With electric mixer at low speed, beat in water and olive oil until smooth. With hands, mix in enough additional flour to make stiff dough.

On lightly floured board, knead dough, adding flour as necessary, until smooth and elastic, 5 minutes. Place in greased bowl; cover with towel. Let rise in warm place (85 degrees), free from drafts, 30 minutes. Spray 12-inch tart pan with vegetable spray.

To make Filling: Place small skillet sprayed with vegetable cooking spray on medium heat. Add oil. Add onion; sauté until soft. Whisk together ricotta cheese, egg substitute, salt, pepper, nutmeg, and Pesto Sauce in medium-size bowl. Add sautéed onion. Spoon into crust. Bake 25 to 30 minutes in 375-degree, preheated oven.

Serves 6

NUTRITIONAL DATA

PER SERVING		EXCHANGES	
calories	409	milk	0.0
% calories from fat	17	vegetable	1.0
fat (gm)	7.5	fruit	0.0
sat. fat (gm)	2.6	bread	3.5
cholesterol (mg)	21.3	meat	2.0
sodium (mg)	734	fat	0.5
protein (gm)	23.7		
carbohydrate (gm)	61.5		

LEEKS AU GRATIN

L eeks have been grown since ancient times and were considered to have healthful characteristics. But today, flavor makes leeks a popular vegetable.

    6 large leeks
    4 cups Vegetable Broth (see index)
    ½ cup Parmesan cheese, freshly grated
    ⅓ cup bread crumbs
       Pepper, freshly ground, to taste

Remove most of green top portion of leeks, and cut off and discard first or second outer leaves if they seem tough. Trim base, keeping leaves attached to it. Cut leeks in half lengthwise, and rinse thoroughly, making sure that all sand and grit caught between layers is washed away.

Pour broth into large, low-sided saucepan, bring to a boil, and add all leeks. Try to have leeks in single layer. Add more broth, if necessary, to cover leeks. Cover, reduce heat to low, and simmer for 5 to 10 minutes, until leeks are cooked but still somewhat firm. Do not overcook, or they will lose their flavor and texture. When cooked, remove leeks carefully from the broth with tongs, and place on plate to cool.

Spray vegetable cooking spray on baking dish large enough for leeks in single layer. Place leeks in baking dish. Combine Parmesan and bread crumbs in mixing bowl, and sprinkle over leeks. Add pepper. Bake for 30 minutes in 375-degree preheated oven until a golden crust forms on top. Serve hot in baking dish.

Serves 6

NUTRITIONAL DATA

PER SERVING		EXCHANGES	
calories	197	milk	0.0
% calories from fat	21	vegetable	3.5
fat (gm)	4.7	fruit	0.0
sat. fat (gm)	1.9	bread	1.0
cholesterol (mg)	6.6	meat	0.0
sodium (mg)	235	fat	0.5
protein (gm)	8		
carbohydrate (gm)	32.6		

ONIONS STUFFED WITH MUSHROOMS

    5   medium red onions
 1½   cups mushrooms, finely chopped
    2   cloves garlic
    4   tablespoons bread crumbs
    3   tablespoons Parmesan cheese, freshly grated
    2   tablespoons parsley, chopped
    2   tablespoons oregano, chopped
    1   teaspoon Spike
   ½   teaspoon pepper, freshly ground

Remove skin and 1 or 2 outer layers of onions. Steam onions until half cooked, about 20 to 30 minutes, depending on size. Test by inserting fork or knife point. It should enter but meet resistance. Drain onions and let cool until they can be handled.

Meanwhile, prepare stuffing by combining remaining ingredients in small mixing bowl.

Cut onions in half across grain. Scoop out pulp in center, leaving solid shell of 3 or 4 layers of onion and bottom intact. Chop ½ cup of pulp fine, and add it to stuffing mixture.

Fill onion halves with stuffing. Place snugly side by side in baking dish sprayed with vegetable cooking spray. Bake for 30 minutes in 350-degree preheated oven. Serve warm or at room temperature.

Serves 6

NUTRITIONAL DATA

PER SERVING		EXCHANGES	
calories	84	milk	0.0
% calories from fat	15	vegetable	3.0
fat (gm)	1.5	fruit	0.0
sat. fat (gm)	0.7	bread	0.0
cholesterol (mg)	2.5	meat	0.0
sodium (mg)	94	fat	0.0
protein (gm)	3.8		
carbohydrate (gm)	15.2		

♥

STUFFED PEPPER ROLLS

T hese bell peppers are filled with capers, currants, pine nuts, onion, and herbs. This is a Mediterranean recipe that makes a wonderful vegetarian meal.

6   green, yellow, and red bell peppers
½   cup bread crumbs
2   tablespoons capers, chopped
1   tablespoon pine nuts
4   tablespoons currants, soaked in water for 30 minutes and drained
2   tablespoons parsley, chopped
2   tablespoons basil, chopped
¼   cup celery, chopped
¼   cup onion, chopped
¼   teaspoon hot pepper flakes
    Spike, to taste
    Pepper, to taste
3   tablespoons Basic Tomato-Basil Sauce (see index) or canned tomato sauce

Wash peppers, cut in half lengthwise, and remove seeds and inner membrane.

In mixing bowl combine bread crumbs, capers, pine nuts, currants, parsley, basil, celery, onion, hot pepper, and Spike and pepper to taste. Mix well, and place 2 or 3 tablespoons of this mixture into each pepper half. Place peppers in baking dish large enough to hold them tightly together in single layer.

Mix tomato sauce with 1 cup water, and pour evenly over the peppers. Place in preheated 350-degree oven for 30 minutes or until peppers are cooked but still firm. Transfer to serving platter, and serve hot.

Serves 8

NUTRITIONAL DATA

PER SERVING		EXCHANGES	
calories	139	milk	0.0
% calories from fat	8	vegetable	0.9
fat (gm)	9.2	fruit	0.2
sat. fat (gm)	1.2	bread	0.3
cholesterol (mg)	0	meat	0.0
sodium (mg)	77	fat	0.1
protein (gm)	3.4		
carbohydrate (gm)	15.6		

POTATOES, FIESOLE STYLE

T hese potatoes make a nice vegetarian main dish and go well with soup and salad.

- 2 lbs. potatoes, peeled or unpeeled, washed and sliced in pieces ¼ inch thick
- 1 medium onion, thinly sliced
- 3 tablespoons Classic Spaghetti Sauce (see index) or canned tomato sauce
- 1 tablespoon oregano, chopped
- 1 tablespoon basil, chopped
- 1 teaspoon Spike
- ½ teaspoon pepper, freshly ground
- ½ lb. mozzarella cheese
- 3 tablespoons bread crumbs

Spray 10-inch-square baking dish with vegetable cooking spray. Place layer of potatoes in bottom of dish and upright along sides. Place layer of onions over potatoes in bottom of dish, cover with thin layer of sauce, sprinkle with oregano, basil, Spike, and pepper, and top with layer of cheese.

Repeat process until all ingredients are used, finishing with layer of cheese. Sprinkle with bread crumbs, cover dish with aluminum foil, and bake in preheated 400-degree oven for 30 minutes. Remove foil, and bake another 15 minutes. Serve potatoes hot from baking dish.

Serves 8

NUTRITIONAL DATA

PER SERVING		EXCHANGES	
calories	203	milk	0.0
% calories from fat	22	vegetable	0.0
fat (gm)	5	fruit	0.0
sat. fat (gm)	3	bread	2.0
cholesterol (mg)	16.8	meat	1.0
sodium (mg)	177	fat	0.0
protein (gm)	10.1		
carbohydrate (gm)	30.3		

POTATOES SAVRIN

*T*hese *potatoes are parboiled, then baked with a milk sauce rather than the traditional rich cream sauce. Serve as a main course with soup and salad.*

2½ lbs. potatoes
 1 teaspoon Spike
 1 teaspoon black pepper, freshly ground, to taste
 4 tablespoons Parmesan cheese, freshly grated
 ½ pound Gruyère cheese, thinly sliced
 3 cups evaporated skim milk

Peel potatoes, and boil them in salted water until almost tender. They should be slightly undercooked. Drain, and set aside.

Spray 10-inch-square baking dish with vegetable cooking spray. Slice potatoes approximately ¼-inch thick. Place layer of potatoes on bottom of baking dish and upright along sides. Sprinkle with Spike, ½ teaspoon pepper, 2 tablespoons of Parmesan, and cover with half slices of Gruyère.

Repeat process, using all remaining ingredients. Last layer should be at least ½-inch below top of baking dish. Pour in milk. It should cover potatoes entirely and just touch top layer of cheese. Bake in 350-degree preheated oven for 1 hour, until brown crust forms and milk is absorbed. Serve hot.

Serves 6–8

NUTRITIONAL DATA

PER SERVING		EXCHANGES	
calories	346	milk	1.0
% calories from fat	27	vegetable	0.0
fat (gm)	10.4	fruit	0.0
sat. fat (gm)	6.1	bread	2.0
cholesterol (mg)	37.2	meat	0.5
sodium (mg)	273	fat	2.0
protein (gm)	20		
carbohydrate (gm)	44		

ZUCCHINI WITH GARLIC AND TOMATO

*T*he secret of this dish is to cook the zucchini *quickly. It should be served a little under-cooked.*

- 1½ lbs. zucchini, washed, trimmed, and sliced into ½-inch rounds
- 4 cloves garlic, minced
- 2 large tomatoes, peeled, seeded, and chopped or 1 cup canned Italian plum tomatoes, drained and chopped
- 1 teaspoon Spike
- 1 tablespoon basil, chopped
- 1 tablespoon oregano, chopped
- 2 tablespoons parsley, chopped

  Pepper, freshly ground, to taste

Spray large skillet with vegetable cooking spray. Add zucchini and garlic, and sauté over medium heat, stirring and turning zucchini so that they color on both sides, for 4 to 5 minutes. Add tomatoes, Spike, basil, oregano, and pepper, and cook for 5 more minutes, stirring occasionally. Turn off heat, and add parsley. The zucchini should still be quite firm and almost crunchy. Serve warm.

Serves 6

NUTRITIONAL DATA

PER SERVING		EXCHANGES	
calories	28	milk	0.0
% calories from fat	6	vegetable	1.0
fat (gm)	0.2	fruit	0.0
sat. fat (gm)	0	bread	0.0
cholesterol (mg)	0	meat	0.0
sodium (mg)	7	fat	0.0
protein (gm)	1.2		
carbohydrate (gm)	6.6		

BEANS WITH VEGETABLES AND HERBS

Y̶ou can use either dried or canned Italian white beans. Both work equally well.

1   cup dried white beans or 2 cups canned Italian white beans
1   tablespoon flour
2   tablespoons olive oil
1   medium onion, chopped
1   medium carrot, chopped
1   stalk celery, finely chopped
1   hot pepper, fresh or dried, seeded and chopped
1   teaspoon dried sage, crushed
2   teaspoons chives, chopped
2   tablespoons parsley, chopped
1   large red or green bell pepper, seeded and diced
    Pepper, freshly ground, to taste

Soak beans for 8 hours in 3 cups water with 1 tablespoon flour. Drain, rinse, and cook in 4 cups water until tender, about 1 hour. Drain, and set aside. If canned beans are used, omit soaking with water and flour and simply drain before assembling rest of dish.

Heat olive oil in large saucepan, add onion, carrot, and celery, and sauté over medium heat, stirring, for 5 minutes. Stir in hot pepper, sage, chives, parsley, and bell pepper, and continue to sauté for another 5 to 7 minutes, until pepper is tender.

Add 2 cups of cooked beans and pepper. Combine well, reduce heat to low, and cook, stirring frequently, for another 5 minutes. Serve hot.

Serves 6

NUTRITIONAL DATA

PER SERVING		EXCHANGES	
calories	149	milk	0.0
% calories from fat	29	vegetable	1.0
fat (gm)	5	fruit	0.0
sat. fat (gm)	0.8	bread	1.0
cholesterol (mg)	0	meat	0.0
sodium (mg)	19	fat	1.0
protein (gm)	6.1		
carbohydrate (gm)	20.9		

12
RICE, RISOTTO, AND POLENTA

Rice

Rice is the most common starch of Lombardy, the Piedmont, and the Veneto. It grows in the *risaie,* the rice fields of the Po plain of northern Italy, which is as flat as the American Midwest. Italian rice dishes are creamy, rather than fluffy like pilafs, and are prepared *al dente.* These dishes are cooked with little liquid at a time; more hot liquid is added slowly only when the rice has absorbed the first. The rice is stirred constantly while cooking, producing a dish with a special texture.

The secret to making rice that is creamy and chewy at the same time is the Italian arborio rice, which can be found in good markets and Italian specialty stores. If it is not available, use long-grain rice, although the results will be less than perfect. Specially treated and precooked rice are not good choices because the former does not absorb liquid properly and the latter is apt to disintegrate.

Risotto

Risotto must be eaten immediately after it is cooked because it does not hold well and cannot be reheated; otherwise it can only be used for croquettes. This is a dish to make after all your guests have arrived so it can be served immediately.

265

Freshly cooked, hot risotto is considered by many to be culinary magic. Don't underestimate its leftover charm as mouthwatering cakes. They are easy to make, crispy on the outside, and creamy on the inside. You can use them as appetizers, serve them with drinks, or serve them for supper.

To make risotto cakes keep risotto mixture chilled. Place seasoned bread crumbs in flat dish. Shape chilled risotto into cakes about 3 inches in diameter and about 1-inch thick. If using for appetizers, make them a little smaller.

One by one, coat cakes evenly in bread crumbs, shaking of excess; place them in single layer on cookie sheet. Refrigerate until you are ready to sauté them.

Coat non-stick skillet with light olive oil. Heat over medium heat. Use a spatula to transfer cakes to skillet; do not crowd them. Cook until browned on both sides, about 8 minutes total, using wide spatula to turn them.

Keep cakes warm in 200-degree oven until all are ready to serve. Serve cakes with a garnish of your favorite red sauce, a melange of fresh herbs, diced fresh tomatoes with basil, sautéed mushrooms, or a sprinkle of freshly grated Parmesan cheese.

Polenta

Today, polenta is made of coarsely ground cornmeal, but it has a special history. The name comes from the Latin *pulmentum,* a mush made from coarsely ground grains that the Romans adapted from the Etruscans.

Corn was introduced into Europe from America at the end of the 15th century but initially received little attention. Two centuries later, it was reintroduced, this time from Turkey, met with much greater success, and became known in Italy as *granturco,* Turkish grain.

At one point in the 19th century, polenta became something of a health hazard. Corn, an otherwise nutritious grain, lacks one of the B vitamins, nicotinic acid. Many poor northern Italian peasants ate a diet that relied heavily on polenta and suffered from pellagra, a disease caused by an acute vitamin deficiency. Conditions are greatly improved since then, and today polenta is very popular, especially in the north.

Most polenta dishes are full of pronounced flavors and could not be called subtle. Polenta is especially welcome in winter, when heartier dishes are preferred. The secret to good polenta is the cornmeal; the fresher the cornmeal, the tastier the polenta.

RICE WITH RAW VEGETABLE SAUCE

2½ cups arborio rice
 4 tomatoes, peeled and seeded
 1 cup celery, finely chopped
 1 cup carrots, finely chopped
 ½ cup red or yellow onion, sliced
 1 clove garlic, finely chopped
 ⅓ cup parsley, finely chopped
 ⅓ cup fresh basil, finely chopped
 2 tablespoons olive oil
   Spike, to taste
   Black pepper, freshly ground, to taste
   Tabasco sauce, few drops

Cook rice al dente in 5 cups of boiling water, and drain.

Prepare sauce by combining all remaining ingredients in bowl. If using a food processor, process a small amount of vegetables at a time to ensure that they remain finely chopped, not pureed. They should be crunchy to contrast with softness of rice.

When rice is cooked, place it in glass serving bowl, and pour raw vegetable sauce over it.

Mix well, and serve. You can also put half the sauce over the rice and pass other half in sauceboat to be added by each diner.

Serves 6

NUTRITIONAL DATA

PER SERVING		EXCHANGES	
calories	360	milk	0.0
% calories from fat	14	vegetable	1.0
fat (gm)	5.4	fruit	0.0
sat. fat (gm)	0.8	bread	4.0
cholesterol (mg)	0	meat	0.0
sodium (mg)	37	fat	1.0
protein (gm)	7		
carbohydrate (gm)	70.4		

♥

TOMATOES STUFFED WITH RICE

T hese tomatoes go well with steak, chicken, or veal. They can also be used to create a salad platter by adding sliced tomatoes, onion, peppers, and cucumbers around the tomato.

- 6 large tomatoes
- 3 tablespoons Basic Tomato-Basil Sauce (see index) divided
- 2 cloves garlic
- 8 large basil leaves, finely chopped
- 1 tablespoon parsley, finely chopped
- 6 tablespoons arborio rice
   Spike, to taste
   Pepper, freshly ground, to taste

Wash tomatoes, place them on cutting board, stem side down, and with sharp knife slice ¼-inch cap off each tomato. Reserve caps, which will serve as tops for stuffed tomatoes. With a paring knife or serrated spoon, remove pulp from tomatoes, creating a shell, taking care to keep bottoms intact, and set them aside. Eliminate seeds from pulp, chop, and place in mixing bowl.

Add to tomato pulp 1 tablespoon of tomato sauce, garlic, basil, parsley, rice, Spike, and pepper. Combine well.

Preheat oven to 375 degrees.

Spray an 8 × 10-inch baking dish (large enough to hold tomatoes without crowding) with vegetable cooking spray, and place tomatoes inside. Sprinkle inside of tomatoes with pinch of Spike, and fill each tomato two-thirds full with rice-and-tomato mixture. Replace caps and drizzle with remaining olive oil. Add a mixture of 2 tablespoons of tomato sauce and enough water to come halfway up sides of tomatoes.

Bake, basting once or twice, until rice is cooked, about 35 to 40 minutes. Transfer tomatoes carefully from baking dish to serving platter or plates. Serve hot or at room temperature.

Serves 6

NUTRITIONAL DATA

PER SERVING		EXCHANGES	
calories	78	milk	0.0
% calories from fat	7	vegetable	2.0
fat (gm)	0.6	fruit	0.0
sat. fat (gm)	0.1	bread	0.5
cholesterol (mg)	0	meat	0.0
sodium (mg)	32	fat	0.0
protein (gm)	2.2		
carbohydrate (gm)	17		

RICE WITH SHRIMP
(Gamberetti Risola)

2 tablespoons olive oil, divided
2 tablespoons red onion, diced
1¼ cups arborio or long-grain white rice
⅓ cup white wine
4 cups unsalted chicken broth, kept hot over low heat
12 oz. shrimp, shelled and deveined
1 cup peas
1 teaspoon lemon rind, cut into julienne strips
3 tablespoons pimiento, chopped
1 tablespoon fresh lemon juice
½ teaspoon Spike
   Pepper, freshly ground, to taste
3 tablespoons fresh basil, finely chopped

Heat 1 tablespoon olive oil in large saucepan over low heat. Add onion. Cook, stirring until tender, 5 minutes. Stir in rice, and coat with oil. Add wine, heat to boiling; stir over high heat until almost evaporated.

Stir in 1 cup of chicken broth. Continue adding broth, about ½ cup at a time, stirring constantly. Each portion should be absorbed before adding the next. With last ½ cup broth, add shrimp, peas, and lemon.

Cook uncovered, stirring constantly, until broth is absorbed and rice is tender to the bite, the dish is moist and creamy, and shrimp are cooked through, 5 to 8 minutes. Add remaining 1 tablespoon olive oil, pimiento, and lemon juice. Stir in Spike and black pepper to taste.

Arrange on a platter and sprinkle with basil.

Serves 4

NUTRITIONAL DATA

PER SERVING		EXCHANGES	
calories	431	milk	0.0
% calories from fat	21	vegetable	1.0
fat (gm)	9.9	fruit	0.0
sat. fat (gm)	1.6	bread	3.5
cholesterol (mg)	132.9	meat	2.0
sodium (mg)	189	fat	1.0
protein (gm)	25.2		
carbohydrate (gm)	55.4		

RICE WITH AUTUMN VEGETABLES

(Riso dell'Autunno)

T his dish combines three late-harvest vegetables—eggplant, celery, and mushrooms—with a traditional Milanese risotto for a wonderful autumn treat.

1 recipe Lemon Risotto (see index)

1 tablespoon olive oil

¼ cup onion, minced

2 tablespoons garlic, minced

1 large eggplant (about 1 lb.), peeled and cut into ½-inch dice

½ teaspoon hot red pepper flakes

½ cup celery, minced

1 cup cooked garbanzo or kidney beans (rinsed and drained, if canned)

1 cup mushrooms, sliced

1 teaspoon fresh rosemary, minced

¼ cup parsley, minced

Spike, to taste

Black pepper, freshly ground, to taste

2 tablespoons Parmesan cheese, freshly grated

Make Lemon Risotto and set aside.

Heat oil in large skillet over moderate heat. Add onion and garlic, and sauté until slightly softened, about 3 minutes. Add eggplant, and brown on all sides. Add hot pepper flakes and celery, and cook an additional 3 minutes. Remove from heat.

Preheat oven to 375 degrees. Stir beans, mushrooms, rosemary, and half of parsley into eggplant mixture. Combine vegetables and risotto. Season to taste with Spike and pepper.

Transfer to a 2-quart casserole, sprayed with vegetable cooking spray, cover, and bake until heated through, about 20 minutes. Serve from casserole, topped with remaining parsley and Parmesan.

Serves 4

NUTRITIONAL DATA

PER SERVING		EXCHANGES	
calories	563	milk	0.0
% calories from fat	29	vegetable	0.5
fat (gm)	18.3	fruit	0.0
sat. fat (gm)	5.2	bread	5.0
cholesterol (mg)	13.5	meat	1.5
sodium (mg)	1187	fat	2.5
protein (gm)	21.4		
carbohydrate (gm)	78.2		

RISOTTO BAKED WITH EGGPLANT

Many food scholars believe that on its way to Italy from Asia, rice first was eaten in Sicily. While risotto has become more firmly established in the north, Sicilian cooks have their own versions, such as this one.

2 lbs. eggplant
　 Spike, to taste
4 tablespoons onion, chopped fine
1½ cups canned Italian plum tomatoes, peeled and cut up, with their juice
2 tablespoons parsley, chopped
2 tablespoons fresh basil, chopped
1 cup beef broth
¾ cup water
1⅓ cups arborio rice
⅔ cup dry white wine
　 Black pepper, freshly ground, to taste
3 tablespoons Romano cheese, freshly grated
3 tablespoons Parmesan cheese, freshly grated
1 cup mozzarella, diced into ¼-inch cubes

Cut off the eggplant's green stems, peel, and cut lengthwise into ¼-inch thick slices. Stand slices along sides of deep colander, sprinkle with Spike, and place colander in a basin. Allow eggplant to rest for at least 30 minutes until most of its liquid runs off.

Spray skillet well with olive-oil flavored vegetable cooking spray, and place on high heat. Pat eggplant slices thoroughly dry on both sides with paper towel, and place them into hot pan. Reduce heat slightly to medium-high, and cook eggplant until it becomes light golden brown. With slotted spoon, transfer eggplant to platter lined with paper towels to drain. When blotted, stack eggplant on dry plate.

Choose heavy-bottomed pot suitable for making risotto, spray with vegetable cooking spray, put in chopped onion, and place over medium-high heat. Sauté onion until it becomes pale gold. Add cut-up tomatoes with their juice, and turn heat to low. Cook for about 5 minutes, stirring well. Add parsley and basil. Stir 2 or 3 times, then transfer a little more than two-thirds of pot's contents to bowl.

Simmer broth in saucepan over medium-low heat. Put rice in pot in which you cooked tomatoes, and turn up heat to medium-high. Stir rice for a few seconds until it is coated, then put in wine.

Cook, uncovered, stirring from time to time until wine has evaporated, then add ½ cup of simmering broth. Stir until broth has evaporated, then ladle another ½ cup of broth into rice and keep stirring. Proceed in this manner, adding broth when necessary, until you run out of broth. Continue with water while stirring constantly to keep rice from sticking to pot, until risotto is done. It should be tender, but firm—al dente. Altogether, it should take 25 to 30 minutes. Add several grindings of pepper and a pinch of Spike, but not too much since cheeses will contribute some saltiness.

Spread the risotto on a platter to cool.

Turn oven to 400 degrees. Spray bottom of deep oven-to-table baking dish well with vegetable cooking spray. Spread 1-inch layer of rice on bottom. Cover rice with eggplant slices. Pour a little sauce from bowl over eggplant, then some Romano, Parmesan, and diced mozzarella. Cover with another layer of rice and with other ingredients in sequence described above. Topmost layer may be either rice or eggplant, but it should be sprinkled with grated Parmesan cheese.

Bake for 10 to 12 minutes on uppermost oven rack until cheese melts and forms a light, golden crust. Let settle for 5 minutes, and serve directly from baking dish.

Serves 6

NUTRITIONAL DATA

PER SERVING		EXCHANGES	
calories	295	milk	0.0
% calories from fat	17	vegetable	0.5
fat (gm)	5.6	fruit	0.0
sat. fat (gm)	2.7	bread	3.0
cholesterol (mg)	16.3	meat	1.0
sodium (mg)	419	fat	0.5
protein (gm)	12		
carbohydrate (gm)	45.5		

LEMON RISOTTO
(Risotto al Limone)

This tangy Roman risotto is excellent before or with a fish course.

- 2 tablespoons olive oil
- ¼ cup onion, minced
- 1 lemon rind, grated
- 1½ cups arborio rice, uncooked
- 4½ cups chicken broth
- ¼ cup plus 2 teaspoons lemon juice
- ½ cup Parmesan cheese, freshly grated
-     Spike, to taste
-     Pepper, to taste

In heavy saucepan over moderately low heat, add olive oil, onion, and lemon rind; sauté slowly for 5 minutes. Add rice; stir to coat with oil. Raise heat to high; toast rice, stirring for 30 seconds.

Immediately add ½ cup broth; reduce heat to medium-low, and stir until broth is absorbed. Add ½ cup at a time, stirring constantly, and adding more only when previous portion has been absorbed. When all stock is absorbed (about 20 to 25 minutes), stir in ¼ cup lemon juice. Rice should be tender. If not, add warm water bit by bit until rice is tender yet firm.

Stir in Parmesan, and cook briefly to blend and melt cheese. Season to taste with Spike and pepper. Add remaining lemon juice; serve immediately in warm bowls.

Serves 4

NUTRITIONAL DATA

PER SERVING		EXCHANGES	
calories	423	milk	0.0
% calories from fat	27	vegetable	0.0
fat (gm)	12.5	fruit	0.0
sat. fat (gm)	3.9	bread	4.0
cholesterol (mg)	11	meat	1.5
sodium (mg)	1109	fat	1.5
protein (gm)	15.9		
carbohydrate (gm)	59.7		

RISOTTO WITH MUSHROOMS

½ oz. dried wild mushrooms *(Boletus edulis)*
2 tablespoons olive oil
½ medium onion, finely chopped
1 tablespoon parsley, finely chopped
1 stalk celery, finely chopped
1 small carrot, finely chopped
1 lb. fresh mushrooms, cleaned, trimmed, and thinly sliced
2 cups arborio rice
   Pinch of Spike
6 cups Vegetable Broth (see index)

Soak dried mushrooms in 1 cup of warm water; remove carefully from water, reserving the liquid. Rinse under cold running water to remove grit and sand, drain, chop coarsely, and set aside.

Strain the soaking liquid through a thick layer of cheesecloth or a coffee filter, and set aside.

Place oil in large, heavy saucepan and add onion, parsley, celery, and carrot. Sauté over medium heat for 5 minutes. Add fresh and dried mushrooms, and sauté for another 2 minutes. Stir in rice and Spike, and cook, stirring, for 2 minutes.

Pour in mushroom liquid, then broth, ½ cup at a time, stirring constantly, until rice is cooked al dente. Do not overcook. Serve immediately.

Serves 6

NUTRITIONAL DATA

PER SERVING		EXCHANGES	
calories	169	milk	0.0
% calories from fat	36	vegetable	2.5
fat (gm)	7.3	fruit	0.0
sat. fat (gm)	1	bread	0.5
cholesterol (mg)	0	meat	0.0
sodium (mg)	35	fat	1.5
protein (gm)	5.2		
carbohydrate (gm)	23.6		

RISOTTO ALLA MILANESE

2 tablespoons olive oil
1 medium onion, finely chopped
3 cups arborio rice
½ cup dry white wine
  Generous pinch saffron
8 cups hot Vegetable Broth (see index)
½ cup Parmesan cheese, freshly grated
  Pinch of Spike
  Truffles (optional)
  Parsley

Heat oil in large, heavy saucepan, add onion, and sauté until transparent. Add rice, and sauté, stirring constantly, for 2 to 3 minutes. Add wine, and cook, stirring until it evaporates. Add saffron and combine well. Add hot vegetable broth, ½ cup at a time, and continue cooking, stirring constantly, until risotto is creamy, smooth, moist, and cooked al dente.

Remove from heat, add Parmesan, and combine. Correct for seasoning. Slice truffles over top if you like, and serve immediately on heated serving platter decorated with parsley.

Serves 8

NUTRITIONAL DATA

PER SERVING		EXCHANGES	
calories	419	milk	0.0
% calories from fat	17	vegetable	1.5
fat (gm)	8.1	fruit	0.0
sat. fat (gm)	2.1	bread	4.0
cholesterol (mg)	4.9	meat	0.5
sodium (mg)	142	fat	1.0
protein (gm)	10.7		
carbohydrate (gm)	73.2		

Basic polenta

P olenta must be watched and stirred continuously as it cooks, but the results are worth the work. It is a thick, creamy, golden pudding that has inspired cooks to many variations. Common throughout northern Italy, polenta can be eaten hot, or it can be cooled until firm and sliced. In that form, it is usually served with meat sauces or mushrooms and cheese. It is often baked until bubbly.

1 cup yellow cornmeal
4 cups water, divided
1 teaspoon salt

Mix cornmeal with 1½ cups of water to smooth paste. Pour remaining water and salt into top part of double boiler. Not using bottom part, bring water to boiling point over direct heat.

Stir cornmeal paste gradually into boiling water. Cook over medium heat, stirring constantly, until mixture reaches boiling point. Then set double-boiler top over bottom pan filled with boiling water. Cook covered, stirring frequently, for 30 to 45 minutes.

Note: Choose Chunky Vegetable Sauce (see index) or butter, honey, maple syrup, cheese, or tomato sauce to serve over this warm dish.

Makes about 4 cups
Serves 6

NUTRITIONAL DATA

PER SERVING		EXCHANGES	
calories	84	milk	0.0
% calories from fat	4	vegetable	0.0
fat (gm)	0.4	fruit	0.0
sat. fat (gm)	0.1	bread	1.0
cholesterol (mg)	0	meat	0.0
sodium (mg)	356	fat	0.0
protein (gm)	2		
carbohydrate (gm)	17.8		

BAKED POLENTA WITH MUSHROOMS

1 medium-size onion, minced

1 clove garlic, minced

2 tablespoons parsley, minced

¾ lb. mushrooms, thinly sliced

⅔ cup canned tomatoes, drained

Spike, to taste

Spike and pepper, to taste

8 cups cooked hot polenta (2 recipes Basic Polenta, see preceding recipe)

¼ cup liquid Butter Buds

1 cup Parmesan cheese, freshly grated

Heat deep skillet sprayed with vegetable cooking spray. Add onion, garlic, and parsley, and cook, stirring constantly, until onion is soft. Add mushrooms and tomatoes. Cook over medium heat for 7 to 10 minutes or until mushrooms have given up almost all of their liquid but are still firm. Season with Spike and pepper to taste.

While polenta is still hot, beat in Butter Buds and Parmesan cheese. Spoon polenta into loaf pan, 9 × 5 × 3 inches, and cool.

Unmold polenta, and cut it in half. Return one part to loaf pan and top with mushroom sauce and remaining polenta.

Bake in 350-degree preheated oven for 30 minutes or until top is golden brown and crusty. Unmold on warm platter, and serve with tossed green salad.

Serves 6

NUTRITIONAL DATA

PER SERVING		EXCHANGES	
calories	276	milk	0.0
% calories from fat	20	vegetable	1.0
fat (gm)	6.1	fruit	0.0
sat. fat (gm)	3.3	bread	2.5
cholesterol (mg)	13.2	meat	1.0
sodium (mg)	1187	fat	0.5
protein (gm)	12.6		
carbohydrate (gm)	42.4		

POLENTA WITH 3 CHEESES

S erve as a main luncheon dish with a salad and dessert or as a side dish to ham, roasted meats, and stews.

    8 cups water
    2 teaspoons salt
 1¾ cups polenta or yellow cornmeal
   ¼ cup low-fat Lorraine cheese, finely diced
   ¼ cup skim mozzarella cheese, finely diced
   ½ cup grated Parmesan cheese
   ¼ cup liquid Butter Buds

Bring water and salt to full rolling boil in heavy 4-quart saucepan. Gradually sprinkle in polenta in thin steady stream, stirring constantly with wooden spoon to prevent lumping. Cook over low heat, stirring constantly, for 4 to 5 minutes. Continue cooking over low heat, without cover, for 15 minutes.

Stir in Lorraine and mozzarella cheese, mixing well. Continue cooking another 15 minutes, stirring frequently.

Turn polenta out on heated serving dish. Sprinkle with Parmesan, and drizzle with Butter Buds.

Serves 6

NUTRITIONAL DATA

PER SERVING		EXCHANGES	
calories	243	milk	0.0
% calories from fat	25	vegetable	0.0
fat (gm)	6.7	fruit	0.0
sat. fat (gm)	4	bread	2.0
cholesterol (mg)	18.6	meat	1.0
sodium (mg)	1164	fat	1.0
protein (gm)	11.8		
carbohydrate (gm)	32.5		

13
DINNER SAUCES

Forget heavy, cream-based sauces. The new sauces are made with vegetables, olive oil, yogurt, or tofuto, a combination of skim milk and tofu that produces a delicious substitute for heavy cream.

Italian cooking uses many sauces, some cooked and some not. It is a mistake to think only of tomato sauce when one thinks of Italy. Regional sauces vary from the *ragu* of Bologna to the *pesto* of Genoa to the *saor* of Venice. Another mistake is to believe that food is generously covered with sauce. In fact, Italians use sauces sparingly, even on pasta.

Unlike many French sauces, Italian sauces are easy to prepare and do not require tedious reducing to get the right consistency. Start with the best seasonal ingredients, and if you are using canned tomatoes, use a good brand.

In sauces such as pesto, only fresh basil will do, but I have substituted dried herbs in some recipes because many people cannot obtain fresh. Be encouraged to give the unfamiliar sauces a try. I think you will like the results.

MOCK BÉCHAMEL SAUCE

2 cups skim milk

3 tablespoons all-purpose flour

½ oz. butter-substitute

¼ teaspoon salt

Pepper, freshly ground, to taste

Combine milk, flour, and butter substitute in saucepan. Heat, stirring constantly, until thickened. Season with salt and pepper. Use when you need a cream sauce, as in pasta or macaroni dishes.

Makes 2 cups

Serves 8

NUTRITIONAL DATA

PER SERVING		EXCHANGES	
calories	33	milk	0.5
% calories from fat	4	vegetable	0.0
fat (gm)	0.1	fruit	0.0
sat. fat (gm)	0.1	bread	0.0
cholesterol (mg)	1	meat	0.0
sodium (mg)	119	fat	0.0
protein (gm)	2.4		
carbohydrate (gm)	5.2		

TANGY DILL SAUCE

T his sauce is delicious with chicken, lamb, and seafood.

¼ cup fat-free mayonnaise

2 tablespoons Dijon mustard

¼ teaspoon black pepper, freshly ground
Pinch of salt

3 tablespoons fresh dill, chopped

2 tablespoons fresh lemon juice

In small bowl, whisk together mayonnaise, mustard, pepper, and salt. Whisk in dill and lemon juice. Use immediately, or cover and refrigerate for up to 1 week.

Makes about 1 cup

Serves 16 (1-tablespoon servings)

NUTRITIONAL DATA

PER SERVING		EXCHANGES	
calories	5	milk	0.0
% calories from fat	18	vegetable	0.0
fat (gm)	0.1	fruit	0.0
sat. fat (gm)	0	bread	0.0
cholesterol (mg)	0	meat	0.0
sodium (mg)	57	fat	0.0
protein (gm)	0.2		
carbohydrate (gm)	1.1		

DIJONAISE SAUCE

1 cup fat-free mayonnaise
3 tablespoons Dijon mustard
1 teaspoon lemon juice

Combine all ingredients, and mix well. Refrigerate before serving. Use on salmon, sandwiches, or chicken. It also works well in potato or tuna salad.

Makes 1 cup
Serves 16 (1-tablespoon servings)

NUTRITIONAL DATA

PER SERVING		EXCHANGES	
calories	11	milk	0.0
% calories from fat	11	vegetable	0.0
fat (gm)	0.2	fruit	0.0
sat. fat (gm)	0	bread	0.0
cholesterol (mg)	0	meat	0.0
sodium (mg)	163	fat	0.0
protein (gm)	0.2		
carbohydrate (gm)	3.2		

FLORENTINE SAUCE FOR PASTA

2 lbs. fresh spinach

2 tablespoons butter substitute

3 tablespoons flour

2 cups skim milk

1¾ cups low-fat cottage cheese or low-fat ricotta cheese

¼ cup Parmesan cheese

Carefully wash spinach, and break off tough ends. Chop spinach leaves, then steam for 2–3 minutes. Drain well. Using paper towels dry well, and set aside.

In top of double boiler over boiling water, heat butter substitute granules. Add flour, stirring constantly for about 2–3 minutes. Add milk, a little at a time, stirring constantly with wire whisk until sauce thickens, about 10 minutes.

Add all other ingredients, including drained spinach. Mix thoroughly, and heat through. Serve over pasta.

Makes 6 cups

Serves 12 (½-cup servings)

NUTRITIONAL DATA

PER SERVING		EXCHANGES	
calories	78	milk	0.0
% calories from fat	18	vegetable	1.0
fat (gm)	1.6	fruit	0.0
sat. fat (gm)	0.9	bread	0.0
cholesterol (mg)	5.1	meat	1.0
sodium (mg)	283	fat	0.0
protein (gm)	9.2		
carbohydrate (gm)	7.5		

HOLLANDAISE SAUCE

2 tablespoons liquid butter substitute
1 tablespoon flour
1 cup boiling water
4 oz. egg substitute, beaten
Juice of ½ lemon

Combine butter-substitute granules and flour in saucepan. Add boiling water, stirring constantly. Cook over low heat.

Beat egg substitute and lemon juice together. Add some of first mixture to this. Then slowly add egg mixture to butter-flavored mixture. Cook until mixture coats spoon. This is delicious, easy to make, and will keep well.

Makes 1½ cups
Serves 6

NUTRITIONAL DATA

PER SERVING		EXCHANGES	
calories	16	milk	0.0
% calories from fat	1	vegetable	0.0
fat (gm)	0	fruit	0.0
sat. fat (gm)	0	bread	0.0
cholesterol (mg)	0	meat	0.0
sodium (mg)	87	fat	0.0
protein (gm)	1.9		
carbohydrate (gm)	1.7		

BASIC MARINARA SAUCE

¼ cup onion, chopped

2 cloves garlic, minced

¼ cup liquid butter substitute

1 6-oz. can tomato paste

¼ cup sherry

1 beef bouillon cube

1 tablespoon sugar

1 tablespoon basil

1 bay leaf

¼ teaspoon black pepper, freshly ground

Sauté garlic and onions for 1 minute in liquid butter-flavored granules. Add tomato paste, wine, bouillon cube, and seasonings. Blend well, and cook for 30 minutes over medium heat. Remove bay leaf, and serve over pasta.

Makes about 2 cups

Serves 4

NUTRITIONAL DATA

PER SERVING		EXCHANGES	
calories	84	milk	0.0
% calories from fat	5	vegetable	3.0
fat (gm)	0.5	fruit	0.0
sat. fat (gm)	0.1	bread	0.0
cholesterol (mg)	0	meat	0.0
sodium (mg)	740	fat	0.0
protein (gm)	2.1		
carbohydrate (gm)	15.1		

NAPOLI PASTA SAUCE

¼ cup fennel bulb, chopped

¼ cup shallot, minced

4 cloves garlic, minced

8 cups tomato, peeled, seeded, and chopped

½ teaspoon Spike

¼ teaspoon pepper, freshly ground

1 tablespoon sugar

½ cup fresh parsley, chopped

2 tablespoons ripe olives, thinly sliced

Coat skillet with cooking spray; place over medium heat until hot. Add fennel, shallot, and garlic; sauté 2 minutes. Add tomato, Spike, and pepper; cook 7 minutes. Strain mixture through a sieve into bowl, reserving 3 cups tomato juice. Place tomato pulp in bowl; set aside.

Combine reserved tomato juice and sugar in large skillet; stir well. Place over high heat, and cook 10 minutes or until reduced to 1½ cups. Add tomato pulp, parsley, and olives; stir well. Reduce heat to medium, and cook 5 minutes or until thoroughly heated. Serve over pasta.

Makes 4 cups

Serves 8 (½-cup servings)

NUTRITIONAL DATA

PER SERVING		EXCHANGES	
calories	67	milk	0.0
% calories from fat	18	vegetable	2.5
fat (gm)	1.5	fruit	0.0
sat. fat (gm)	0.2	bread	0.0
cholesterol (mg)	0	meat	0.0
sodium (mg)	96	fat	0.0
protein (gm)	2.3		
carbohydrate (gm)	13.7		

SWEET PEPPERS AND TOMATO SAUCE

2 large cloves garlic, chopped

1 medium onion, chopped

1 lb. red bell peppers, seeded and chopped

2 lbs. firm ripe tomatoes, cored, seeded, and chopped

2 tablespoons tomato paste

1 tablespoon dried basil

1 tablespoon dried oregano

1 teaspoon sugar

1 teaspoon Spike

⅛ teaspoon black pepper, freshly ground

⅛ teaspoon red pepper flakes (optional)

Place garlic and onion in large skillet sprayed with vegetable cooking spray. Sauté on medium-high heat about 10 minutes or until tender. Add remaining ingredients, and simmer on medium heat about 20 minutes. Let cool.

Place pepper mixture in blender and process slightly, leaving chunks in mixture. Mixture can be frozen at this point. Reheat before using.

Makes about 3½ cups

Serves 7

NUTRITIONAL DATA

PER SERVING		EXCHANGES	
calories	62	milk	0.0
% calories from fat	9	vegetable	2.5
fat (gm)	0.7	fruit	0.0
sat. fat (gm)	0.1	bread	0.0
cholesterol (mg)	0	meat	0.0
sodium (mg)	51	fat	0.0
protein (gm)	2.3		
carbohydrate (gm)	14.2		

PESTO SAUCE

This is a speedy low-fat version of traditional Italian pesto made without oil!

2   cups fresh basil leaves, thoroughly washed and patted dry
4   large cloves garlic, peeled and chopped
½   cup low-salt chicken broth
    Black pepper, freshly ground, to taste

Combine basil and garlic by chopping in food processor, or halve recipe and use blender. Leave motor running, and add chicken broth in slow, steady stream. Shut motor off, and add liberal grinding of pepper. Process briefly to combine, then scrape out into bowl. Cover until ready to use. Use pine nuts for garnish on pasta.

Note: A combination of Parmesan and Romano cheese is delicious in this sauce if you can afford the calories and the fat. I use about ½ cup combined. (Cheese not included in Nutritional Data.)
    Serves 8

NUTRITIONAL DATA

PER SERVING		EXCHANGES	
calories	20	milk	0.0
% calories from fat	12	vegetable	0.5
fat (gm)	0.3	fruit	0.0
sat. fat (gm)	0	bread	0.0
cholesterol (mg)	0	meat	0.0
sodium (mg)	62	fat	0.0
protein (gm)	1		
carbohydrate (gm)	4		

Classic Spaghetti Sauce

¾ lb. ground lean turkey

1 cup onion, chopped

½ cup green bell pepper, chopped

¼ cup celery, chopped

2 cloves garlic, minced

2 16-oz. cans tomatoes, cut up

1 6-oz. can tomato paste

⅓ cup water

2 tablespoons fresh parsley, chopped

1 teaspoon sugar

1 tablespoon fresh basil, chopped

1 teaspoon fresh oregano, chopped

½ teaspoon fresh marjoram, crushed

¼ teaspoon black pepper, freshly ground

In large saucepan or Dutch oven, cook ground turkey, green pepper, celery, and garlic till meat is brown. Drain fat. Carefully stir in undrained tomatoes, tomato paste, water, parsley, sugar, basil, oregano, marjoram, and pepper.

Bring to boil; reduce heat. Cover, and simmer for 30 minutes. Uncover, and simmer for 10 to 15 minutes more or to desired consistency, stirring occasionally.

Makes about 4 cups

Serves 8

NUTRITIONAL DATA

PER SERVING		EXCHANGES	
calories	109	milk	0.0
% calories from fat	29	vegetable	2.5
fat (gm)	3.7	fruit	0.0
sat. fat (gm)	0.9	bread	0.0
cholesterol (mg)	15.8	meat	1.0
sodium (mg)	376	fat	0.0
protein (gm)	8		
carbohydrate (gm)	12.7		

SPINACH AND MUSHROOM SAUCE

This sauce can be used over pasta, scallops, fish, lamb, or chicken.

- ¼ oz. dried porcini mushrooms
- ⅓ cup boiling water
- 2 large shallots
- 8 large mushrooms, stems trimmed
- Fresh spinach, medium bunches (about 1 lb. total), stems removed
- 1 cup evaporated skim milk
- ½ cup beef broth or bouillon
- 1 teaspoon fresh lemon juice
- 1 teaspoon Spike
- Pepper, freshly ground, to taste
- 2 tablespoons parsley, minced

Place dried mushrooms in small bowl, and cover with boiling water. Let stand 20 minutes to soften. Remove mushrooms from liquid. Strain liquid through sieve lined with dampened cheesecloth or paper towel; reserve. Cut mushrooms into thin strips; set aside.

With food processor running, drop shallots through feed tube; process until minced. Leave in work bowl. Stack mushrooms in feed tube. Slice, using very little pressure. Transfer to medium bowl. Stuff spinach leaves in feed tube in batches. Slice, using light pressure.

Place heavy skillet sprayed with vegetable cooking spray over medium-high heat. Add porcini and fresh mushroom mixture. Cook until shallots are tender, stirring frequently, about 5 minutes. Add milk, broth, and reserved mushroom-soaking liquid. Boil until reduced to thick sauce, stirring occasionally, about 10 minutes. Remove sauce from heat.

Add spinach. Sauté until wilted and all liquid evaporates, about 3 minutes. Add sauce, lemon juice, and Spike. Season with pepper.

This sauce can be prepared 1 day ahead. Cover and refrigerate. Mix in parsley before serving.

Makes about 2 cups

Serves 8

NUTRITIONAL DATA

PER SERVING		EXCHANGES	
calories	47	milk	0.5
% calories from fat	7	vegetable	0.0
fat (gm)	0.4	fruit	0.0
sat. fat (gm)	0.1	bread	0.0
cholesterol (mg)	1.3	meat	0.0
sodium (mg)	131	fat	0.0
protein (gm)	4.7		
carbohydrate (gm)	7.3		

CILANTRO TOMATO SAUCE

S erve as a substitute for purchased tomato sauce.

- ½ lb. plum tomatoes or regular tomatoes
- 3 sprigs fresh cilantro
- 1 shallot or green onion
- 1 clove garlic
- 1 tablespoon orange rind, grated
- 1 teaspoon cornstarch
- 1 teaspoon oregano
- 1 teaspoon Spike
- ½ teaspoon black pepper, freshly ground

In a blender, container, or food processor bowl combine ingredients; cover, and process till smooth. Place a sieve over a saucepan; pour tomato mixture into sieve, pressing with the back of a spoon. Discard seeds, skin, and anything left in sieve.

In the saucepan cook and stir the tomato mixture till thickened and bubbly. Cook and stir for 5 minutes more. Season to taste with Spike and black pepper.

Makes about ¾ cup
Serves 6

NUTRITIONAL DATA

PER SERVING		EXCHANGES	
calories	13	milk	0.0
% calories from fat	10	vegetable	0.5
fat (gm)	0.2	fruit	0.0
sat. fat (gm)	0.03	bread	0.0
cholesterol (mg)	0	meat	0.0
sodium (mg)	4	fat	0.0
protein (gm)	0.4		
carbohydrate (gm)	2.9		

♥

BASIC TOMATO-BASIL SAUCE

I should call this "September" sauce because September usually finds me up to my elbows in fresh tomatoes and basil. This is a basic tomato sauce that I use on everything, so I make a lot each September.

- 2 teaspoons olive oil
- 1 cup onion, finely chopped
- 3 cloves garlic, minced
- 10–12 fresh tomatoes, chopped, or 2 28-oz. cans plum tomatoes, undrained, chopped
- ¼ cup fresh basil, chopped
- 3 teaspoons fresh oregano, minced
- ¼ teaspoon pepper, freshly grated

Heat oil in large skillet over medium heat until hot. Add onion and garlic, and sauté until tender. Stir in tomatoes, and bring to boil. Add remaining ingredients; stir well.

Reduce heat to low, and cook, uncovered, 1 hour and 20 minutes or until thickened, stirring frequently. Serve over cooked pasta, in casseroles, or any time you need a good tomato sauce.

Makes 4 cups
Serves 8 (½-cup servings)

NUTRITIONAL DATA

PER SERVING		EXCHANGES	
calories	60	milk	0.0
% calories from fat	22	vegetable	2.0
fat (gm)	1.6	fruit	0.0
sat. fat (gm)	0.2	bread	0.0
cholesterol (mg)	0	meat	0.0
sodium (mg)	325	fat	0.0
protein (gm)	2.2		
carbohydrate (gm)	10.9		

Tomato-Mushroom Sauce: Follow recipe above, but add 2 cups sliced fresh mushrooms to sautéed onion-garlic mixture before stirring in tomatoes.

NUTRITIONAL DATA

PER SERVING		EXCHANGES	
calories	66	milk	0.0
% calories from fat	21	vegetable	2.0
fat (gm)	1.7	fruit	0.0
sat. fat (gm)	0.3	bread	0.0
cholesterol (mg)	0	meat	0.0
sodium (mg)	325	fat	0.0
protein (gm)	2.6		
carbohydrate (gm)	12		

TOMATO-EGGPLANT SAUCE

E ggplant is the base of a sauce that combines sun-dried and fresh tomatoes. This is a very versatile sauce. Use it on pasta, rice, lasagna, shrimp, fish, chicken breasts, or baked potatoes.
1 medium eggplant (about 1 lb.), cut into ¾-inch dice

- 1½ teaspoons Spike, divided
- 3 large cloves garlic
- 1 medium onion, chopped
- 1 cup chicken broth, canned
- ⅓ recipe Sun-Dried Tomatoes (see index), drained and finely chopped
- 4 large plum tomatoes (about 9 oz.), seeded and diced
- ¼ cup tomato paste
- 2 tablespoons balsamic vinegar or other red wine vinegar
- 10 fresh basil leaves, cut julienne
- 2 tablespoons fresh oregano, chopped

Place eggplant in colander. Sprinkle with 1 teaspoon Spike; toss well. Let stand 30 minutes to drain.

With food processor running, drop garlic through feed tube, and process until minced. Scrape down sides of work bowl. Add onion to work bowl, and mince by turning on and off.

Rinse eggplant. Pat dry with paper towels. Heat heavy, large skillet sprayed with vegetable cooking spray over medium-high heat. Add eggplant. Cook until beginning to soften, stirring frequently, about 10 minutes. Add garlic and onion. Stir until heated through, about 2 minutes.

Mix stock, plum tomatoes, sun-dried tomatoes, tomato paste, vinegar, and remaining ½ teaspoon Spike into eggplant. Bring to boil. Reduce heat, and simmer until eggplant is tender, stirring occasionally, about 10 minutes.

This can be prepared 3 days ahead. Cover and refrigerate. Adjust seasoning, and stir in basil and oregano just before serving.

Makes about 4 cups
Serves 8

NUTRITIONAL DATA

PER SERVING		EXCHANGES	
calories	78	milk	0.0
% calories from fat	15	vegetable	3.0
fat (gm)	1.5	fruit	0.0
sat. fat (gm)	0.7	bread	0.0
cholesterol (mg)	2.3	meat	0.0
sodium (mg)	207	fat	0.0
protein (gm)	2.8		
carbohydrate (gm)	16.2		

ITALIAN TOFUTO

T his sauce can serve any purpose of heavy cream, only better. Gone is most fat and cholesterol. Soups made with it have the same velvety texture and creamy taste as if made with heavy cream.

⅔ cup tofu

¾ cup skim milk

1 teaspoon dry mustard

In blender set at high speed or food processor with metal blade, process tofu and milk 1 minute or until creamy. Add dry mustard, and blend again. Make just before using for best results.

Note: If using for a dessert recipe, substitute 1 teaspoon lemon juice for dry mustard.

Serves 6

NUTRITIONAL DATA

PER SERVING		EXCHANGES	
calories	32	milk	0.0
% calories from fat	38	vegetable	0.0
fat (gm)	1.4	fruit	0.0
sat. fat (gm)	0.2	bread	0.0
cholesterol (mg)	0.5	meat	0.5
sodium (mg)	29	fat	0.0
protein (gm)	3.3		
carbohydrate (gm)	2.1		

TOMATO PUREE

2 tablespoons shallot, minced
1 clove garlic, minced
2 cups tomato, peeled, seeded, and chopped
¼ teaspoon salt
⅛ teaspoon ground red pepper
1½ teaspoons cornstarch
¼ cup evaporated skim milk
1 teaspoon fresh dill, chopped

Coat heavy saucepan with cooking spray; place over medium heat until hot. Add shallot and garlic; sauté 2 minutes. Add tomato, salt, and pepper; sauté 5 minutes.

Position knife blade in food processor bowl; add tomato mixture. Process until smooth.

Return tomato puree to saucepan; cook over medium-low heat 5 minutes or until reduced to 1 cup, stirring constantly.

Place cornstarch in separate mixing bowl; gradually add milk, stirring with wire whisk until blended. Add to tomato mixture; bring to boil over medium heat, and cook 1 minute, stirring constantly.

Remove from heat; stir in dill. Serve with fish, chicken, or on bruschetta or pizza.

Note: Store in airtight container in refrigerator for up to 2 weeks.
Makes 1¼ cups
Serves 5 (¼-cup servings)

NUTRITIONAL DATA

PER SERVING		EXCHANGES	
calories	36	milk	0.0
% calories from fat	8	vegetable	**1.5**
fat (gm)	0.3	fruit	0.0
sat. fat (gm)	0.1	bread	0.0
cholesterol (mg)	0.5	meat	0.0
sodium (mg)	130	fat	0.0
protein (gm)	1.9		
carbohydrate (gm)	7.2		

WHITE CLAM SAUCE

  2 dozen littleneck clams, scrubbed
  5 tablespoons olive oil, divided
  2 large cloves garlic, sliced paper thin
1½ tablespoons Italian parsley, chopped
  2 teaspoons jalapeño peppers, chopped
  2 large plum tomatoes, seeded and cut in ½-inch dice (1 cup)
  ½ cup dry white wine
    Spike, to taste
  1 lb. pasta, preferably spaghetti or fettuccine
  6 fresh basil leaves

Discard any clams that are broken or that do not clamp shut under water. In large skillet, arrange clams in even layer. Cover, and cook over high heat, shaking pan occasionally, until clams open, about 4 minutes. Transfer open clams to large bowl. If some clams are only partially opened, cover and continue cooking, removing each clam as it opens fully.

Pour clam liquid into small bowl. Detach clam meat from shells, and gently rinse each clam in clam liquid to remove any sand. Cut clams into bite-size pieces, and place in small bowl. Pour 2 table-spoons of olive oil on top, cover, and set aside at room temperature.

Line sieve with paper towel, and strain reserved clam juices into another bowl; set aside.

In large skillet or flameproof casserole, heat remaining 3 table-spoons olive oil with garlic over moderately high heat. Cook, stirring, for a few seconds, until fragrant. Stir in parsley and jalapeño. Add tomatoes, and cook, stirring occasionally, for 1 to 2 minutes. Add wine, and cook until slightly reduced, about 1 minute.

When ready to serve, reheat tomato sauce over high heat. Add pasta along with strained clam juice, and cook, tossing and stirring with forks, until all the liquid has been absorbed and pasta is al dente, about 1 minute.

Add basil and reserved clams with their oil, and toss. Transfer to platter, and serve at once.

Makes about 2 cups
Serves 4

NUTRITIONAL DATA

PER SERVING		EXCHANGES	
calories	706	milk	0.0
% calories from fat	27	vegetable	1.0
fat (gm)	21.1	fruit	0.0
sat. fat (gm)	3	bread	5.0
cholesterol (mg)	57	meat	3.0
sodium (mg)	132	fat	3.5
protein (gm)	38		
carbohydrate (gm)	83.3		

CHUNKY VEGETABLE SAUCE

This tangy sauce is suitable for fish, vegetables, and frittatas.

1 Spanish onion, sliced

2 cloves garlic, minced

2 green bell peppers, halved, seeded, and cut into 1-inch squares

2 red bell peppers, halved, seeded, and cut into 1-inch squares

1 eggplant, cubed, salted, and drained for 30 minutes

3 medium-sized tomatoes, peeled, seeded, and diced

Sauté onion in skillet sprayed with vegetable cooking spray. Add peppers; cook for 8 minutes, then add eggplant. After cooking mixture for 5 minutes, add tomatoes. Cook sauce for 15 minutes, until all vegetables are soft and any excess liquid has evaporated.

Makes 2½ cups

Serves 10 (¼-cup servings)

NUTRITIONAL DATA

PER SERVING		EXCHANGES	
calories	33	milk	0.0
% calories from fat	7	vegetable	1.5
fat (gm)	0.3	fruit	0.0
sat. fat (gm)	0	bread	0.0
cholesterol (mg)	0	meat	0.0
sodium (mg)	6	fat	0.0
protein (gm)	1.1		
carbohydrate (gm)	7.6		

14
BREADS
(PANE)

Italians eat a great deal of bread. In Italy, you will find bread at every meal; it is used in soups, with antipasti, and even in desserts. Each area of the country has its own bread, rolls, bread sticks, etc. Bread is easy to make, and since it contains no salt and no oil, it is well suited for use in other dishes. I hope you will try these recipes and use them in other recipes that call for bread; the results will amaze you.

BREAD DRESS UPS

You can add style to any meal by enhancing the bread you serve. The next time you're in a hurry and can't bake bread from scratch, try one of these quick and easy ideas.

Italian Herb Rolls

Unroll package (8) refrigerated bread sticks without separating. Sprinkle ¼ cup finely chopped onion and 1 teaspoon Italian herbs over dough. Roll up, starting from a short side. Slice where perforated. Place coils in a greased 9 × 1½-inch-round baking pan. Bake in 375-degree oven for 15 to 17 minutes or till golden.

Twisted Bread Sticks

Separate package of refrigerated bread sticks. Uncoil, and cut each bread stick in half. Twist dough. In small bowl, combine some grated Parmesan or Romano cheese and a few dashes red pepper flakes. Brush dough with beaten egg white, then spinkle with cheese mixture. Bake according to package directions.

Tomato Biscuits

Separate package (8) refrigerated biscuits. Pat or roll each to 3-inch circle. Place on ungreased baking sheet. Lightly brush circles with olive oil. Place thin tomato slice in center of each circle. Sprinkle lightly with mixture of oregano, basil, and Parmesan cheese. Bake in 400-degree oven for 8 to 10 minutes or till golden.

Italian Bread with Basil

Brush 1 side of ¾-inch-thick slices of Italian bread with melted margarine or butter. Sprinkle with crushed, dried basil and grated Parmesan cheese. Place bread slices, cheese side up, on unheated rack of broiler pan. Broil 4 to 5 inches from heat for 2 to 3 minutes or till cheese is golden.

Garlic Bread

Brush 1 side of ¾-inch-thick slices of Italian bread with melted margarine or butter. Sprinkle lightly with garlic powder. Generously sprinkle with shredded mozzarella cheese. Place bread slices, cheese side up, on unheated rack of broiler pan. Broil 4 to 5 inches from heat for 2 to 3 minutes or till cheese is golden and bubbly.

Pesto Bread

Cut 16-oz. loaf of Italian bread (about 14 inches long) in half horizontally. In small mixing bowl, stir together ⅔ cup low-cal mayonnaise or salad dressing, ½ cup grated Parmesan or Romano cheese, and 1 tablespoon Pesto Sauce (see index) or purchased pesto. Spread over cut sides of bread. Place bread, pesto side up, on unheated rack of broiler pan. Broil 4 to 5 inches from heat for 2 to 3 minutes or till bubbly. Sprinkle with Italian herbs. Cut diagonally into 2-inch slices.

FLORENTINE SNACK BREAD

This flat "pizza" bread is scented with rosemary, oregano, oil, and garlic, which will fill the house with tantalizing aromas when it's baked. Cut it into "fingers," and serve it as a snack with a glass of red wine or iced tea. You can slip it into your picnic basket with roast chicken and antipasti.

- 1 package active dry yeast
- 1 teaspoon salt
- 3 cups unbleached flour
- 1 cup warm (105 degrees) water
- 3 tablespoons olive oil plus olive oil for brushing crust
- 1 tablespoon garlic, minced
  Cornmeal
  Coarse salt
- 1 teaspoon fresh rosemary, minced
- 1 teaspoon fresh oregano, minced

Combine yeast, salt, and flour in large bowl. Combine water and oil in small bowl. Add liquid to dry ingredients, and mix until they form a rough mass.

Knead mixture in bowl with hands until it holds together, then turn it out onto lightly floured surface and knead in garlic. Continue kneading until dough is smooth and elastic, about 8 minutes. Form into ball, and let rest on lightly floured surface, covered, for 1 hour.

Roll dough into a 12 × 14-inch rectangle, and transfer to baking sheet sprinkled with cornmeal. Use fingertips to make indentations in dough at 2-inch intervals. Sprinkle dough lightly with coarse salt, and drizzle olive oil over top. Sprinkle with rosemary and oregano.

Bake at 375 degrees (preheated) until golden, about 15 minutes. Remove from oven and brush with olive oil. Cool slightly on rack; serve warm. Makes one 12 × 14-inch rectangle.

Serves 24

NUTRITIONAL DATA

PER SERVING		EXCHANGES	
calories	78	milk	0.0
% calories from fat	23	vegetable	0.0
fat (gm)	2	fruit	0.0
sat. fat (gm)	0.3	bread	1.0
cholesterol (mg)	0	meat	0.0
sodium (mg)	89	fat	0.0
protein (gm)	2.2		
carbohydrate (gm)	12.7		

BREAD FOR SOUP
(Pane per la Zuppa)

T his Neapolitan version of French toast goes well with soup or stew.

- 1 teaspoon garlic, minced
- 1 tablespoon fennel seed, lightly crushed in a mortar
- 1 tablespoon black pepper, freshly ground
- 1 teaspoon salt
  Egg substitute equal to 5 or 6 eggs
- 3 tablespoons olive oil
- 1 loaf Italian bread cut in ¾-inch slices
- 2 tablespoons Parmesan cheese, freshly grated

Combine garlic, fennel, pepper, and salt in small bowl, and set aside.

Whisk together egg substitute and 3 tablespoons olive oil. Dip bread slice in egg mixture one at a time and let them soak briefly to absorb some egg. Arrange bread slices on large, lightly oiled baking sheet. If bread is slightly stale, you may need additional egg substitute. Dust bread slices with half the fennel mixture.

Bake 10 minutes at 350 degrees (preheated). Turn slices, brush with remaining fennel mixture, and bake 10 minutes more. Sprinkle with Parmesan, and bake an additional 5 minutes or until bread is golden. Serve hot with soup or stew.

Makes 12 slices

Serves 6

NUTRITIONAL DATA

PER SERVING		EXCHANGES	
calories	254	milk	0.0
% calories from fat	29	vegetable	0.0
fat (gm)	8.3	fruit	0.0
sat. fat (gm)	1.5	bread	2.0
cholesterol (mg)	1.6	meat	1.0
sodium (mg)	465	fat	1.0
protein (gm)	10.7		
carbohydrate (gm)	33.8		

POLENTA BREAD

This cornbread from northern Italy bears a strong resemblance to American Spoon Bread, lightened with egg whites and baked to resemble a pudding. The addition of red peppers and garlic definitely makes it Italian.

    2 tablespoons garlic, minced
    1 cup polenta (coarse yellow cornmeal)
 1½ teaspoons salt
    1 cup red bell peppers, chopped
    3 eggs, separated
    2 cups skim milk
  ½ cup evaporated skim milk
    1 tablespoon fresh basil, minced
  ½ teaspoon red pepper flakes
  ¼ cup liquid Butter Buds

In small skillet sprayed with vegetable cooking spray, over moderately low heat, sauté garlic until fragrant. Remove from heat. Combine polenta, salt, and bell pepper in bowl, and set aside.

Put egg yolks, skim milk, and evaporated milk in saucepan, and whisk well. Bring to boil, whisking constantly. Add cornmeal mixture gradually, then add garlic, basil, and red pepper flakes. Cook 2 minutes, stirring constantly with wooden spoon. Add Butter Buds, and cook additional 2 minutes.

Spray an 8-cup souffle dish or casserole with vegetable spray. Place dish in 375-degree preheated oven 5 minutes to warm it.

Beat egg whites with pinch of salt until stiff peaks form. Gently fold whites into thickened cornmeal. Pour mixture into hot souffle dish. Bake until puffed and golden, about 30 minutes. Serve immediately.

Serves 8

NUTRITIONAL DATA

PER SERVING		EXCHANGES	
calories	144	milk	0.5
% calories from fat	15	vegetable	0.5
fat (gm)	2.4	fruit	0.0
sat. fat (gm)	0.7	bread	1.0
cholesterol (mg)	81.5	meat	0.0
sodium (mg)	564	fat	0.5
protein (gm)	7.8		
carbohydrate (gm)	22.3		

SICILIAN MORNING BREAD

T ry this subtly sweet egg bread, fragrant with lemon, Marsala, and fennel, instead of a Danish. If you are having this for breakfast, make it a day ahead and reheat it in the morning. Delicious with lemon curd for an afternoon snack.

- 1 teaspoon olive oil
- 1 package active dry yeast
- ½ cup plus 1 teaspoon sugar
- 1⅓ cups milk, scalded and cooled to 100 degrees
- 6½ cups (about) unbleached flour
- ¼ cup dried currants
- ⅓ cup golden raisins
- ⅓ cup Marsala wine
- ½ cup unsalted butter
- 3 tablespoons shortening
- 1½ teaspoons fennel seed
- 4 eggs
- 1 tablespoon lemon rind, grated
- ½ teaspoon salt

EGG WASH

- 1 egg white, lightly beaten
- 1 teaspoon water
- ½ tablespoon Marsala wine

Brush olive oil over surface of large stainless-steel bowl. Put yeast and 1 teaspoon of sugar in bottom of bowl. Add 1 cup of scalded milk, and stir to dissolve yeast. Set aside for 10 minutes, then add 1½ cups flour and remaining milk.

Knead by hand or with mixer and dough hook until dough is soft and silky, about 7 or 8 minutes. Cover, and let rise 5 hours. While dough rises, soak currants and raisins in Marsala for at least 1 hour.

In saucepan over low heat, melt butter and 2 tablespoons of shortening. Add fennel seeds, remove from heat, and let stand until cool. Add eggs to fennel seed mixture one at a time, blending well after each addition, then add lemon rind and remaining sugar. Set aside.

When dough has risen 5 hours, add fennel seed mixture, and mix well. Add salt, and begin adding remaining flour ½ cup at a time. When dough is firm enough to knead, turn out onto lightly floured board, and knead until smooth and soft, about 10 to 15 minutes, adding as much flour as necessary to prevent sticking. During final 5 minutes, knead in raisins and currants.

Form dough into 2 loaves. Use remaining shortening to grease two 9-inch loaf pans. Place dough in pans, cover, and let rise until doubled in size. This may take as long as 3 hours. (Dough may also be formed into 1 large round loaf and baked free-form.)

To make Egg Wash: Mix ingredients together. Brush on loaves 5 minutes before baking. Brush again immediately before baking. Bake at 375 degrees (preheated) until loaves are golden brown and sound hollow when tapped, about 35 minutes. Cool on racks.

Makes 2, 9-inch loaves or 1 large round loaf
Serves 32 (16 slices per loaf)

NUTRITIONAL DATA

PER SERVING		EXCHANGES	
calories	177	milk	0.0
% calories from fat	29	vegetable	0.0
fat (gm)	5.7	fruit	0.5
sat. fat (gm)	2.7	bread	1.5
cholesterol (mg)	35.6	meat	0.0
sodium (mg)	51	fat	1.0
protein (gm)	4.8		
carbohydrate (gm)	26.2		

♥

15
BISCOTTI

Biscotto (biscotti is plural) means twice-cooked and refers to the double-baking process that produces a crunchy cookie with a long shelf life. In Italy, biscotti can mean any of a wide assortment of cookies, but it usually refers to an almond-studded biscuit that has been produced in Prato for centuries. The dough is shaped into a log and baked; then it is sliced, and the cookies are returned to a slow oven to dry out.

In Italy, where cookies come in many fanciful shapes and sizes, most have symbolic meaning in some part of the country. Weddings and holidays require special cookies. Italian knot cookies and marriage cookies for the bride and honey balls for Easter are memorable.

One surprise is that cookies are often eaten in the morning, especially the harder ones. Italy has no breakfast as Americans know it. Most Italians stop at the neighborhood pastry shop for a quick biscotto on the way to school or work.

Some of these recipes are quite low in calories, which makes them an ideal snack. If you have never had biscotti, you are in for a treat.

Baking Tips

To keep biscotti from sticking, spray baking sheet with light coating of vegetable cooking spray or line with parchment.

Place logs of dough at least 4 inches apart on baking sheet because dough spreads during baking.

After first baking, cool logs of dough for about 10 minutes before slicing them with serrated knife, using a gentle sawing motion.

For second baking, be sure to leave space between cookies so heat can circulate around them. Biscotti crisp as they cool.

To maintain crispness, biscotti should be cooled completely before being stored in airtight container. They stay fresh for 1 month and can be frozen for up to 3 months.

ANISE BISCOTTI

2 cups unbleached all-purpose flour

1 cup sugar

1 tablespoon anise seeds, crushed

1 teaspoon baking powder

½ teaspoon baking soda

¼ teaspoon salt

2 large eggs

2 large egg whites

2 tablespoons lemon zest, grated

1 tablespoon fresh lemon juice

Combine flour, sugar, anise seeds, baking powder, baking soda, and salt. Whisk together eggs, egg whites, lemon zest, and lemon juice, and add to dry ingredients. Mix well.

Working on floured surface with damp hands, shape dough into 2 logs, each about 14 inches long and 1½ inches thick. Set logs on baking sheet lined with foil and lightly coated with vegetable cooking spray, and bake at 325 degrees (preheated) for 20 to 25 minutes or until firm to touch. Transfer logs to rack to cool.

Cut logs diagonally into ½-inch-thick slices. Stand slices upright on baking sheet, and bake at 300 degrees for 40 minutes. Let cool before storing.

Makes about 4 dozen

Serves 48

NUTRITIONAL DATA

PER SERVING		EXCHANGES	
calories	39	milk	0.0
% calories from fat	6	vegetable	0.0
fat (gm)	0.3	fruit	0.0
sat. fat (gm)	0.1	bread	0.5
cholesterol (mg)	8.9	meat	0.0
sodium (mg)	32	fat	0.0
protein (gm)	1		
carbohydrate (gm)	8.2		

♥

CAPPUCCINO BISCOTTI

    2 cups unbleached all-purpose flour
    1 cup sugar
    ½ teaspoon baking soda
    ½ teaspoon double-acting baking powder
    ½ teaspoon salt
    2 teaspoons instant coffee crystals
    ¼ cup plus 1 tablespoon strong-brewed espresso,
       cooled
    1 tablespoon skim milk
    1 large egg yolk
    1 teaspoon mocha extract
    ¾ cup hazelnuts, toasted, skinned, and chopped
       coarse
    ½ cup semisweet chocolate chips

In bowl, combine flour, sugar, baking soda, baking powder, salt, and instant coffee; mix well.

In small bowl, whisk together espresso, milk, yolk, and the mocha extract; add mixture to the flour mixture, beating until dough is formed. Stir in hazelnuts and chocolate chips.

Turn dough out onto floured surface, knead it several times, and halve it. With floured hands, form each piece of dough into log 12 inches long and 2 inches wide, and arrange logs at least 4 inches apart on baking sheet lined with foil and lightly coated with vegetable cooking spray. Bake logs in middle of preheated 350-degree oven for 35 minutes, and let them cool on baking sheet on rack for 10 minutes.

On cutting board, cut logs diagonally crosswise into ¾-inch-thick slices. Arrange biscotti, cut sides down, on baking sheet, and bake at 300 degrees (preheated) for 5 to 6 minutes on each side, or until they are pale golden.

Transfer biscotti to racks to cool, and store them in airtight containers.

Makes about 32
Serves 32

NUTRITIONAL DATA

PER SERVING		EXCHANGES	
calories	92	milk	0.0
% calories from fat	30	vegetable	0.0
fat (gm)	3.2	fruit	0.0
sat. fat (gm)	0.2	bread	1.0
cholesterol (mg)	6.7	meat	0.0
sodium (mg)	81	fat	0.5
protein (gm)	1.4		
carbohydrate (gm)	15.2		

CHOCOLATE BISCOTTI

2½ cups unbleached all-purpose flour

1 cup sugar

1 teaspoon baking soda

½ teaspoon salt

1 teaspoon allspice

2 tablespoons unsweetened cocoa powder (preferably Dutch process)

½ teaspoon chocolate extract

3 eggs

1¼ cups blanched whole almonds, toasted lightly and chopped coarsely

In large bowl, combine flour, sugar, baking soda, salt, allspice, and cocoa powder. Mix well.

In small bowl, whisk together chocolate extract and eggs; add mixture to flour mixture, beating until dough is formed. Stir in almonds.

Turn dough out onto lightly floured surface, knead it several times, and divide it into thirds. With floured hands, form each piece of dough into log 10 inches long by 2½ inches wide, and arrange logs at least 4 inches apart on baking sheet lined with foil and lightly coated with vegetable cooking spray.

Bake the logs in middle of preheated 350-degree oven for 25 minutes, and let them cool on baking sheet on rack for 10 minutes.

On cutting board, cut logs diagonally crosswise into ¾-inch-thick slices. Arrange biscotti, cut sides down, on baking sheet, and bake in 350-degree oven for 5 minutes on each side.

Transfer biscotti to racks to cool, and store in airtight containers.
Makes 36
Serves 36

NUTRITIONAL DATA

PER SERVING		EXCHANGES	
calories	84	milk	0.0
% calories from fat	27	vegetable	0.0
fat (gm)	2.6	fruit	0.0
sat. fat (gm)	0.3	bread	1.0
cholesterol (mg)	17.7	meat	0.0
sodium (mg)	71	fat	0.5
protein (gm)	2.3		
carbohydrate (gm)	13.3		

CRANBERRY-ALMOND BISCOTTI

1⅓ cups (about ¼ lb.) dried cranberries
2½ cups unbleached all-purpose flour
1 cup sugar
½ teaspoon baking soda
½ teaspoon double-acting baking powder
½ teaspoon salt
3 large eggs
1 teaspoon vanilla extract
1 cup shelled almonds, chopped
Egg wash made by beating together 1 large egg and 1 teaspoon water

In bowl, cover cranberries with hot water, and soak for 5 minutes. Drain cranberries well, and pat dry with paper towels.

In bowl, combine flour, sugar, baking soda, baking powder, and salt; mix well. Add eggs and vanilla, beating until dough is formed. Stir in cranberries and almonds.

Turn dough out onto lightly floured surface, knead it several times, and halve it. With floured hands, form each piece of dough into log 13 inches long and 2 inches wide. Arrange logs at least 4 inches apart on baking sheet lined with foil and lightly coated with vegetable cooking spray, and brush them with egg wash.

Bake logs in middle of preheated 325-degree oven for 30 minutes, and let them cool on baking sheet on rack for 10 minutes.

On cutting board, cut logs diagonally crosswise into ¾-inch-thick slices. Arrange biscotti, cut sides down, on baking sheet, and bake them in 325-degree oven for 10 to 12 minutes on each side, or until they are pale golden.

Transfer biscotti to racks to cool, and store them in airtight containers.

Makes 36
Serves 36

NUTRITIONAL DATA

PER SERVING		EXCHANGES	
calories	95	milk	0.0
% calories from fat	21	vegetable	0.0
fat (gm)	2.2	fruit	0.0
sat. fat (gm)	0.3	bread	1.0
cholesterol (mg)	17.8	meat	0.0
sodium (mg)	47	fat	0.5
protein (gm)	3.3		
carbohydrate (gm)	15.9		

BISCOTTI DI PRATO

3¾ cups unbleached all-purpose flour

2 cups sugar

1 teaspoon double-acting baking powder

¼ teaspoon salt

4 large eggs

2 large egg yolks

1 teaspoon almond extract

1⅔ cups unblanched whole almonds, toasted lightly and chopped coarse

Egg wash made by beating together 1 large egg and 1 teaspoon water

In bowl, combine flour, sugar, baking powder, and salt; mix well.

In small bowl, whisk together whole eggs, yolks, and almond extract and add mixture to flour mixture. Beat until dough is formed, and stir in almonds.

Turn dough out onto lightly floured surface, knead it several times, and divide it into fourths. With floured hands, form each piece of dough into log 11 inches long and 2 inches wide. Arrange logs at least 4 inches apart on 2 baking sheets lined with foil and lightly coated with vegetable cooking spray, and brush them with egg wash.

Bake in preheated 350-degree oven for 25 minutes, and let logs cool on baking sheets on racks for 10 minutes.

On cutting board cut logs diagonally crosswise into ¾-inch-thick slices. Arrange biscotti, cut sides down, on baking sheets, and bake at 350 degrees for 5 to 7 minutes on each side, or until they are pale golden.

Transfer biscotti to racks to cool, and store in airtight containers.

Makes 56

Serves 56

NUTRITIONAL DATA

PER SERVING		EXCHANGES	
calories	84	milk	0.0
% calories from fat	25	vegetable	0.0
fat (gm)	2.4	fruit	0.0
sat. fat (gm)	0.4	bread	1.0
cholesterol (mg)	22.8	meat	0.0
sodium (mg)	15	fat	0.5
protein (gm)	2.1		
carbohydrate (gm)	14.1		

MOCHA BISCOTTI

*I*n *this cookie, half the dough is almond-flavored like the traditional biscotti di Prato, and the other half is chocolate/coffee-flavored.*

½ cup whole unblanched almonds

2 cups unbleached all-purpose flour

1 cup sugar

1 teaspoon baking powder

½ teaspoon baking soda

¼ teaspoon salt

2 large eggs

2 large egg whites

2 teaspoons mocha extract, divided

1 tablespoon unsweetened cocoa powder

2 teaspoons instant coffee powder

1 oz. unsweetened chocolate, melted

Spread almonds on baking sheet, and bake in preheated oven at 325 degrees for 12 to 14 minutes or until lightly toasted. Set aside.

Stir together flour, sugar, baking powder, baking soda, and salt. Whisk together eggs, egg whites, and 1 teaspoon mocha extract, and add to dry ingredients. Mix just until smooth.

In small bowl, combine cocoa, instant coffee, and 4 teaspoons water.

Divide dough in half. To half, add cocoa mixture and melted chocolate. Mix just until incorporated. To other half, stir in 1 teaspoon mocha extract and almonds.

Place half of almond dough on well-floured work surface. Roll into cylinder, then roll cylinder back and forth to form 14-inch log. Repeat with remaining doughs. Place logs on baking sheet lined with foil and lightly coated with vegetable cooking spray. Bake at 325 degrees preheated for 20 to 25 minutes or until firm to touch. Transfer logs to rack to cool.

Cut logs diagonally into ½-inch-thick slices. Stand slices upright on baking sheet, and bake at 300 degrees for 40 minutes. Let cool before storing.

Makes 4 dozen

Serves 48

NUTRITIONAL DATA

PER SERVING		EXCHANGES	
calories	49	milk	0.0
% calories from fat	22	vegetable	0.0
fat (gm)	1.2	fruit	0.0
sat. fat (gm)	0.3	bread	0.5
cholesterol (mg)	8.9	meat	0.0
sodium (mg)	32	fat	0.5
protein (gm)	1.3		
carbohydrate (gm)	8.6		

16
DESSERTS
(DOLCI)

In Italy desserts are often reserved for weekends and holidays. The most common desserts eaten during the week include cheese, ices, almond cookies, and always fresh fruit. Remember to keep the fancy desserts for special occasions when a spectacular dolci and coffee will set the occasion apart from everyday meals. Moderation is the key to enjoying desserts that will pamper your taste buds and satisfy your emotions.

Coffee is an important part of Italian desserts and has a special page at the end of this book. Be sure to serve coffee with any Italian dessert because the supreme indulgence, dessert, should be lingered over and enjoyed.

APPLES WITH RASPBERRY SAUCE

U*sually this dessert is made with fermented raspberries that have been aged in fruit wood for at least six months. A good raspberry vinegar works just as well.*

  2 cups raspberries (fresh or unsweetened frozen)
  3 tablespoons raspberry jam
  2 tablespoons sugar
  ¼ cup light dessert wine (such as Moscato)
  1 tablespoon raspberry vinegar
  8 medium Golden Delicious apples, peeled, cored, and thinly sliced
  ½ cup tofu or purchased low-calorie whipped topping

In food processor or blender, puree raspberries. Add jam and sugar, and pulse to blend. Add wine and vinegar, and blend well.

Put apple slices in large bowl, pour sauce over, and mix gently to coat apple slice. Cover bowl, and refrigerate for 1 hour.

Spoon fruit with its sauce into individual dessert bowls, and top with a dollop of tofu.

Serve immediately.

Serves 10

NUTRITIONAL DATA

PER SERVING		EXCHANGES	
calories	120	milk	0.0
% calories from fat	8	vegetable	0.0
fat (gm)	1.1	fruit	2.0
sat. fat (gm)	0.2	bread	0.0
cholesterol (mg)	0.2	meat	0.0
sodium (mg)	17	fat	0.0
protein (gm)	1.8		
carbohydrate (gm)	27.3		

BELLINI PEACHES WITH RASPBERRIES

SAUCE

> 3 medium peaches, peeled, quartered, and pitted
> 2 teaspoons lemon juice
> ¼ cup sugar

FRUIT

> 4 large peaches, peeled or not, cut into ½-inch-wide slices
> 2 teaspoons lemon juice
> 2 tablespoons sugar

> 1½ cups chilled Champagne or sparkling wine*
> ½ pint fresh raspberries

To make Sauce: Puree peeled peaches in food processor or blender with 2 teaspoons lemon juice. Put puree in small bowl with sugar. Mix well. Cover, and chill several hours.

To make Fruit: Mix sliced peaches with lemon juice and sugar. Chill for several hours.

To serve, combine puree with Champagne. Taste for sweetness. Adjust sugar as needed. Arrange sliced peaches in chilled shallow serving bowls. Pour Champagne-peach sauce over, dividing evenly. Sprinkle each with raspberries. Serve immediately. Serve remaining Champagne in flutes with dessert if desired.

*Note: A nonalcoholic sparkling beverage may be used in place of the Champagne.

Serves 4

NUTRITIONAL DATA

PER SERVING		EXCHANGES	
calories	209	milk	0.0
% calories from fat	1	vegetable	0.0
fat (gm)	0.3	fruit	3.5
sat. fat (gm)	0	bread	0.0
cholesterol (mg)	0	meat	0.0
sodium (mg)	0.2	fat	0.0
protein (gm)	1.5		
carbohydrate (gm)	41		

BERRY-CHOCOLATE MANICOTTI

This is an elegant dessert that can be prepared ahead for the most important occasions.

   6 packaged manicotti or cannelloni shells
1½ cups low-fat ricotta cheese
   1 3-oz. package cream cheese, softened
   ¼ cup sugar
   1 teaspoon almond extract
   1 cup strawberries, sliced
   ¼ cup semisweet chocolate chips
   3 tablespoons strong brewed coffee
   ¼ cup evaporated skim milk

In large saucepan cook pasta shells in boiling water for 20 minutes. Drain. Rinse with cold water; drain well.

For filling, in medium mixing bowl combine ricotta cheese, cream cheese, sugar, and almond extract. Beat with electric mixer on low to medium speed till creamy. Fold in berries.

Using small spoon, stuff about ½ cup of filling into each cooked shell. Chill well for up to 5 hours.

For sauce, in heavy saucepan heat chocolate and corn syrup over low heat till chocolate melts, stirring constantly. Gradually stir in milk. Remove from heat. Chill well.

Place filled shells on dessert plates. Drizzle with sauce. Garnish with berries.

Note: Raspberries, blueberries, or blackberries may be used in place of strawberries.

Serves 6

NUTRITIONAL DATA

PER SERVING		EXCHANGES	
calories	286	milk	0.0
% calories from fat	31	vegetable	0.0
fat (gm)	9.9	fruit	0.0
sat. fat (gm)	3.3	bread	2.5
cholesterol (mg)	24	meat	0.0
sodium (mg)	103	fat	1.5
protein (gm)	11.5		
carbohydrate (gm)	39.4		

CANNOLI

This is a light version of an old favorite.

- 2 cups low-fat ricotta cheese
- ¼ cup sugar
- 1 teaspoon vanilla extract
- ¼ cup semisweet chocolate chips
- 1 tablespoon dried apricots, chopped (optional)
- 12 purchased cannoli cones

For filling, in medium bowl combine ricotta cheese, sugar, and vanilla. Stir or beat until smooth. Fold in chocolate chips and if desired apricot pieces (not included in Nutritional Data). Cover, and chill.

Spoon filling into decorating bag fitted with large tip. Pipe filling into cones. Chill up to 1 hour.

Serves 12

NUTRITIONAL DATA

PER SERVING		EXCHANGES	
calories	123	milk	0.0
% calories from fat	20	vegetable	0.0
fat (gm)	2.7	fruit	0.0
sat. fat (gm)	0	bread	1.5
cholesterol (mg)	5.3	meat	0.0
sodium (mg)	63	fat	0.5
protein (gm)	5.1		
carbohydrate (gm)	20.3		

CASSATA SICILIANA

Layers of angel food cake, ricotta cheese, chocolate, and candied fruit comprise Cassata Siciliana. In Sicily this cake is served at Christmas and Easter.

CASSATA

- 1 cup low-fat ricotta cheese
- ¼ cup sugar
- ¼ cup mixed candied fruit (citron, lemon peel, orange peel, pineapple, and/or cherries), chopped
- 1 oz. semisweet chocolate, chopped
- 1 teaspoon orange rind, grated
- 1 angel food loaf cake, 10 oz., homemade or purchased
- ¼ cup dark rum

CHOCOLATE SAUCE

- ⅓ cup unsweetened cocoa powder
- 2 tablespoons cornstarch
- 2 tablespoons sugar
- ½ cup strong brewed coffee
- ⅓ cup skim milk
- 2 teaspoons vanilla extract
- 1 teaspoon vegetable oil

To make Cassata: Line 9 x 5-inch loaf pan with plastic wrap. In medium-size bowl, whisk together ricotta and sugar. Stir in candied fruit, chocolate, and orange zest.

Slice angel food cake horizontally with a serrated knife into ½-inch-thick slices. Use largest slice to line bottom of loaf pan, filling in with small pieces if necessary. Brush with ⅓ of rum. Spread with ½ of ricotta filling.

Arrange second layer of cake slices on top, brush with ½ of the remaining rum, and spread remaining filling over top. Arrange remaining slices over top, and brush with remaining rum. Cover with plastic wrap, and weight down with another loaf pan and heavy can. Refrigerate overnight.

To make Chocolate Sauce: In small, heavy saucepan, combine cocoa, cornstarch, and sugar. Gradually whisk in coffee and milk. Stirring constantly, bring to boil over medium heat for 30 seconds. Remove from heat, and whisk in vanilla and oil.

Let cool, and serve at room temperature or chilled. Sauce may be prepared ahead and stored, covered, in refrigerator for up to 1 week.

To serve Cassata: Invert loaf pan onto serving dish. Remove plastic wrap. Slice, and serve with chocolate sauce.

Serves 8

NUTRITIONAL DATA

PER SERVING		EXCHANGES	
calories	233	milk	0.0
% calories from fat	10	vegetable	0.0
fat (gm)	2.8	fruit	0.0
sat. fat (gm)	0.2	bread	3.0
cholesterol (mg)	4.1	meat	0.0
sodium (mg)	126	fat	0.5
protein (gm)	6.7		
carbohydrate (gm)	44.1		

CHOCOLATE SORBET

*T his is so decadent and delicious that no one
will believe it is low fat!*

- ½ cup sugar or to taste
- 1¼ cups unsweetened cocoa
- 2 cups warm water
- ⅓ cup Madeira or port wine

Mix sugar and cocoa in bowl. Whisk in water, a little at a time, until smooth. Add wine. Process sorbet in ice cream maker according to manufacturer's instructions. If not using it immediately, freeze sorbet, and then process for a few seconds in food processor to soften before serving.

Serves 6

NUTRITIONAL DATA

PER SERVING		EXCHANGES	
calories	108	milk	0.0
% calories from fat	11	vegetable	0.0
fat (gm)	1.7	fruit	0.0
sat. fat (gm)	0.4	bread	1.5
cholesterol (mg)	0	meat	0.0
sodium (mg)	12	fat	0.0
protein (gm)	3.5		
carbohydrate (gm)	26.3		

ITALIAN KNOT COOKIES

*T*hese cookies were thought to be ideal for a wedding reception because they symbolize two people whose lives were about to become entwined.

COOKIES

   3 cups unbleached all-purpose flour
2¼ teaspoons baking powder
   ½ teaspoon baking soda
   ½ teaspoon salt
   4 tablespoons unsalted butter, softened
   ½ cup sugar
   3 large eggs
   ½ cup orange juice
   2 tablespoons orange zest

FROSTING

1½ cups confectioners' sugar, sifted
   4 tablespoons skim milk
   1 teaspoon almond extract
     Yellow food coloring (optional)
     Yellow sugar sprinkles (optional)

To make Cookies: Sift flour, baking powder, baking soda, and salt together. Set aside.

In large bowl, cream butter and sugar until light and fluffy. Add eggs 1 at a time, beating well after each addition. Beat in orange zest and juice. Beat in dry ingredients gradually, and mix well. Dough will be soft; wrap it in waxed paper and refrigerate it for 1 hour to make it easier to handle.

Place dough on well-floured surface. Pinch off egg-size pieces of dough, and roll each piece into rope about 7 inches long and ½ inch thick. Tie each into loose knot, and place 1 inch apart on cookie sheets sprayed with vegetable cooking spray.

Bake at 350 degrees (preheated) for 12 to 15 minutes or until lightly browned. Transfer cookies to wire racks to cool slightly. Frost when still slightly warm.

To make Frosting: Combine sugar and milk in bowl, and beat until smooth. Add milk if necessary to make thin frosting. Beat in almond extract. Add food coloring if desired.

Dip top of each cookie into frosting, shaking off excess. Place them on racks, and top with colored sprinkles (not included in Nutritional Data). Let frosting dry before storing. These will keep in airtight container for up to 1 week, or freeze them for up to 3 months.

Makes 42

Serves 42

NUTRITIONAL DATA

PER SERVING		EXCHANGES	
calories	73	milk	0.0
% calories from fat	20	vegetable	0.0
fat (gm)	1.6	fruit	0.0
sat. fat (gm)	0.9	bread	1.0
cholesterol (mg)	18.4	meat	0.0
sodium (mg)	58	fat	0.0
protein (gm)	1.5		
carbohydrate (gm)	13.3		

MARRIAGE COOKIES

COOKIES

1¾ cups unbleached all-purpose flour, sifted

8 tablespoons (1 stick) butter or shortening

¾ cup sugar

½ teaspoon allspice

½ teaspoon baking powder

¾ teaspoon baking soda

¼ cup Dutch process cocoa

¼ cup walnuts, coarsely ground

1 cup raisins, coarsely chopped

½ cup skim milk

FROSTING

1½ cups confectioners' sugar, sifted

2½ tablespoons evaporated skim milk

1 teaspoon butter or margarine, softened

1 teaspoon rum extract

Pastel-colored sugar sprinkles

To make Cookies: Beat flour and butter or shortening in bowl until well blended. Beat in sugar, allspice, baking powder, baking soda, cocoa, nuts, and raisins. Stir in milk, and mix well to make soft dough.

Drop teaspoonfuls of dough about 1 inch apart onto 2 cookie sheets sprayed with vegetable cooking spray. Bake at 350 degrees (preheated) for 10 minutes or until firm. Transfer to wire racks to cool.

To make Frosting: Combine all frosting ingredients in bowl, and beat until smooth. Dip top of each cookie into frosting. Place cookies on racks, and top with colored sprinkles (not included in Nutritional Data). Let frosting dry before storing. These will keep in airtight container for up to 2 weeks, or they can be frozen for 3 to 4 months.

Makes 48

Serves 48

NUTRITIONAL DATA

PER SERVING		EXCHANGES	
calories	72	milk	0.0
% calories from fat	28	vegetable	0.0
fat (gm)	2.3	fruit	0.5
sat. fat (gm)	1.3	bread	0.0
cholesterol (mg)	5.4	meat	0.0
sodium (mg)	39	fat	0.5
protein (gm)	0.9		
carbohydrate (gm)	12.6		

SICILIAN FIG COOKIES

I n Sicily fig-filled cookies are an absolute "must have."

COOKIES

   4 cups unbleached all-purpose flour
1½ tablespoons baking powder
   ¼ teaspoon salt
   ½ cup sugar
   1 cup vegetable shortening
   1 large egg
   1 tablespoon orange extract
   ½ cup skim milk

FILLING

   2 cups dried figs
   2 cups dried dates, pitted
   ½ cup raisins
   ½ cup honey
   1 teaspoon allspice
   ½ cup orange marmalade
      Egg wash made with 1 large egg white beaten with
      1 tablespoon water

To make Cookies: Sift flour, baking powder, and salt together into large bowl. Add sugar, and stir well. Cut in shortening with fork and work the mixture until it looks like cornmeal.

Beat egg, orange extract, and milk together in bowl. Add to flour mixture and work mixture with hands into rough dough.

Turn dough out onto floured surface, and knead for 5 minutes or until smooth. Dough will be soft.

Cut dough into 4 pieces, wrap each piece in plastic wrap, and chill for 45 minutes.

To make Filling: Grind figs, dates, and raisins in food processor until coarse, or coarsely chop. Place mixture in bowl, add remaining filling ingredients; mix well. Mixture will be thick. Set aside.

Work with 1 piece of dough at a time, keeping remaining dough covered. On floured surface, roll out each piece of dough to 12-inch square. Cut dough into 4 x 3-inch rectangles, and spoon 2 tablespoons of filling mixture into center of each rectangle.

Carefully fold over long edges of each rectangle to meet, then pinch seam to close it securely, and turn the cookie seam side down. Pinch ends closed, and fold them under.

Shape cookies into crescents, and place seam side down on cookie sheets sprayed with vegetable cooking spray. Make 2 or 3 diagonal slits in top of each crescent with scissors.

Brush with egg wash, and bake at 375 degrees (preheated) for 25 minutes or until golden brown. Transfer to wire racks to cool. These cookies can be frozen for up to 3 months.

Note: These cookies make wonderful gifts. Wrap each cookie in plastic wrap, twist the ends, and tie them with colored ribbons.

Makes 48

Serves 48

NUTRITIONAL DATA

PER SERVING		EXCHANGES	
calories	153	milk	0.0
% calories from fat	26	vegetable	0.0
fat (gm)	4.6	fruit	1.0
sat. fat (gm)	1.2	bread	0.5
cholesterol (mg)	4.5	meat	0.0
sodium (mg)	47	fat	1.0
protein (gm)	1.8		
carbohydrate (gm)	27.5		

Spicy Cookie Balls

COOKIES

3¼ cups unbleached all-purpose flour

1½ cups sugar

  1 tablespoon baking powder

¼ cup spicy cocoa*

  1 teaspoon black pepper, freshly ground

  1 teaspoon ground cinnamon

¾ cup vegetable shortening

½ teaspoon salt

½ cup skim milk

¼ cup chopped walnuts

FROSTING

1½ cups confectioners' sugar, sifted

  3 tablespoons skim milk

  1 teaspoon rum extract

    Colored Sprinkles (optional)

To make Cookies: Sift first 6 ingredients together into large bowl. Work in shortening with your hands until mixture resembles coarse meal. Add salt, milk, and nuts, and mix well with hands until blended.

Pinch off 1-inch pieces of dough, and roll them into balls. Place them 1 inch apart on 2 cookie sheets sprayed with vegetable cooking spray, and bake at 350 degrees (preheated) for 15 to 20 minutes or until firm.

While cookies are baking, make frosting.

To make Frosting: In bowl, combine confectioners' sugar, 3 tablespoons of milk, and rum extract and beat until smooth. Add milk if necessary to make thin frosting.

Remove cookies from oven, and dip tops of warm cookies into icing.

Place on wire racks, and top with colored sprinkles (not included in Nutritional Data). Let frosting dry before storing. These will keep in airtight container for up to 1 week or can be frozen for up to 2 months.

*Note: Spicy cocoa is used for baking and hot drinks. It is flavored with allspice and nutmeg. If you cannot find spicy cocoa, use regular baking cocoa mixed with ½ teaspoon each allspice and nutmeg.

Makes 54

Serves 54

NUTRITIONAL DATA

PER SERVING		EXCHANGES	
calories	88	milk	0.0
% calories from fat	31	vegetable	0.0
fat (gm)	3.1	fruit	0.0
sat. fat (gm)	0.8	bread	1.0
cholesterol (mg)	0.1	meat	0.0
sodium (mg)	40	fat	0.5
protein (gm)	1.1		
carbohydrate (gm)	14.4		

ITALIAN RUM CAKE

T his cake is very popular during holiday time in Italy. Many versions can be found in different regions.

CAKE

⅓ cup diet margarine

⅓ cup vegetable oil

1½ cups sugar

3 eggs

3 cups all-purpose flour

1½ tablespoons baking powder

1 teaspoon salt

1⅓ cups skim milk

½ cup walnuts, chopped

2 teaspoons vanilla extract

RUM SAUCE

6 oz. apricot nectar

½ cup sugar

½ cup light rum

To make Cake: Cream margarine and oil; gradually add sugar, beating well at medium speed of electric mixer. Add eggs, one at a time, beating after each addition.

Combine flour, baking powder, and salt; add to creamed mixture alternately with milk, beginning and ending with flour mixture. Mix just until blended after each addition. Stir in walnuts and vanilla. Pour batter into greased and floured 12-cup bundt pan.

Bake at 350 degrees for 44 to 60 minutes or until a wooden pick inserted in center comes out clean. Let cool in pan 10 minutes; remove from pan, and let cool completely on a wire rack.

To make Rum Sauce: Combine nectar and sugar in saucepan. Bring to boil over medium heat; stirring frequently, reduce heat, and simmer 5 minutes. Remove from heat, and stir in rum. Let cool slightly. Pour 1 cup rum sauce over cake; serve with remaining cup of sauce.

Makes 1, 10-inch cake

Serves 10

NUTRITIONAL DATA

PER SERVING		EXCHANGES	
calories	483	milk	0.0
% calories from fat	29	vegetable	0.0
fat (gm)	16	fruit	2.0
sat. fat (gm)	2.4	bread	3.0
cholesterol (mg)	64.4	meat	0.0
sodium (mg)	468	fat	3.0
protein (gm)	7.8		
carbohydrate (gm)	73		

LEMON FARINA CHEESECAKE

½ cup almonds, slivered

¾ cup sugar

1¼ cups creamed low-fat cottage cheese

3 tablespoons lemon juice

2 teaspoons lemon peel, freshly grated

⅓ cup uncooked instant farina

¼ cup liquid Butter Buds

3 large egg whites

½ cup golden raisins

Strawberries, raspberries, or blueberries

Grease 8- or 9-inch round cake pan; line bottom with waxed paper. Grease paper, and lightly flour paper and pan.

In blender or food processor, process almonds with sugar until ground fine. Add cottage cheese, juice, and peel. Process until smooth. Add farina and Butter Buds; process until thoroughly blended.

Beat egg whites in medium-size bowl with electric mixer until soft peaks form when beaters are lifted. Pour cheese mixture into egg whites and add raisins. Fold ingredients gently with rubber spatula until no whites are visible. Pour into prepared pan.

Bake at 325 degrees (preheated) 40 to 45 minutes until top of cake looks dry and pick inserted near center comes out clean. Cool in pan on rack. Invert onto serving plate. Peel off waxed paper. Refrigerate if not serving within 1 hour. To serve, garnish with berries.

Serves 8

NUTRITIONAL DATA

PER SERVING		EXCHANGES	
calories	211	milk	0.0
% calories from fat	19	vegetable	0.0
fat (gm)	4.5	fruit	2.0
sat. fat (gm)	0.8	bread	0.5
cholesterol (mg)	3	meat	0.5
sodium (mg)	255	fat	0.5
protein (gm)	8.8		
carbohydrate (gm)	35.6		

LEMON ICE

½ cup sugar
½ cup boiling water
1 cup cold water
¼ teaspoon lemon peel, finely grated
½ cup lemon juice
12 mint leaves

Dissolve sugar in boiling water. Add cold water, lemon peel, and lemon juice. Pour into 9 x 5 x 3-inch loaf pan. Freeze about 4 hours or till icy.

Stir lemon mixture, then freeze 1 to 3 hours more or till nearly firm, stirring every 30 minutes.

Or freeze overnight without stirring till nearly firm. Then place lemon ice mixture in blender container or food processor bowl. Cover and blend or process till fluffy, stopping once or twice to scrape the sides.

Spoon lemon ice into small stemmed glasses. Garnish with mint leaves.

Serves 6

NUTRITIONAL DATA

PER SERVING		EXCHANGES	
calories	65	milk	0.0
% calories from fat	0	vegetable	0.0
fat (gm)	0	fruit	1.0
sat. fat (gm)	0	bread	0.0
cholesterol (mg)	0	meat	0.0
sodium (mg)	0.3	fat	0.0
protein (gm)	0.1		
carbohydrate (gm)	17.8		

Peaches in Chianti

This is a recipe from Tuscany that is simple and supremely refreshing in summer.

8 medium to large freestone peaches, ripe but firm
2 tablespoons lemon juice
3 tablespoons sugar
1 cup Chianti wine
Biscotti di Prato (see index) or biscotti of choice

Peel peaches, and cut into eighths. Place in stainless steel, glass, or ceramic bowl. Add lemon and sugar, and mix gently but well. Let stand 5 minutes. Pour wine over peaches, and cover. Refrigerate 8 hours or overnight.

To serve, arrange peach segments in wine glasses or wide-mouthed dessert glasses, and spoon a little wine into each glass. Serve with biscotti.

Serves 8

NUTRITIONAL DATA

PER SERVING		EXCHANGES	
calories	66	milk	0.0
% calories from fat	1	vegetable	0.0
fat (gm)	0.1	fruit	1.0
sat. fat (gm)	0	bread	0.0
cholesterol (mg)	0	meat	0.0
sodium (mg)	10	fat	0.0
protein (gm)	0.7		
carbohydrate (gm)	14.7		

PEARS, CARDINAL STYLE

Pears are a favorite fruit in Italy, and many desserts are made with them. This dessert is named for the robes worn by the cardinals of Firenze. It is usually made with alkermes, a liqueur made from cinnamon, vanilla, and cochineal, which has a vivid red color that stains very easily. You can buy it in specialty shops or by mail order through food catalogs.

 6 slightly underripe Anjou or Bartlett pears
 6 tablespoons plus ½ cup sugar
 ½ cup cranberry juice cocktail or alkermes
 3 cups dry red wine
   Confectioners' sugar
   Fresh mint leaves

Remove small slice from bottom of each pear to make it stand upright. Using vegetable peeler, remove 4 or 5 long narrow strips of skin from each pear to create striped effect. Place pears upright in 3-inch deep baking dish just large enough to hold pears snugly.

Sprinkle each pear with 1 tablespoon sugar. Drizzle cranberry juice over them, and add enough wine to almost cover pears.

Bake, uncovered, in preheated 350-degree oven for about 35 minutes or until they are soft and easily pierced with knife. Do not overcook, or they will collapse and be mushy.

Transfer pears to serving dish, and pour cooking liquid into saucepan. You should have about 2 cups of liquid; if necessary, add wine to equal 2 cups. Add ½ cup sugar, stir and bring to boil. Reduce heat to medium, and cook until liquid is reduced by half. Pour this sauce over pears.

Baste pears frequently with sauce as it cools; sauce will thicken and glaze pears. Refrigerate pears for 1 hour before serving. Place pears on individual serving dishes, spoon some sauce around bottom of each pear, and sprinkle pears with confectioners' sugar. Garnish each plate with a mint leaf, and serve.

Serves 6

NUTRITIONAL DATA

PER SERVING		EXCHANGES	
calories	319	milk	0.0
% calories from fat	2	vegetable	0.0
fat (gm)	0.8	fruit	5.5
sat. fat (gm)	0.1	bread	0.0
cholesterol (mg)	0	meat	0.0
sodium (mg)	78	fat	0.0
protein (gm)	1.2		
carbohydrate (gm)	63.1		

POLENTA POUND CAKE

*Y*ou can use this golden loaf cake as the basis *for strawberry shortcake or many other desserts. You can slice and toast it, then top it with berries. The use of polenta marks this as a northern Italian dish.*

⅔ cup sugar

3 tablespoons margarine, softened

3 egg whites

1 egg yolk

1¾ cups yellow cornmeal

¾ cup all-purpose flour

2 teaspoons baking powder

1 teaspoon baking soda

½ teaspoon salt

1 cup buttermilk

Raspberry Sauce (see index)

Fresh fruit, such as peach slices, strawberries, raspberries, blueberries, or blackberries

Low-calorie whipped topping

Cream sugar, margarine, and eggs at medium speed with electric mixer until light and fluffy.

Combine cornmeal, flour, baking powder, baking soda, and salt. With mixer at low speed, add this mixture to creamed mixture alternately with buttermilk, beginning and ending with cornmeal mixture. Pour into 9-inch round cake pan coated with cooking spray.

Bake at 350 degrees for 40 minutes or until wooden pick inserted in center comes out clean. Cool in pan 10 minutes; remove from pan, and cool on rack.

Serve with Raspberry Sauce or fresh fruit and whipped topping (none of which are included in Nutritional Data).

Makes 9-inch loaf

Serves 8

NUTRITIONAL DATA

PER SERVING		EXCHANGES	
calories	278	milk	0.0
% calories from fat	19	vegetable	0.0
fat (gm)	5.8	fruit	0.0
sat. fat (gm)	1.3	bread	3.0
cholesterol (mg)	27.8	meat	0.0
sodium (mg)	422	fat	1.0
protein (gm)	6.5		
carbohydrate (gm)	50.3		

♥

STRAWBERRIES AND FIGS

P eople seem to love this dessert. Be sure the figs are fresh. I know they are expensive, but I think that they are well worth the money. This is an effortless, elegant dessert.

- 1 12-oz. package frozen strawberries, thawed
- ½ cup refined sugar
- 12 fresh figs, washed and cut in half
- 4 dollops (2 oz.) vanilla yogurt
- Fresh mint sprigs

Place strawberries and sugar in food processor, and puree them. On each of 4 dessert plates, place 6 fig halves (open side up). Pour strawberry puree on top. Add dollop of yogurt. Place sprig of mint on top.

Serves 4

NUTRITIONAL DATA

PER SERVING		EXCHANGES	
calories	246	milk	0.0
% calories from fat	3	vegetable	0.0
fat (gm)	0.8	fruit	4.0
sat. fat (gm)	0.2	bread	0.0
cholesterol (mg)	0.8	meat	0.0
sodium (mg)	15	fat	0.0
protein (gm)	2.6		
carbohydrate (gm)	62.9		

TIRAMISU

Tiramisu means "pick-me-up" in Italian, and this dessert certainly lives up to its name. There are many versions of this dessert, but I have tried to give you a low-fat recipe that is close to the original.

3 large egg yolks
½ cup sugar
1 tablespoon plus 1 cup strong coffee
2 tablespoons cognac
½ cup low-fat ricotta cheese
8 oz. Kraft Free cream cheese
1 tablespoon buttermilk
About 20 ladyfingers (5 oz.), toasted
2 tablespoons Dutch-process cocoa

In bowl, combine egg yolks, ½ cup sugar, 1 tablespoon coffee, and cognac. Beat mixture with rotary beater until foamy, 2 to 3 minutes.

In food processor or blender process ricotta, cream cheese, and buttermilk until smooth. Add to egg mixture. Set filling aside.

Pour 1 cup coffee into shallow bowl. Dip in both sides of each ladyfinger quickly. Arrange layer of 6 or 7 ladyfingers on bottom of decorative serving bowl. Spread about one-third of filling mixture over ladyfingers.

Continue layering ladyfingers and filling, finishing with layer of filling. Sift cocoa over top, and refrigerate for 1 hour before serving.

To serve, spoon into individual dessert dishes.

Serves 8

NUTRITIONAL DATA

PER SERVING		EXCHANGES	
calories	190	milk	0.0
% calories from fat	19	vegetable	0.0
fat (gm)	4.1	fruit	0.0
sat. fat (gm)	1.1	bread	2.0
cholesterol (mg)	149.4	meat	1.0
sodium (mg)	246	fat	0.0
protein (gm)	9.7		
carbohydrate (gm)	27		

17
Sweet Sauces

Summer's delicious fruits and berries produce a wealth of luscious sauces. Make dessert something special by adding one of these easy sauces to frozen yogurt, fruit sherbet, angel cake, or even fresh fruit. You can even use them on top of pancakes or waffles for a brunch treat.

To save time, microwave the sauces in a glass measure, and use the same bowl for storage. Frozen and canned fruit in a "no-sugar" pack may be used when fresh is not available. Defrost frozen fruit according to package directions, and drain canned fruit before using it in recipes.

CHAMPAGNE SABAYON SAUCE

This delicate sauce can be served over ice cream, sherbet, fresh fruit, cold pudding, or mousse.

1 cup white or pink Champagne

5 egg yolks

¾ cup sugar

Place egg yolks and Champagne in top of double boiler or in heatproof bowl and set it over simmering (not boiling) water. Water should not touch vessel containing ingredients. Whisk egg yolks and Champagne gently for 8 to 10 minutes; mixture should not expand. Its temperature should be kept at 115 degrees; use cooking thermometer to check it.

Pour mixture into bowl, and add sugar. Using electric mixer set at medium speed, beat mixture for 5 minutes, then beat it at low speed or with whisk for an additional 5 minutes.

Makes about 3¾ cups

Serves 15 (¼-cup servings)

NUTRITIONAL DATA

PER SERVING		EXCHANGES	
calories	66	milk	0.0
% calories from fat	22	vegetable	0.0
fat (gm)	1.7	fruit	1.0
sat. fat (gm)	0.5	bread	0.0
cholesterol (mg)	71	meat	0.0
sodium (mg)	2	fat	0.0
protein (gm)	1		
carbohydrate (gm)	10.1		

CHERRY SAUCE WITH GRAND MARNIER

⅓ cup sugar

1 tablespoon cornstarch

¼ cup orange juice

1 lb. fresh sweet cherries, pitted

3 tablespoons Grand Marnier or other orange-flavored liqueur

½ teaspoon orange rind, grated

Combine first 2 ingredients in a 2-quart glass measure. Gradually add orange juice, stirring with wire whisk. Stir in cherries. Cover with heavy-duty plastic wrap, and vent.

Microwave at high 6 to 7 minutes or until thickened and bubbly, stirring every 3 minutes. Partially mash cherries; stir in remaining ingredients. Serve warm over fresh orange sections or orange sherbert.

Makes 2 cups

Serves 32 (1-tablespoon servings)

NUTRITIONAL DATA

PER SERVING		EXCHANGES	
calories	24	milk	0.0
% calories from fat	5	vegetable	0.0
fat (gm)	0.1	fruit	0.5
sat. fat (gm)	0	bread	0.0
cholesterol (mg)	0	meat	0.0
sodium (mg)	0.1	fat	0.0
protein (gm)	0.2		
carbohydrate (gm)	5.3		

HOT LEMON SAUCE

Serve this sauce hot or warm over puddings and cakes.

- ½ cup sugar
- 2 tablespoons cornstarch
- ¼ teaspoon water
- 3 tablespoons fresh lemon juice
- 1½ teaspoons lemon peel, grated
- 1½ tablespoons butter

In saucepan, combine sugar and cornstarch. Stir in water. Stirring constantly, cook over low heat until mixture thickens and becomes clear. Add lemon juice, lemon peel, and butter.

Makes about 1½ cups

Serves 6 (¼-cup servings)

NUTRITIONAL DATA

PER SERVING		EXCHANGES	
calories	97	milk	0.0
% calories from fat	25	vegetable	0.0
fat (gm)	2.9	fruit	1.0
sat. fat (gm)	1.8	bread	0.0
cholesterol (mg)	7.7	meat	0.0
sodium (mg)	29	fat	0.5
protein (gm)	0.1		
carbohydrate (gm)	19.2		

ORANGE DESSERT SAUCE

T *his sauce is excellent for angel food cake, ice cream, or sherbert.*

2 tablespoons orange peel, grated

2 tablespoons cornstarch

1 tablespoon sugar

1 cup fresh orange juice

1 egg yolk

In heavy pot (not aluminum), stir orange peel, cornstarch, and sugar together. Gradually pour in orange juice while stirring with whisk to keep mixture smooth. Over medium heat, stir the sauce for 3 or 4 minutes, until it thickens.

Place egg yolk in small bowl, and beat it as you slowly pour in hot sauce. Scrape in all sauce from pot, then transfer contents of bowl to pot.

Return sauce to heat for half a minute while continuing to beat it. Chill before serving.

Makes about 1 cup

Serves 8 (2-tablespoon servings)

NUTRITIONAL DATA

PER SERVING		EXCHANGES	
calories	36	milk	0.0
% calories from fat	17	vegetable	0.0
fat (gm)	0.7	fruit	0.5
sat. fat (gm)	0.2	bread	0.0
cholesterol (mg)	26.6	meat	0.0
sodium (mg)	1.3	fat	0.0
protein (gm)	0.6		
carbohydrate (gm)	7		

PEACH-LEAF CUSTARD

*This delicately flavored sauce will comple-
ment hot or cold poached fruits. Scented
geranium leaves can be substituted for the peach
leaves.*

6 peach leaves

3 cups skim milk

5 egg yolks

1 cup sugar

Cornstarch

In heavy saucepan, bring milk to boil with peach leaves, then set
mixture aside to infuse for 15 minutes.

In large bowl, beat egg yolks and sugar together until yolks are
pale and light. Stir in pinch of cornstarch. Bring milk to boil again.
Stirring constantly, pour it into egg yolks a little at a time.

Pour custard mixture into saucepan, and place it over low heat.
Cook custard for about 3 minutes, stirring with wooden spoon. As
soon as custard thickens, remove it from heat. Discard peach
leaves, and let custard cool.

Makes 4 cups

Serves 16 (¼-cup servings)

NUTRITIONAL DATA

PER SERVING		EXCHANGES	
calories	80	milk	1.0
% calories from fat	18	vegetable	0.0
fat (gm)	1.7	fruit	0.0
sat. fat (gm)	0.6	bread	0.0
cholesterol (mg)	67.3	meat	0.0
sodium (mg)	26	fat	0.0
protein (gm)	2.4		
carbohydrate (gm)	14.3		

RASPBERRY SAUCE

T his sauce is usually served with strawberries or raspberries. it also goes well with poached fruit, angel food cake, pound cake, ice cream, or sherbet.

1½ cups ripe raspberries

¼ cup sugar

3 tablespoons fresh lemon juice

1 tablespoon raspberry liqueur

Puree raspberries in blender. Stir in sugar, Flavor with lemon juice and raspberry liqueur. Strain puree through a fine-mesh sieve to remove seeds.

Makes about 1 cup

Serves 8 (2-tablespoon servings)

NUTRITIONAL DATA

PER SERVING		EXCHANGES	
calories	41	milk	0.0
% calories from fat	3	vegetable	0.0
fat (gm)	0.1	fruit	0.5
sat. fat (gm)	0	bread	0.0
cholesterol (mg)	0	meat	0.0
sodium (mg)	0.2	fat	0.0
protein (gm)	0.2		
carbohydrate (gm)	9.9		

Vanilla "Cream"

This thick sauce is suitable for baked or steamed pudding and for baked or poached fruit.

4 tablespoons cornstarch
4 cups skim milk
½ cup sugar
1 vanilla bean
Egg substitute equal to 4 eggs

Place cornstarch in 1-quart saucepan. Whisk in a little milk to dissolve cornstarch. Whisk in remaining milk and sugar. Add vanilla bean. Cook over medium heat, stirring constantly, for 5 to 10 minutes or until mixture boils and thickens.

Remove from heat, and whisk in egg substitute. Return to heat, and cook, stirring constantly, for 5 minutes. When custard is thick enough to coat spoon, strain it through fine sieve into large bowl. Let cool before serving.

Makes about 6 cups
Serves 24 (¼-cup servings)

NUTRITIONAL DATA

PER SERVING		EXCHANGES	
calories	39	milk	0.5
% calories from fat	2	vegetable	0.0
fat (gm)	0.1	fruit	0.0
sat. fat (gm)	0	bread	0.0
cholesterol (mg)	0.7	meat	0.0
sodium (mg)	35	fat	0.0
protein (gm)	23		
carbohydrate (gm)	7.4		

18
COFFEE
(ITALIAN STYLE)

The bittersweet flavor of strong Italian coffee is an acquired taste for many Americans. Italians love their coffee and have it daily, sometime several times a day.

Few Italian homes have a powerful steam-generating machine to make true espresso. At home, the after-dinner coffee is usually made in a *napoletana,* a three-part coffee pot that sits on the stove burner. Water goes into the bottom part, and coffee into a basket in the middle. The top part, which has a spout, is screwed on spout side down. When the water in the bottom begins to boil, the whole contraption is turned upside down to allow the hot water to drip through. The coffee is dark, rich, and less bitter than steam-made espresso.

While coffee is reserved for the end of the meal and not served with dessert unless you ask for it, most Italians begin their morning with a cup of coffee. The morning coffee is a gentler brew. Caffe latte, one part espresso to three parts steamed milk, is the usual morning beverage.

Italians also like coffee in the afternoon as a pick-me-up, which provides an opportunity to gather in cafes for coffee, conversation, and a little something sweet.

The Perfect Cup of Espresso

Espresso originated in the early 1900s because an impatient gentleman in Naples hated waiting for his coffee to brew and asked an engineer to speed up the process by forcing water through the coffee grounds with pressure. According to espresso experts, body, aroma, and froth are the essences of good espresso. A good cup should have: strong flavor, rich aroma, a pleasing after taste, and thick, long-lasting, creamy froth. The way the beans are roasted and ground, the espresso machine, and the coffee maker's skill are all important factors.

To brew espresso for your Italian menu, purchase a finely ground, dark-roast coffee at the supermarket or at a coffee shop. Use an espresso maker, which brews quickly, under pressure, to produce coffee with a foamy head. (If you don't have an espresso maker, you can compromise and brew espresso in a drip coffee maker; or even use instant espresso coffee crystals.) Espresso is usually served in tiny cups with sugar and a twist of lemon peel.

Cappuccino is another popular Italian coffee. It is a blend of one-third espresso and two-thirds steamed milk.

Americano, on the other hand, is simply a traditionally sized espresso expanded in volume to a full cup by the addition of hot water.

INDEX